The Odds Almanac

A. James Fix, Ph.D.
and
David Daughton

Follett Publishing Company / Chicago

Library of Congress Cataloging in Publication Data
Fix, A. James, 1941–
 The odds almanac.
  1. Curiosities and wonders. 2. Probabilities—Popular works. I. Daughton, David, 1944–   joint author. II. Title.
AG243.F59   031′ . 02   80-36693
ISBN 0-695-81438-9

Second Printing

to our parents
who were there when we needed them

to Laurelee and Barbara
to whom not just this book but our lives are dedicated

to Kim
who taught laughter

to Deke
who knows integrity and compassion

to Joan
who shares with others her precious gift of life

to Irving Kass, M.D.
who gave the very best and expected the very best

Contents

Preface

   We have gathered all our odds from the best studies that we could find in each field that we have covered. Most of the odds come from the scientific and business journals that we comb each month. We have organized our own studies to uncover various unpublished odds. Some odds have been computer generated in various parts of the world to provide greater accuracy than several hardworking researchers could hope to achieve.

We have made decisions along the way in selecting which items to include and in determining which of two or three competing estimates about the same phenomenon we would accept.

In gathering the odds, we have looked for permanence. For the most part we have avoided public opinion surveys as sources. Public opinion changes; we wanted odds that we can count on—probabilities that will tell us something enduring about the world in which we live. Even though we have used this general rule, we have admittedly broken it when an item reflected a trend likely to endure or when it was just too much fun to leave out.

We have generally avoided interactive odds—those that apply only when more than one or two factors come together. We have also avoided odds that do not apply equally to both sexes. This choice reflects our belief that most such odds will not stand the test of time. We have made two exceptions to this. In our chapter on the sexes, we have compiled odds that reflect the different experiences or capacities of men and women in our culture or that illustrate important aspects of the relations between the sexes. We have also included odds that reflect important differences between the sexes, for instance, their risks of suicide.

Because we are part of the academic and scientific communities, we are most comfortable reporting the references upon which we base each of our statements. At first we had planned to document every item in this book. We quickly recognized, however, that to do this would require much space that could be put to better use, and although we will never entirely overcome our old habits, we have at least restrained them for this one time.

In spite of this decision, however, our credibility still rests largely on the credibility of our sources. And we will be happy to share these sources with any of our readers. Our publisher—Follett Publishing Company, 1010 West Washington Boulevard, Chicago, Illinois 60607—has supported us in this and has offered to receive all questions from readers and relay them to us. When a self-addressed stamped envelope is included, we will provide references for any item that we have presented.

We are always searching for important, well-documented, "new" odds to update our collection, and in future volumes we hope to credit those who alert us to additional material.

Acknowledgments

We have collected and interpreted the odds. But this sort of effort in itself does not produce a book. These people helped us along the way, and we want them to know how grateful we are. We thank Elaine Goldberg for her confidence in us; William Maxey for the drudgery of editing thousands of disconnected items; Mark Frazel for his help in organizing the entries; and Erika Hugo for patient, level-headed good judgment, and an easy smile during tense times.

Two other sources of emotional support and encouragement (outside those constant life-giving doses from our families) were our two work colleagues Susan Kiger and Rebecca Gogetap. Thank you, friends.

Introduction

We both saw it when it was new. The place was Seattle, in 1962, at what is now the Civic Center, near the Space Needle. It was called a Probability Machine.

It's like a pinball machine tilted on end. It holds hundreds of rubber balls, each waiting its turn to be dropped into the motionless field of spokes through which it will bounce erratically, finally falling into one of the columns at the bottom. Because each ball drops from a middle point, it is most likely to end in one of the central columns. Some do bounce errantly and end up in a column near one side or the other. But most, after hopping their way through the spoke-forest, always come to rest in one of the center columns.

Time after time the center column grows tallest while the columns farther from the center stack up more slowly. The process invariably produces what statisticians call a normal distribution curve—tall in the center and diminishing in size at the sides. The machine, built to sense when this has been achieved, triumphantly announces its accomplishment with a clanging and then empties and begins all over again.

It is still there, this deceptive, perennially successful, and very noisy piece of statistical gimmickry. It may be only a passing curiosity to most people, but in a simple yet dramatic way, this machine illustrates all the fundamental concepts of chance, random events, and probability. Had scientific consultants never constructed that rude and impertinent gadget, we might never have attempted to give others the same simple but profound insights that that machine represents for us.

The machine cannot predict where each individual rubber ball will end up. It is not programmed to worry, nor need it ever be concerned about the final outcome. Scientists and mathematicians are so certain of this that they talk about the "laws" (that is, absolute certainties) of probability.

The individual faces risks. But where the sum of thousands of millions of events is considered, few risks exist; virtually everything is certain. Businesses as diverse as casino gambling and home insurance are based on this individual-uncertainty–group-certainty principle. In Las Vegas, Reno, or Atlantic City, no casino operator can say which customers will leave as winners, which as losers. But casino executives never lose sleep over that because there is no chance— none at all—that they will lose money from gambling. From fires, perhaps, or thefts, or earthquakes, but from gambling? Never. And the final score is always Casinos: winners; Gamblers: losers.

The individual-uncertainty–group-certainty contradiction has another side. We call it the lottery phenomenon. In all honest lotteries, the individual has only a small chance of winning. Yet it is almost certain that *someone* will win. Most of us enjoy lotteries because of this certainty that there will in the end be a winner.

Most people do not realize that a large part of our knowledge in several very important fields is merely "probability knowledge." Most biological, medical, social-scientific, and even physical and biochemical knowledge is of this sort. Does a new drug help prevent heart attacks? Does a food or chemical cause cancer? Will it snow in Aspen tomorrow? Do special preschool educational programs improve children's future academic success? Did naturalists for years place the wrong fossil skull on brontosaurus skeletons in museums? Will the earth grow warmer or colder during the next century? Will the ozone layer in the upper atmosphere diminish, and will that lead to more skin cancer on Earth?

We don't know. No one really knows these things, at least not in the sense of absolute certainty. Many of us grew up learning in our science courses about the "laws" of science, the "scientific facts" that we believed all scientists agreed upon. To some extent most scientists do agree upon some "laws" and some "facts," but most people would be amazed at the amount of uncertainty that scientists themselves would be the first to confess.

Take any of the questions about chemicals, drugs, meteorology, social influences, or anything else that scientists study. Only on rare and exciting occasions do scientists find a basic new fact in answer to any of them. What they usually find are probabilities. Few things at the expanding edge of knowledge ever approach the degree of certainty shown by polio immunization, for example, or for that matter, moon shots. What we are left with, usually, is a best guess based on probability. This drug appears to help most people. This chemical appears to harm some people. Which people? Well, we're not sure yet, but we're working on it.

But even these probabilities will not remain stable, of course. Odds are often based upon the best scientific knowledge and technology currently available. Tomorrow's odds will depend on tomorrow's best estimates. Improved mathematical analyses or deeper scientific scrutiny can change our odds just by providing more precise perceptions of reality. The U.S. Weather Service constantly updates its statistical formulas to improve our guesses on tomorrow's, next month's, and, we hope, eventually, next year's, weather.

Technological changes affect the odds, too, almost like changes in the rules affect performance probabilities in sports. In 1979, for the first time in history, the probability of any human's contracting smallpox fell to 0. Today's odds on surviving leukemia are several times greater than those of a decade ago, and we are promised that tomorrow's will be greater yet.

The figures presented in *The Odds Almanac* represent the most accurate probabilities at one moment in time and should provide not only a fascinating perspective on many areas of modern life but some insight into the nature of ever-present probability. In your daily life, the word *probably* may take on an entirely new aspect.

1   The United States

The United States is home to one of the most heterogeneous populations in the world. From the beginning, Native Americans, European settlers from diverse stocks, and Africans provided the materials for a new culture. As the nation grew, periodic waves of immigrants from all parts of the world contributed to the development of an "American" lifestyle as well as an American gene pool.

Most of us see only a small piece of our collective way of life. A couple of friendly wagers will probably be enough to convince you that most of us have a somewhat inaccurate perception of our fellow Americans and "our" own way of life. What are the odds that any one of us lives alone, has blue eyes, drives a truck for a living, or reads more than twenty books a year? These probabilities, as well as some intriguing ones about our fifty states, our home and family life, and our ethnic makeup, are found in the pages that follow.

POPULATION

If you are a U.S. citizen, you are one among more than 220 million. If a lottery among the entire population were held, your chances of winning would therefore be approximately 1 in 220 million. Imagine that we hold such an American Sweepstakes and select one U.S. citizen. What are the chances that the grand prize winner. . . ?

lives in a state bordering on the 17,000-mile U.S. coastline	3 in 4	75 in 100
lives in an urban area	3 in 4	73.5 in 100

In 1800, 95 percent of the U.S. population lived in rural areas. It is anticipated that 85 percent of the population will live in cities and suburbs by the year 2000.

lives in a town of 2,500 people or more	2 in 3	68 in 100
is a member of an organized religion	3 in 5	61 in 100
will take a vacation next year	3 in 5	58 in 100
is female	1 in 2	51.4 in 100
has tooth decay	1 in 2	51 in 100
sleeps 7½ hours or less a night	1 in 2	50 in 100
ate 1,450 pounds or more of food last year	1 in 2	50 in 100

The average food consumption of a teenager in the USA is nearly a ton (1,920 pounds) per year.

will drink alcohol at some time during the next year	1 in 2	48 in 100
attends a church service once a week	2 in 5	41 in 100
is shy	2 in 5	40 in 100

Approximately 30 percent of the population feels shy more than half the time, and 4 percent feels shy all the time.

has brown eyes	2 in 5	40 in 100
lives in a suburb	2 in 5	39 in 100
has blue eyes	1 in 3	33 in 100
will be interviewed next year by a professional polling organization	1 in 3	32 in 100

is twenty-one to forty-four years old	1 in 3	32	in 100
lives in a central city area	2 in 7	28	in 100
lives in an apartment	2 in 7	28	in 100
is a student	1 in 4	25	in 100
is not allergic to poison ivy	1 in 4	25	in 100
read more than twenty books last year	1 in 4	25	in 100
is Roman Catholic	1 in 4	23	in 100
is less than sixteen years of age	1 in 4	23	in 100
receives government payments for social security, welfare, or supplemental income	1 in 5	22	in 100
lives alone	1 in 5	21	in 100
is forty-five to sixty-five years old	1 in 5	20	in 100
is an immigrant or has a parent who is an immigrant	1 in 5	19	in 100
has tried marijuana at least once	1 in 5	19	in 100
lives in either California or New York	1 in 6	17.5	in 100
works for federal, state, city, or county government	1 in 6	17	in 100
has a "wandering eye" caused by a weak ocular muscle	1 in 6	17	in 100
plays a musical instrument	1 in 6	17	in 100
receives a monthly social security check	1 in 6	17	in 100
has straight hair	1 in 7	14	in 100
is Baptist	1 in 8	13	in 100
is of English ancestry	1 in 8	12	in 100
has dyed hair	1 in 9	12	in 100
attended a convention last year	1 in 9	12	in 100
is black	1 in 9	11	in 100
is sixty-five or older	1 in 9	11	in 100

In 1900, there was only a 4-percent chance of selecting someone sixty-five or older. At the beginning of the twentieth century, life expectancy was forty-seven years. Today, it is seventy-three years. By 2050, 1 in 6 persons in the USA will be sixty-five or older.

is left-handed	1 in 10	10	in 100
is of German ancestry	1 in 10	10	in 100

does not use English as his or her primary language	1 in 10	10 in 100
is Hispanic	1 in 11	9 in 100
currently smokes marijuana	1 in 14	7 in 100
is less than five years old	1 in 14	7 in 100
is named George, David, John, James, William, or Charles	1 in 16	6 in 100
lives in either New York City, Chicago, or Los Angeles	1 in 18	6 in 100
plays the piano	1 in 18	6 in 100
is a Swedish-American	1 in 18	5.5 in 100
is an only child	1 in 20	5 in 100
was born in another country	1 in 20	5 in 100
is a college student	1 in 20	5 in 100
is an Italian-American	1 in 20	5 in 100
has red hair	1 in 25	4 in 100
is Jewish	1 in 30	3 in 100
is an adult woman with naturally blond hair	1 in 30	3 in 100
is institutionalized	1 in 33	3 in 100
is a farmer	1 in 33	3 in 100

In the early 1900s, 1 in 3 persons in the USA farmed.

is a secretary or typist	1 in 50	2 in 100
is a blue-eyed piano player	1 in 54	1.8 in 100
is a Polish-American	1 in 55	1.8 in 100
is of Greek ancestry	1 in 75	1.3 in 100
is a teacher	1 in 80	1.25 in 100
cannot read or write	1 in 80	1.25 in 100

Illiteracy can be defined in many ways. This particular probability counts only the poorest readers among us. Some data indicate that more than 10 percent of us are unable to read or write well enough to function fully in society.

is named Smith	1 in 92	1.1 in 100
cooks or waits on tables for a living	1 in 95	1.1 in 100
is a retail salesperson	1 in 100	1 in 100
drives a truck for a living	1 in 110	

will die next year   1 in 114

Infant mortality keeps this figure high. If a baby survives infancy, the chances of long life markedly increase. People sixty-five or older account for 80 percent of the deaths in the USA.

is a bookkeeper   1 in 120
is a Johnson   1 in 120
is a Brown   1 in 165
is a Jones   1 in 168
works on an assembly line   1 in 185
is a Miller   1 in 190
is a registered nurse   1 in 200
works for AT&T   1 in 200
is a Davis   1 in 210
is a construction laborer   1 in 230
is listed in *Who's Who in America*   1 in 250
wears dentures   1 in 250
is a Wilson   1 in 275
can fly an airplane   1 in 300
works for the U.S. Postal Service   1 in 334
is a Jackson   1 in 350
is a Clark   1 in 399
is a millionaire   1 in 400

In 1968, 1 in 900 citizens was a millionaire. If inflation averages 10 percent over the next decade, 1 in 300 will be a millionaire by 1990.

is a Hungarian-American   1 in 400
is a Japanese-American   1 in 400
is a Lewis   1 in 442
is a prostitute   1 in 500
wears mildly radioactive dentures   1 in 500

The porcelain compound in some prosthetic teeth is laced with uranium to glow slightly so that the teeth will not appear dull green.

is a physician   1 in 535
is a manufacturer's sales
    representative   1 in 600
is a Carter   1 in 630
is a social worker   1 in 650

lives in Wyoming	1 in 650
is a computer programmer	1 in 800
works as a bartender	1 in 800
has a parent who was born in Ireland	1 in 1,000
will file for bankruptcy next year	1 in 1,000
is a psychologist	1 in 2,000
belongs to a nudist colony	1 in 4,000
works for United Airlines	1 in 4,000
is a bartender named George, David, John, James, William, or Charles	1 in 12,800
is a Smith who wears mildly radioactive dentures	1 in 75,000
is a left-handed nudist with tooth decay	1 in 80,000

Senior Citizens

Characteristics   An individual in the USA is at least sixty-five years old. What are the chances that he or she wears corrective lenses? 95 in 100

is mobile and self-sufficient	80 in 100
lives in his or her own home	77 in 100
lives with a spouse	51 in 100
has some form of arthritis	44 in 100
has hypertension	35 in 100
lives alone	26 in 100
survives on an income below the official federal poverty level	13 in 100
has a college degree	10 in 100
is senile	8 in 100
lives in a nursing home	4 in 100
will fracture a hip next year	1 in 120

Gender   Choose at random an individual in the USA who is sixty-five years of age or older. What are the chances that this person is a woman?   59 in 100
Of those eighty-five years old or older, 68.4 percent are women.

Ethnic Backgrounds
Median Ages A Jewish American lives in the USA. What are the chances that he or she is less than forty-five years old?   1 in 2
In contrast, half of all Irish-Americans are younger than thirty-seven; half of all Italian-Americans, under thirty-six; half of all black Americans, under twenty-four; and half of all Mexican-Americans, under twenty-one. The median age of the entire U.S. population is thirty.

Hungarian-Americans A person is a Hungarian-American. What are the chances that he or she lives in New York City?   15 in 100
   in California   10 in 100

Italian-Americans A person is an Italian-American. What are the chances that he or she lives within 250 miles of New York City?
43 in 100

New York City, 1890 What are the chances that a person residing in New York City in 1890 was either an immigrant or the son or daughter of at least one immigrant parent?   84 in 100
The majority of laborers, tailors, carpenters, and bricklayers were immigrants.

DAILY LIVING

Family Life
Family Size Two-person families comprise 38.5 percent of all U.S. families. What are the chances that a given U.S. family is composed of three persons?   21 in 100
   of four persons   19.9 in 100
   of five or more persons   21   in 100
The average household in the USA in 1980 consists of fewer than three people (2.81). In 1890, the average was five people per household.

Annual Income Choose at random any family living in the USA. What are the chances that the annual family income is greater than $16,000 a year?   1 in 2

In the last fifty years, the median family income has risen to this level from less than $2,000. In 1940, the figure was $5,000; in 1960, $9,400. Today, however, 63 percent of U.S. families have two wage earners, while in 1929, only 10 percent did.

AFDC Payments   A family receives AFDC (Aid to Families with Dependent Children). What are the chances that the family lives in one of the nation's six largest cities?   14 in 100
   is white   53 in 100

Children Under Eighteen   A U.S. youth is less than eighteen years old. What are the chances that he or she is being raised by a single parent?   18 in 100
The majority of U.S. households (53%) contain no children less than eighteen years old.

A child is born in the United States. What are the chances that he or she will live with both natural parents until his or her eighteenth birthday?   52 in 100

A child attends school in the USA. What are the chances that he or she lives with both natural parents?   74 in 100
   with his or her mother only   15 in 100
   with one natural parent and a
     stepparent   9 in 100
   with his or her father only   1 in 100

Child Custody   A child's parents divorce. What are the chances that custody of the child will be awarded to the mother?   9 in 10

Discipline   What is the probability that a parent in the USA will use physical means to discipline his or her children?   9 in 10

Parent-Child Interaction   At any given waking moment, what is the probability that a one-year-old child is attempting to interact with his or her parent?   1 in 10

Comic-Book Readers   A child is between eight and ten years old.

What are the chances that he or she is a comic-book reader?
92 in 100
Even among five-to-seven-year-olds, 82 percent regularly read comic books.

Inoculations   A child in the USA is within a year of kindergarten. What are the chances that the child has been properly inoculated against the major childhood diseases?   3 in 5

Dental Visits   A child less than seventeen years old lives in the USA. What are the chances that he or she has never been to a dentist? 3 in 10

Life Insurance   A family is headed by a married couple. What are the chances that they own at least one life insurance policy?   9 in 10

Automobiles   A person lives in a suburban community in the USA. What are the chances that his or her home maintains two automobiles?   54 in 100

Marijuana   A person living in the USA is over fifty. What are the chances that he or she has smoked marijuana at least once?   1 in 33
Among those eighteen to twenty-five, the figure is 2 in 3, while for college students, 3 in 4 admit having tried marijuana at some point.

Home Accidents   What are any given individual's chances of dying from an accident in his or her home this year?   1 in 10,000

Shopping   A shopper checks out of a supermarket in the USA. What are the chances that he or she bought milk?   42 in 100
spices or sugar	22 in 100
soft drinks	19 in 100
canned soup	18 in 100
baking supplies	17 in 100
frozen juice	16 in 100
dry dog food	7 in 100

The average shopper spends 27 minutes inside the supermarket for each trip there. Six of these minutes (22%) are spent going through the checkout process.

Sugar Sources   A person in the USA consumes a gram of sugar. What are the chances that it comes from a fruit or vegetable? 12.5 in 100

from a dairy product	12.5 in 100
from sugar added to food	75 in 100

Garbage   A can filled with perfectly average trash and garbage stands outside a home somewhere in the USA. What are the chances that any given portion of its contents is made of paper?   33 in 100

is yard waste	19 in 100
is food leftovers	17 in 100
is made of glass	10 in 100

Objects of metal and plastic comprise most of the remainder.

Homes

Characteristics   Choose at random any home in the USA. What are the odds that the people there serve coffee?   98 in 100

Among U.S. adults, 25 percent drink five or more cups of coffee each day, and 10 percent drink ten or more.

receive a newspaper	4 in 5	82 in 100
own a color TV set	4 in 5	78 in 100
include a husband and wife	2 in 3	70 in 100

It is expected that by 1990, married couples will comprise less than 60 percent of U.S. households.

are all adults	1 in 2	53 in 100
spend at least $2,000 a year on food	1 in 2	50 in 100
own two or more TV sets	1 in 2	49 in 100
have a gun in their home	1 in 2	47 in 100

This proportion remains remarkably stable year after year.

served potatoes yesterday	2 in 5	43 in 100
had a garden last year	2 in 5	42 in 100
are married but have no children in the home	3 in 10	30 in 100
are a family with a husband as breadwinner and a wife as homemaker	1 in 5	20 in 100

are a parent and one child or more	1 in 5	18	in 100
do not own an automobile	1 in 6	16	in 100
are a family with a breadwinning father, a housewife mother, and two children living at home	1 in 14	6.8	in 100
receive AFDC (Aid to Families with Dependent Children)	1 in 25	4	in 100
are an unmarried couple		1	in 100

The majority of unmarried couples living together (70%) are more than twenty-five years old.

Home Heating Randomly select a house in the USA. What are the chances that it is heated with natural gas?   58 in 100
  with fuel oil or kerosene   21 in 100
  with electricity   12 in 100

FHA Homes The U.S. Federal Housing Administration (FHA) provides mortgage insurance to help a family purchase a house. What are the chances that the house has more than one bath?   75 in 100
  has central air conditioning   64 in 100
  has an attached garage   53 in 100
  has a full basement   16 in 100
The average single-family home contains 1,600 square feet. By the year 2000, this same type of home is expected to contain only 1,300 square feet.

Appliances Someone walks into an unfamiliar house in the USA today. What are the chances that he or she will find a dishwasher there? 38 in 100
  a freezer   40 in 100
  a garbage disposal   41 in 100
  a clothes dryer   74 in 100
  a clothes washer   76 in 100
  a steam iron   98 in 100
  a vacuum cleaner   98 in 100

Farms
Size Select any farm in the USA. What are the chances that it covers more than 360 acres?   1 in 2

In 1940, the size of the average farm was less than 170 acres.

Ownership What are the odds that any given farm is owned by an individual or by a husband and wife?   3 in 4   74 in 100

by a retired person	1 in 6	17 in 100
by a family partnership	1 in 8	12 in 100
by a family corporation	1 in 16	6 in 100
by a primarily nonfarm corporation	1 in 42	2.4 in 100
by a nonfamily partnership	1 in 50	2 in 100

Most U.S. farms (56%) are still operated by their owners.

LAND

Federal Ownership What is the probability that any given acre of land in the USA is owned by the federal government?   33.5 in 100
The total land owned by the federal government is greater than the combined area of all states east of the Mississippi River. Here is the breakdown (chances in 100) by state:

Alaska	96.4	West Virginia	6.9
Nevada	86.6	Minnesota	6.7
Utah	66.1	South Dakota	6.7
Idaho	63.7	Tennessee	6.7
Oregon	52.6	North Carolina	6.3
Wyoming	47.8	Georgia	6.0
Arizona	42.8	South Carolina	5.9
California	42.5	Mississippi	5.5
Colorado	36.1	Kentucky	5.3
New Mexico	33.6	North Dakota	5.2
Montana	29.7	Wisconsin	5.2
Washington	29.5	Missouri	4.9
District of Columbia	26.2	Vermont	4.7
New Hampshire	12.3	Louisiana	3.7
Florida	10.1	Oklahoma	3.5
Hawaii	9.9	Alabama	3.4
Arkansas	9.7	Delaware	3.2
Michigan	9.4	Maryland	3.2
Virginia	9.4	New Jersey	2.7

Pennsylvania	2.3	Ohio	1.3
Indiana	2.1	Rhode Island	1.1
Texas	1.9	New York	0.8
Massachusetts	1.7	Maine	0.7
Illinois	1.6	Iowa	0.6
Kansas	1.4	Connecticut	0.3
Nebraska	1.4		

STATES

Alabama
Farm Size   A farmer works the soil in Alabama. What are the chances that his farm covers 2,000 acres or more?   1 in 100
The average Alabama farm contains slightly more than 200 acres.

Frost-free Days   A person visits Mobile, Alabama. What are the chances that there will be no frost on the day that he or she arrives? 82 in 100

Alaska
People   A person lives in Alaska. What are the chances that this person was not born there?   60 in 100
   is male   53 in 100
   is an Eskimo   9 in 100
   is a pilot   2 in 100

Undiscovered Oil   Oil lies underground in the USA, waiting to be discovered. What are the chances that it is in Alaska?   3 in 5
This, of course, is speculation. No one knows where oil exists until it is discovered. Experts estimate, however, that the majority of U.S. oil discoveries in future years will be in our largest and northernmost state.

Arkansas
Diamonds   A tourist looks for diamonds at the Crater of Diamonds State Park. What are the chances that he or she will find one? 1 in 489
Arkansas has the only diamond mine in the United States.

Governors   Pick any governor of Arkansas between 1874 and 1980. What are the chances that you selected a Democrat?   97 in 100 Of the thirty men elected governor of Arkansas during this period, Winthrop Rockefeller was the only Republican.

High School Graduates   What are the chances that any given adult in Arkansas never graduated from high school?   1 in 2

Arizona
Weather   What are the chances that tomorrow will be a sunny day in a randomly selected location in Arizona?   4 in 5

California
Land   Throw a dart at a map of California. What are the chances that the point will strike a spot representing desert?   25 in 100
 forestland   42 in 100

Natives   A person lives in California. What are the chances that he or she was not born there?   1 in 2

Wine Production   A bottle of wine is produced in the USA. What are the chances that it comes from California?   7 in 10
California also produces 60 percent of the peaches and almost all the lemons in the USA.

Colorado
House Values   A new house is being built in Denver, Colorado. What are the chances that it will sell for more than $72,000?   1 in 2
The average price of new houses nationwide is expected to rise to $125,000 by 1990.

Land   Throw a dart at a map of Colorado. What are the chances that it will hit a spot representing farmland?   54 in 100
 pastureland   36 in 100
 forestland   33 in 100
 irrigated cropland 4 in 100

Population Centers   A person is from Colorado. What are the chances that he or she lives in the Denver, Colorado Springs, or Pueblo metropolitan area?   7 in 10

Connecticut
Manufacturers   A Connecticut factory worker begins a workday. What are the odds that he or she makes metal products?   3 in 4

Forestland   What are the chances that a given acre of land in Connecticut is in a forest?   69 in 100

Tobacco   What are the chances that a given acre of Connecticut cropland is used to raise tobacco?   1 in 20
Tobacco is Connecticut's major money crop. Most of this tobacco is used to make wrapper leaves for cigars.

Delaware
Broilers   Without checking where it was packaged, a U.S. shopper buys a broiler chicken in a local food store. What are the chances that it was raised in Delaware?   1 in 25
Broiler-raising is a major industry in Delaware.

Soybeans   A farmer plants an acre of Delaware cropland. What are the chances that the crop is soybeans?   1 in 3

Forestland   Throw a dart at a map of Delaware. What are the chances that it will hit a spot representing forestland?   31 in 100

Industries   A person is employed in Delaware. What are the chances that he or she is engaged in manufacturing?   33 in 100
   in wholesale or retail trade   17 in 100

District of Columbia
Metrorail   The Washington, D.C., Metrorail is scheduled to be at one of its destinations at a specific time. What are the chances that it will be on time?   98 in 100

Lawyers   A lawyer practices in the USA. What are the chances that his or her practice is in Washington, D.C.?   1 in 25

Florida
Oranges   An American eats an orange. What are the chances that it comes from Florida?   3 in 4
Florida also produces more than 30 percent of the U.S. watermelon crop.

Senior Citizens   A Floridian greets another morning. What are the chances that he or she is sixty-five or older?   15 in 100

Trees   Take a look at any tree native to the USA. What are the chances that the species grows in Florida?   nearly 1 in 2

Thunderstorms   What are the chances that a thunderstorm will occur somewhere in central Florida tomorrow?   27 in 100
Central Florida has more thunderstorms than any other area in the USA.

Miami Rain   What are the chances that it will rain in Miami on any given day in February?   17 in 100
   on any given day in September   60 in 100

Georgia
Broilers   A broiler chicken grows up somewhere in the USA. What are the chances that it is being raised in Georgia?   14 in 100
Georgia and Arkansas vie annually for the title of champion broiler-raising state. Georgia also leads the nation in peanut production.

Workers   You meet an employed Georgian. What are the chances that he or she lives in Atlanta?   30 in 100
   belongs to a labor union   15 in 100

Hawaii
Homes   A Hawaiian resident owns a home. What are the chances that the homeowner does not own the land under the home?   1 in 4

Land Ownership   What are the chances that any given spot of land in Hawaii is owned by the government or one of eighteen corporations? 88 in 100
   by fewer than forty nongovernment owners   44 in 100
   by the government   30 in 100
   by the Bishop Estate   9 in 100

Ancestry A person lives in Hawaii. What are the chances that he or she is of Hawaiian ancestry?   17 in 100
   is pureblood Hawaiian   1 in 100
Approximately 6 percent of Hawaiians have little or no comprehension of English. Nearly 30 percent of those sixty-five and older speak no English.

Waikiki Tourists A tourist heads toward a vacation in Hawaii. What are the chances that all or part of his or her stay will be in Waikiki? 9 in 10

Idaho
Millionaires A person lives in Idaho. What are the chances that he or she is a millionaire?   2.7 in 100
Idaho has the highest proportion of millionaires to population of any state.

Potatoes What are the chances that any given potato product in the USA originated in Idaho?   3 in 5

Illinois
Swiss Cheese A person in the USA eats a serving of Swiss cheese. What are the chances that it was produced in Illinois?   2 in 5

Cook County A person lives in Illinois. What are the chances that he or she resides in Cook County (where Chicago is located)?
48 in 100

Indiana
Natives What are the chances that any given resident of Indiana was born there?   72 in 100

Forestland What are the chances that any given acre of Indiana land is forested?   1 in 6
In the eighteenth century, 88 percent was forestland.

Limestone Limestone is used in construction in the USA. What is the probability that it originated in Indiana?   4 in 5

Iowa
Farmland   What are the chances that a given parcel of Iowa land is being farmed?   95 in 100

Natives   A person lives in Iowa. What are the chances that he or she is Iowa-born?   4 in 5

Soil   A soil sample of Grade I U.S. agricultural land is on display. What are the chances that it is from Iowa?   1 in 4

Kansas
Airplanes   What are the chances that any given privately owned airplane was manufactured in Wichita, Kansas?   3 in 5

Kentucky
Weather   What are the odds of rain in Lexington, Kentucky, on any given day in August?   1 in 3

Louisiana
Sugarcane   A person eats some cane sugar from the USA. What are the chances that it comes from cane grown in Louisiana?   3 in 10

Wild Ducks   In your imagination, follow a wild duck all the way from Canada to its southern destination. What are the chances that it settles in the bayous or salt marshes of Louisiana?   1 in 5

Maine
Blueberries   A person in the USA eats a blueberry. What are the chances that the berry comes from Maine?   3 in 4

Forestland   What are the chances that a given acre of land in Maine
is forested?   85 in 100
   is owned by a pulp or paper company   33 in 100

State Name   Put the names of the fifty states into a hat and draw one out. What are your chances of selecting a state with a one-syllable name?   1 in 50
Only *Maine* has one syllable.

Maryland
Softwoods   A tree grows in Maryland. What are the chances that it is a softwood?   2 in 5

Massachusetts
Cranberries   A cranberry is grown in the USA. What are the chances that it comes from Massachusetts?   3 in 5

Money Paper   Pull any federal reserve note out of your pocket. What are the chances that the paper for the bill was made in Dalton, Massachusetts?   better than 3 in 4

Michigan
Automobiles   What are the chances that a given automobile made in the USA was manufactured in Michigan?   85 in 100

Cherries   A person in the USA eats a tart cherry. What are the chances that it was grown in Michigan's Traverse City area?   2 in 5 This area also produces 23 percent of the nation's sweet cherries.

Residence   A person lives in Michigan. What are the chances that he or she lives on the Upper Peninsula?   4 in 100

Minnesota
Land   What are the chances that a given acre of land in Minnesota is part of an inland lake?   5 in 100
   is part of a forest   40 in 100

Iron Ore   A worker mines a ton of iron ore somewhere in the USA. What are the chances that it is pulled from Minnesota earth?   2 in 3

Mississippi
Land   What are the chances that an acre of Mississippi land is forested?   56 in 100
   is cropland   18 in 100
   By growing cotton almost continuously from 1800 to 1920, Mississippi's farmers unfortunately robbed the cropland of much of its fertility. Today soybeans and cotton share the honors as Mississippi's principal crops.

Missouri
Trees   A tree grows in a forest in Missouri. What are the odds that it grows in the Ozarks?   2 in 3

Montana
Coal   What are the chances that any given county in Montana produces coal?   89 in 100

Elevation   Choose a spot in Montana. What are the chances that it is more than 3,000 feet above sea level?   3 in 4

Farm Size   A farmer in Montana takes a break and looks out over the land. What are the chances that the farm covers more than 2,000 acres?   32 in 100
The size of the average farm in Montana is 2,665 acres.

Physicians   A doctor practices in Montana. What are the chances that his or her practice is located in one of Montana's three major cities—Billings, Great Falls, or Missoula?   52 in 100

Nebraska
Football Fever   A University of Nebraska football game has just been completed. What are the chances that any given person in Nebraska heard at least part of the radio broadcast of the game?   88 in 100
Actually, 82 percent of the people in Nebraska actively listen to each game; 6 percent are "exposed." More Nebraskans listen to longtime sportscaster Lyell Bremser and competitor Joe Patrick than tune in Walter Cronkite, Howard Cosell, or the president of the USA.

Land Ownership   Randomly select a parcel of Nebraska land. What are the chances that it is privately owned?   97 in 100

Legislature   Draw the name of one of the fifty states from a hat. What are the chances that you have selected one with a unicameral (one-house) legislature?   1 in 50
Nebraska is the only state with a one-house legislative body.

Urbanites   A person lives in Nebraska. What are the odds that he or she lives in an urban area?   2 in 3

Nevada

Ghost Towns   A tumbleweed rolls quietly into a Nevada town. What are the odds that it has found a ghost town—a town without people?
2 in 5

Land Ownership   Throw a dart at a Nevada state map. What are the chances that it will hit a spot representing a publicly owned area?
9 in 10

Residents   A person lives in Nevada. What are the chances that he or she lives within 50 miles of Las Vegas?   51 in 100
   lives within 30 miles of Las Vegas   25 in 100
   is a member of a family dependent
     upon tourist dollars   34 in 100
   Tourists spend more than a billion dollars a year in Nevada on gambling, recreation, lodging, and entertainment.

New Hampshire

Forestland   Randomly select an acre of New Hampshire land. What are the chances that it is forested?   9 in 10

New Jersey

Industry   Pick one of the seventy-five largest industries in the USA. What are the odds that the company has a branch in New Jersey?
4 in 5

Residence   A person lives in New Jersey. What are the chances that he or she lives in an urban area?   89 in 100
   lives within 30 miles of
     New York City   66 in 100
   lives on a farm   2 in 100

New Mexico

Uranium   An ounce of uranium is mined in the USA. What are the chances that it comes from New Mexico earth?   47 in 100

Water Area   What are the chances that a lake or a river covers any given spot in New Mexico?   1 in 500

New York

Book Publishers   A new book arrives at a U.S. bookstore. What are the chances that it was published in New York City?   2 in 5
The Odds Almanac comes from Chicago.

City Dwellers   A person lives in New York City. What are the chances that he or she resides in an apartment or a hotel?   90 in 100

is Hispanic	25 in 100
is black	21 in 100
is Jewish	20 in 100
was born in another country	20 in 100
is Italian	15 in 100
is Puerto Rican	11 in 100
is Irish	10 in 100

Bites   A citizen of New York City rushes to a hospital emergency room to be treated for an animal bite. What are the chances that the bite was inflicted by a dog?   90 in 100

by a cat	5 in 100
by a human being	4 in 100
by a rat	1 in 100

New Yorkers are four times as likely to be bitten by other New Yorkers than by rats. New Yorkers sink their teeth into more of their fellow citizens during spring and early summer than at any other time. They show their greatest restraint during January and February.

North Carolina

Crops   Choose a crop grown in the USA. What are the chances that this type of crop is raised in North Carolina?   100 in 100
North Carolina is the only state that produces every type of crop grown in the USA.

Tobacco   What are the chances that the tobacco in any given cigarette comes from North Carolina?   42 in 100

Wooden Furniture   A piece of wooden furniture is taken home by its new owner. What are the odds that it was made in North Carolina? better than 1 in 2

North Dakota
Forestland   Throw a dart at a map of North Dakota. What are the chances that it will hit a spot representing a forested area?   1 in 100

Wheat   Visit any county in North Dakota. What are the chances that there is at least one wheat farm in the county?   100 in 100
The average size of a North Dakota farm is 1,000 acres.

Ohio
Land   A bird lands on Ohio soil. What are the chances that the surface it lands on is glaciated?   75 in 100
   is farmland   60 in 100
   is crop-growing farmland   40 in 100
   is forestland   25 in 100
   In 1800, 95 percent of Ohio's land was forested.

Oklahoma
Indians   A Native American lives in the USA. What are the chances that he or she makes a home in Oklahoma?   1 in 3

Oil   Choose one of Oklahoma's seventy-seven counties. What are the chances that oil or natural gas has already been found in this county? 94 in 100

Oregon
Filberts   A person in the USA eats a filbert nut. What are the chances that it came from Oregon?   96 in 100

Plywood   A person in the USA uses a piece of plywood in construction. What are the chances that it was manufactured in Oregon?
1 in 2

Weather   What are the chances that it will rain or snow in Portland, Oregon, on any given day in January?   61 in 100

Pennsylvania
Steel   Steel is used in U.S. construction. What are the chances that it was manufactured in Pennsylvania?   1 in 4

Nuclear Risk   A Philadelphian lives within 5 miles of two petroleum refineries supplying a substantial amount of fuel to the northeastern United States. If nuclear missiles ever score direct hits on these two refineries, what are the chances that the Philadelphian will be killed instantly?   52 in 100

Rhode Island
Lace   Someone purchases lace made in the USA. What are the chances that it was produced in Rhode Island?   45 in 100

Residence   A person lives in Rhode Island. What are the chances that he or she lives within 25 miles of the state border?   100 in 100
   lives in an urban area   88 in 100
   At the turn of the century, 90 percent of Rhode Island's population lived in urban areas.

South Carolina
Hurricanes   What are South Carolina's chances of being hit by a hurricane next year?   1 in 10

Pines   A tree grows in South Carolina. What are the chances that it is a pine?   3 in 5

South Dakota
Gold   An ounce of gold is mined in the USA. What are the chances that it comes from South Dakota earth?   1 in 4
The Homestake Mine in the Black Hills of South Dakota has yielded 10 percent of all the gold ever mined in the USA.

Land   What are the chances that any given acre of South Dakota land is owned by Native Americans?   1 in 10

Residents   A person lives in South Dakota. What are the chances that he or she resides in the capital city of Pierre?   1 in 60
   is a descendant of Sioux Indians   1 in 20
   is a physician   1 in 940
   South Dakota has the lowest ratio of physicians to total population of any state.

Tennessee
Arable Land   What are the chances that any given acre of Tennessee land is poor or unfit for cultivation?   70 in 100
   is good for cultivation   2 in 100

Texas
Speeders   A car travels along a major Texas highway. What are the chances that the driver is exceeding the speed limit of 55 miles per hour?   77 in 100

Oil   A barrel of oil is produced in the USA. What are the chances that it comes from Texas?   38 in 100
Texas wells produce more oil than those of any other state in the nation.

Mexican-Americans   A person lives in Texas. What are the chances that he or she is a Mexican-American?   18 in 100

Utah
Land   Choose an acre of land in Utah. What are the chances that it is owned and administered by the federal government?   7 in 10
   that the land is arable   10 in 100
   that the land is forested   29 in 100

Mormons   A person lives in Utah. What are the chances that he or she is Mormon?   7 in 10

Vermont
Country Dwellers   A person lives in Vermont. What are the chances that he or she lives in a rural area?   7 in 10
Vermont has the highest percentage of rural population of any state.

Virginia
Harbors   An export leaves a U.S. harbor. What are the chances that the harbor is in Virginia?   15 in 100

Jamestown Colonists   In 1607, the first colonists landed at Jamestown. What are the chances that any one particular colonist did not live to see 1609?   2 in 3

Washington
Apples   An apple is eaten in the USA. What are the chances that it was grown in the state of Washington?   1 in 4

Hydroelectric Power   A U.S. home uses hydroelectric power. What are the chances that the electricity was generated in the state of Washington?   1 in 4

West Virginia
Country Dwellers   A person lives in West Virginia. What are the chances that his or her home is in a rural area?   61 in 100

Wisconsin
Cheese and Butter   A person in the USA eats a helping of cheese. What are the chances that it came from Wisconsin?   2 in 5
Wisconsin also produces 20 percent of all butter consumed in the USA.

Wyoming
Land   Pick an acre of land in Wyoming at random. What are the chances that it is used for grazing?   4 in 5
    that it has coal beneath it   2 in 5

2   Media

Television, newspapers, radio, magazines, and books are a part of our everyday lives. These media reflect many trends in society and create others. For this reason they are a powerful and valuable tool for diverse groups—advertisers, consumers, pollsters, politicians. Many gambles are made in this area; every new book, every new television program, every new advertising campaign is a gamble. The odds against having a best seller or a box office hit are tremendous. Sometimes the odds are ignored and there's a spectacular win; sometimes there is an incredible loss. Many producers and publishers hedge their bets. Changes in content, format, and emphasis are made only after the most careful study of the probabilities that readers or viewers will accept or reject them. Advertisers design their materials and place them in accordance with the odds that their target consumers will be exposed to them. But media odds are not only important to producers and advertisers; they also tell us—often surprising things—about ourselves as media consumers.

BOOKS

The Product

Fiction   What are the chances that the very next book published in the USA will be a work of fiction?   1 in 10

Sales Potential   What are the chances that the next book published in the USA will sell more than 100,000 copies?   1 in 25,000
In other words, 99.996 percent of all books published never crack the 100,000-copy barrier.

Profits   An author has completed a book-length manuscript and has overcome the 90-percent rejection rate to have his or her manuscript accepted by a publisher. Perhaps a year later, the book enters the marketplace. What are the chances that the sales of the book will recover production and promotion costs and that the publisher will make money from this book?   4 in 10
   will break even   3 in 10
   will lose money   3 in 10

Buying: Who, Where, Why

Purchase Incidence   What are the chances that any given adult in the USA will buy a book (other than a textbook) for personal pleasure or information next year?   2 in 5

Personal Spending   A person buys at least two books a year. What are the chances that he or she spends more than $50 a year on books?   37 in 100
This is equivalent to about 14 percent of the entire adult U.S. population (1 person in 7). This figure is based on 1978 prices.

Best Buyers   A dollar finds its way into the income of a book publishing house. What are the chances that it comes from one of the 6 percent of the U.S. population who spend more than $100 per year on books?   1 in 2
Some 58 percent of all book buyers are women, and as often as not, the books that they purchase are for gifts.

Outlets   Despite the increasing number of outlets for book sales, most books are still bought in retail bookstores. To illustrate the relative power of bookstores in the book marketplace, consider someone who plans to buy a book today. What are the chances that he or she will buy it in a bookstore rather than in a supermarket or drugstore? 2 to 1   67 in 100

rather than through a book club	3 to 1	73 in 100
rather than at a newsstand	4.5 to 1	82 in 100
rather than at a garage sale, flea market, or bazaar	5 to 1	84 in 100
rather than by mail order	7 to 1	88 in 100
rather than at an airport, bus terminal, or train station	10 to 1	91 in 100

Book Clubs   What are the chances that any given adult in the USA belongs to a book club?   9 in 100

What are the chances that a book club member belongs to only one book club?   88 in 100

to the Reader's Digest Book Club	31 in 100
to the Literary Guild	21 in 100
to the Book of the Month Club	16 in 100
to a mystery club	4 in 100
to the Quality Paperback Book Club	2 in 100

Although each book club represents only a small portion of the book marketplace, the members are generally loyal and active, buying an average of one book each month.

Reviews   How important are book reviews? A person buys a book. What are the chances that a review has influenced him or her to buy? 6 in 100

The author is about twice as important as a review in selling books. Surveys show that 11 percent of books are purchased by people who have liked a previous book by the same author. The most important influences on book purchases, however, are friends and relatives. Their recommendations lead to 19 percent of book purchases.

Book Digest   A person reads *Book Digest*. What are the chances that he or she will buy a book seen first in that magazine?   32 in 100

Readers

Age   An adult in the USA reads at least two books each year. What are the chances that he or she is less than forty years old?   60 in 100
    is under fifty   75 in 100
Book reading drops sharply among people in their fifties and beyond.

Television Watching   One person reads two or more books every year. Another never reads books. At this moment, one of these persons is watching television. What are the chances that it is the book reader?   48 in 100
Book readers tend to watch almost as much television as nonreaders.

Activities   One person reads two or more books a year. Another seldom reads a book. One of the two engages in one of the following activities. In each case, what are the chances that the participant is the reader?

Visiting a museum	78 in 100
Taking part in a civic or political activity	73 in 100
Working as a volunteer	73 in 100
Attending a movie, play, or other theatrical event	70 in 100
Attending a sports event	64 in 100
Keeping fit with exercise, jogging, swimming, cycling, or walking	61 in 100
Working on a mechanical project	50 in 100

Heinz Steinberg has summed up the research on people's reading habits this way: "Modern readers do not need to escape from the world, but to live in it better." While this may be true, part of the reason that the activities listed favor readers so highly is that, on average, readers are younger than nonreaders.

Bathroom Reading   A person reads part of a book today. What are the chances that he or she reads it in the bathroom?   6 in 100
The study that uncovered this fact also suggests that books have about an equal chance with magazines and newspapers of being read in the bathroom. Sears catalogs, once the mainstay of bathroom readers, have more competition nowadays.

Miscellany

Scientific Love   The *Index Medicus* lists most scientific articles about medicine published in the world. If you opened it at random and let your finger find one title, what are the chances that it would be one concerning "love"?   1 in 33,000

Posthumous Publication   Select any poem by Emily Dickinson. What are the chances that it was published while she was still alive?
1 in 225
After Emily Dickinson's death, her sister found her handwritten works and arranged for their publication. The result was artistic immortality for Emily Dickinson.

Koranic Camels   The Koran is the holy book of Islam. A scholar reads it carefully, searching for a passage containing a reference to camels. What are the chances that he or she will be able to find one?   0
The fact that the Koran never mentions camels has been used to illustrate a general concept: Most great works of spiritual literature concern eternal values and human problems and for this reason often say little about the specific lands and cultures in which they were written.

The Bible forms a contrast to this idea, however, because, while it does concern the eternal human condition, it is highly specific about events and cultural patterns that occurred over several centuries. The Bible contains thirty-seven references to camels—thirty-two in the Old Testament and five in the New Testament.

Technical Words   Any given book uses only a small proportion of the approximately 800,000 words in the English language. What are the chances that any one of these words is a technical term?   38 in 100

Key Letters   Open any book written in English and randomly select a word. What are the chances that the word begins with a *t, a, o, s,* or *w?* greater than 1 in 2

MAGAZINES

Readers   A person living in the USA is chosen at random. What are the chances that he or she will read part of a magazine today?   1 in 4

Subscriptions A person sits down to read a magazine. What are the chances that it came by subscription?   1 in 2

This figure fluctuates somewhat with postage rates. When rates are low, publishers push to increase subscription lists. As postal costs rise, publishers find newsstand outlets more appealing. Some magazines—seasonal sports publications and many comic books, for example—sell no subscriptions at all.

Newsstand Sales A person in the USA obtains a copy of a magazine with a circulation of more than 300,000. What are the chances that the copy was purchased at a newsstand rather than through a subscription?   52 in 100

Highest Circulation Choose at random a person reading one of the more than 16,000 magazines published in the USA. What are the chances that the magazine that he or she is reading is *TV Guide?* 1 in 50

TV Guide has the highest weekly circulation of any U.S. magazine, while *Reader's Digest* has the largest monthly circulation.

MOVIES

The Product

Most Profitable A motion picture ranks among the top twenty most profitable films of all time. What are the chances that it was produced after 1940?   95 in 100

Gone With the Wind, produced in 1939, is the only pre-1940 film still among the top money-makers. The top five, as of January 1980, were all produced during the 1970s: *Star Wars* (1977), *Jaws* (1975), *Grease* (1978), *The Exorcist* (1973), and *The Godfather* (1972).

Gross Income What are the chances that the next film released in the USA will gross at least $8 million?   21 in 100

Of the 188 feature-length films released in 1978, only 40 reached the $8-million level of box-office gross.

G Ratings A movie was released in 1977. What are the chances that the movie carries a G (general audience) rating?   12 in 100

In 1968, 40 percent of the movies that were released received G ratings.

Home Box Office   Home Box Office, a program-leasing service for cable television, provides a first-run film for its viewers. What are the odds that this movie is rated R (restricted audience)?   1 in 3
This is essentially the same overall ratio as for movies released within the traditional theater exhibition network.

Viewing Milieu
Audience Age   Select a person from the audience of a movie in the USA. What are the chances that this individual is less than twenty-four years old?   68 in 100
   is between thirteen and twenty-five   50 in 100

Audience Evaluation   A reader of *Consumer Reports* participates in the magazine's movie poll. What are the chances that the next movie that he or she rates will be graded as "excellent"?   31.6 in 100
   as "good"   37.7 in 100
   as "fair"   21.2 in 100
   as "poor"   9.5 in 100
Movies may be better than ever. On the other hand, *Consumer Reports* readers may be easy film graders or rather discriminating in the films that they attend.

Adult Theaters   Choose a U.S. movie theater at random from a phone book. What are the chances that the one that you select is an adult movie house?   1 in 25

Academy Awards
Best Actors   A male actor receives his first Academy Award for Best Actor. What are the chances that he will win the award again?
9 in 100
Spencer Tracy, Frederic March, Gary Cooper, and Marlon Brando are among the elite society of repeat Best Actor winners.

Best Actresses   An actress receives her first Academy Award for Best Actress. What are the chances that she will someday repeat this achievement?   19 in 100
Bette Davis, Vivien Leigh, Ingrid Bergman, Katharine Hepburn, Olivia de Havilland, Elizabeth Taylor, Glenda Jackson, and Jane Fonda have all won the award at least twice.

Repeat winners are also common in the Best Director category. John Ford won four Best Director awards, and there is a 50–50 chance that next year's Oscar winner for Best Director either will have previously won or will someday win again.

Best Pictures   What are the chances that the movie that wins the Oscar for Best Picture will feature the performance of the woman named as Best Actress?   11 in 100
   of the man named as Best Actor   35 in 100

What are the chances that the Best Picture will be directed by the year's Best Director?   71 in 100

NEWSPAPERS

The Product
English-language   What are the chances that any given newspaper in the world is printed in English?   1 in 2

Frequency of Publication   Choose at random a newspaper published in the USA. What are the chances that it is published daily?
16 in 100
The majority of U.S. newspapers (80%) are weeklies, and 4 percent are published two to three times a week.

Ownership   A daily newspaper is published in the USA. What are the chances that it is owned by a newspaper chain?   72 in 100

Technical Articles   The editor of a local newspaper approves an article for publication in the next issue. What are the chances that the article concerns science, technology, or medicine?   1 in 20

Horoscopes   Pick up a U.S. newspaper at random. What is the probability that there will be horoscope listings in it?   83 in 100

Advertisements   What are the chances that any given space in a daily newspaper is occupied by an advertisement?   55 in 100

Readers and Preferences

Advice Seekers   A person writes to newspaper advice columnist Ann Landers. What are the chances that the writer is less than eighteen years old?   25 in 100

between eighteen and thirty	15 in 100
over thirty	60 in 100

Gender   A man and a woman both work. After they get home, we look in on each of them and find one reading a newspaper. What are the chances that the woman is the reader?   54 in 100

Employed women average 30 minutes a day with the newspaper, while employed men give the paper about 25 minutes.

Sunday Editions   A person somewhere in the USA wakes up on Sunday morning and opens a newspaper. What are the chances that this individual is reading the *New York Daily News*, the nation's largest-selling newspaper?   6 in 100

Were you to guess that the person reads the *Daily News* as opposed to each of the following papers, here are the chances that you would be correct:

the *New York Times*	1.75 to 1	64 in 100
the *Los Angeles Times*	1.75 to 1	64 in 100
the *Chicago Tribune*	2 to 1	67 in 100
the *Philadelphia Inquirer*	2.75 to 1	73 in 100
the *Boston Globe*	3.5 to 1	77 in 100

Congressional Record Insertions   A member of the U.S. Congress places a newspaper item in the *Congressional Record.* What are the chances that it came from the *New York Times* or the *Washington Post?*   greater than 1 in 2

RADIO

Stations

English-language   Randomly select a radio station anywhere on Earth. What are the chances that it broadcasts primarily in English? 58 in 100

More than one third of the radio stations in the world are in the USA.

Network Affiliations   There are ten national radio networks in the USA. Spin your radio dial and turn on the receiver. What are the chances that the first station that you hear is affiliated with a network? 44 in 100

Types   The U.S. Federal Communications Commission renews a radio station's broadcast license. What are the chances that the license belongs to a commercial AM station?   53 in 100
   to a commercial FM station   36 in 100
   to an educational FM station   12 in 100

FM Audience   A person more than twelve years old turns on a radio in the USA. What are the chances that he or she will listen to an FM broadcast?   1 in 2
The rapid growth of the FM market was perhaps the most dramatic media trend of the 1970s. In 1973, FM had only 27 percent of the radio audience. Today FM broadcasts reach at least half of all listeners. FM also dominates certain markets, capturing 59 percent of 7-p.m.-to-midnight listeners and, in some areas, nearly 100 percent of blacks, Spanish-speaking people, and classical music devotees.

Programming
Science   A program on the radio is produced by National Public Radio. What are the chances that it deals with a scientific topic?
1 in 20

Entertainment and Information   Spin a radio dial and turn the set on. What are the chances that the first program that you receive is an entertainment presentation?   88 in 100
   an informational program   12 in 100

Commercial Length   When the next commercial is broadcast over a radio station, what are the chances that it will last 60 seconds?
76 in 100
   30 seconds   20.9 in 100

Impact
USA   A person listens to a radio somewhere in the world. What are the chances that the individual lives in the USA?   1 in 20

Wake-up   A person more than seven years old wakes up in the USA. What are the chances that he or she awakes to the sound of a radio? 4 in 5

Automobiles   What are the chances that any given automobile in the USA has a radio?   95 in 100
In 1952, only 55 percent of the automobiles on the road had radios.

RECORDINGS

Album Percentage   A dollar is spent on a musical recording. What are the odds that it is spent on an album rather than on a single? 4 to 1

Profits   A recording company produces, promotes, and distributes a sound recording. What are the chances that the company will make money from the recording?   1 in 10

Precious Records   What are the chances that the next record album released in the USA will be certified a "gold" record, signifying sales in excess of 500,000 copies?   1 in 50
   will be certified "platinum," signifying sales in
      excess of 1 million copies   1 in 200
Single recordings must sell a million copies for a "gold" and 2 million for a "platinum."

Defects   An individual buys a record. What are the chances that it is defective?   1 in 10
Albums are made primarily from petroleum-derived plastics. Oil shortages have caused some conservation attempts within the music industry and, consequently, a nearly tenfold increase in the defect rate. Industry spokespersons believe that improved manufacturing techniques could virtually eliminate such imperfections.

Disco   Select one of the 100 top-rated songs of 1978 at random. What are the chances that it is a disco song?   1 in 5

TELEVISION

Station Types   A TV station begins another broadcast day. What are the chances that the station is commercially run and uses very high frequency (VHF) transmission (channels 2 to 13)?   52 in 100

is a commercial ultrahigh frequency (UHF) station	22 in 100
is a noncommercial UHF station	16 in 100
is a noncommercial VHF station	10 in 100

It has been argued that the USA could have twenty to sixty stations in virtually every community if UHF potential were fully developed.

Programming

1958   Select one of the Nielsen top-20 rated shows of 1958. What are the chances that the show was a western?   1 in 2

"Gunsmoke," "Wagon Train," "Have Gun, Will Travel," and "The Rifleman" were Nielsen's highest-rated shows of 1958.

1967   Choose one of the Nielsen top-20 rated shows of 1967. What are the chances that your selection was a comedy or a show about rural America?   55 in 100

"The Andy Griffith Show," which combined both qualities, was the top show of 1967.

1975   Choose a number from 1 to 20. What are the chances that the show that was in that Nielsen position in 1975 was a western?   0

was staged in an urban setting   65 in 100

"All in the Family" was Nielsen's top-rated show of 1975.

"Sesame Street"   A three-year-old child lives in New York's Bedford-Stuyvesant neighborhood. What are the chances that the child will watch "Sesame Street" at least once next year?   95 in 100

News Sources   National network news is being aired in the USA. What are the chances that at any given moment the news being reported emanates from Washington, D.C.?   1 in 2

The only other areas that seem to merit a significant amount of national news attention are California, with 9 percent, and New York, with about 6 percent.

Science   What are the chances that the next story reported on a TV news program will deal with science, technology, or medicine? 3 in 1,000

Pilots   A TV pilot is produced. What are the chances that the pilot will be successful enough to launch a series?   1 in 40

Actors and Roles
Representation   Pick at random an actor or actress who acted in a dramatic program during the 1975–1977 TV seasons. What are the chances that this person is a white male?   62.7 in 100

a white female	24.1 in 100
a minority male	9.6 in 100
a minority female	3.6 in 100

Females, both white and minority, tend to be underrepresented on commercial television.

Women's Roles   A woman played a role in a first-run serialized TV crime drama during the 1976–1977 TV season. What are the chances that her role was that of a prostitute as opposed to a secretary? 2 to 1   67 in 100

to a policewoman	2.2 to 1	69 in 100
to a nurse	2.3 to 1	70 in 100
to a waitress	2.3 to 1	70 in 100
to a singer	4 to 1	80 in 100

Villains   A person watches a prime-time program. What are the chances that the next character that he or she sees on the screen (excluding commercials) will be a crook?   17 in 100

Commercials and Advertising
Frequency   An individual turns on a TV set to a network channel. What are the chances that the first thing that he or she sees will be a commercial?   10 in 100

a public service announcement or program promotion	4 in 100

Length   What are the chances that the next commercial that appears on TV will last 30 seconds?   83 in 100

| 10 seconds | 8 in 100 |
| 60 seconds | 5 in 100 |

Two forces came together in the 1970s to shorten TV commercials. Advertisers discovered that the attention span of viewers toward ads peaked in less than a minute and that a shorter commercial could deliver a message with equal impact. Simultaneously, network and local TV executives realized that, by reducing the length of each commercial, more could be presented per hour. Even at lower rates per "spot," more commercials per hour means more income for TV stations. In 1965, most commercials (77%) lasted a full 60 seconds.

Children's Shows   It is time for a Saturday morning TV commercial. What are the chances that it will advertise a game, toy, or hobbycraft? 35 in 100

| a highly sugared cereal | 27 in 100 |
| candy | 13 in 100 |

News Program Income   A dollar is earned by a local TV station. What are the chances that it is income generated from advertising during the local news program?   1 in 2

Advertisers   A local station brings in a dollar from advertising. What are the chances that it comes from a restaurant or a fast-food chain? 18 in 100

from a bank or savings and loan association	12 in 100
from an auto dealer	12 in 100
from a supermarket	12 in 100
from a department store	11 in 100
from a motion picture promotion	7.5 in 100

Network Standards   An advertising agency produces a commercial for airing on network TV. A network standards committee reviews the commercial. What are the chances that the committee will reject it? 3 in 10

Ad Challenges   The National Advertising Division of the Council of Better Business Bureaus receives a formal challenge of a TV commercial's accuracy. What are the chances that the council will find the challenge groundless and not censure the advertiser?   39 in 100

Viewing

Popularity   What are the chances that in any given home in the USA there is a TV set?   98 in 100

there are two TV sets	35 in 100
TV is watched every day	67 in 100
TV is never watched	2 in 100

Children   A three-year-old child is engaged in one of his or her many daily activities. What are the chances that the child is watching TV? 18 in 100

Gender   We look in on a married couple in the USA, one of whom is watching television. What are the chances that the viewer is the husband?   61 in 100
If the wife does not hold a job outside the home, the chances are about 50–50 that she will be watching TV at any given time.

Market Areas   A person watches a TV program in the USA. What are the chances that the viewer lives in the market area centered in New York City?   8.4 in 100

Los Angeles	5.3 in 100
Chicago	3.8 in 100
Philadelphia	3.2 in 100
Miles City–Glendioc, Montana	less than 1 in 1,000

Political Viewing   What is the probability that any specific adult in the USA will watch a 30-minute TV program concerning presidential candidates?   1 in 20
Among the "least informed" adults, this likelihood falls to 1 in 35.

Alternatives   An adult in the USA is either watching television or reading. What are the odds that he or she is watching TV as opposed to reading a newspaper?   3 to 1   75 in 100

to reading a book	14 to 1	93 in 100
to reading a magazine	17 to 1	94 in 100

Nielsen   A TV viewer questions how a certain show gets such a high Nielsen rating and wishes out loud that the A. C. Nielsen Company would pick him or her as one of their TV viewers. What are this viewer's chances of becoming a Nielsen viewer?   1 in 33,000

By hooking up little black boxes to TV sets in 2,600 U.S. homes and having several thousand families fill out weekly viewing diaries, the Nielsen Company monitors the TV viewing habits of 84 million households.

Waste   A TV set is turned on during the daytime. What are the chances that no one is watching it?   1 in 25

3   Transportation

In these days of concern about fuel efficiency, safety, and quality of service in transportation, relevant statistics are of interest to a variety of people. The odds on risks are important to the traveler. Most of us could not come close to estimating the real statistical risks of air travel, nor could we assess the change in risk when we decide to take a private rather than commercial flight. The odds on accident causes are important to purchasers and manufacturers alike. As more people turn to public transportation, smaller cars, and cycles of various types, and as competition is stimulated by the deregulation of fares, the odds may begin to shift as they reflect new trends in the world of transportation.

How likely is it that your car will be stolen? What causes most motorcycle accidents? Are teenage drivers the least careful group? How well are trucks utilized in shipping goods? Transportation odds help answer these questions.

AIRPLANES

Ownership   An airplane sits on a runway in the USA. What are the chances that it belongs to a scheduled commercial air carrier?
1 in 100

O'Hare International   An airplane lands at Chicago's O'Hare Airport. What are the chances that it is an international flight?   3.5 in 100

Mishaps and Mayhaps
Overbooking   A would-be passenger purchases a ticket for a commercial airline flight. What are the chances that he or she will ultimately be bumped from the flight because it has been overbooked?
1 in 1,250

Hijackings   What are the chances that any given commercial flight will be hijacked?   1 in 180,000

Lost Luggage   In the course of a journey, an airline passenger takes three interconnecting flights. What are the chances that at least one piece of luggage will not be with him or her at the final destination?
1 in 10

Deficient Airports   The International Federation of Airline Pilots has given "black star" ratings to the world's twenty-two most critically deficient airports. What are the chances that any given black-star airport is in the USA?   1 in 22
The only black-star airport in the USA is Los Angeles International.

Accidents
Risks   A passenger takes off on a commercial airliner. What are his or her risks of being killed on the flight?   1 in 100,000
This is roughly equivalent to one fatal crash in more than six years of actual time in the air.

on a noncommercial flight   1 in 54,945

Domestic Airline Safety   Two commercial airliners take to the air. One is operated by a U.S. airline corporation; the second is based in an-

other country. One of the two planes crashes. What are the chances
that it is the U.S. aircraft?   18 in 100
Eastern European airlines have the worst safety records of all.

When and Where   A fatal air crash occurs somewhere in the world.
What are the chances that it happens during takeoff and climb or
during landing?   39 in 100
Studies have shown that most airplane crashes (86%) occur within a
30-mile radius of an airport.

AUTOMOBILES

Intercity Travel   A person travels from one U.S. city to another. What
is the probability that the trip is by automobile?   9 in 10

The Machine
Producers   Select at random an automobile built in the USA. What
are the chances that it was produced by General Motors?   57 in 100
   by Ford   28 in 100
   by Chrysler   13 in 100
   by American Motors   2 in 100
Imports began to make great inroads in the U.S. market in the 1960s. In
1963, only 1 in 17 cars (6%) sold in the USA was imported, but by 1968,
that figure had increased to 1 in 5 (20%).

Imports   Pick at random a General Motors vehicle currently on the
road in the USA. What are the chances that it was manufactured
abroad?   2 in 10
   A Chrysler vehicle   3 in 10

Mercedes-Benz Colors   Somewhere in the world a person orders a
new Mercedes-Benz car. What are the chances that it will be white?
19.9 in 100
   Caledonia green   9   in 100
   mimosa yellow   6.3 in 100
   astral silver metallic   5.6 in 100

Fuel
Inefficiency   A penny's worth of fuel is used by a car with a V-8 engine driving at 50 miles per hour. What are the chances that the fuel is eaten up by engine friction?   35 in 100
  in a car with a V-6 engine   30 in 100

Engine Knock   Choose any U.S.-built car from the years 1975 through 1978. What are the chances that this auto will develop knock and ping after using unleaded regular gasoline for 10,000 miles? 35 in 100
  for 20,000 miles   50 in 100

Early Fuels   Talk to a person whose parents or grandparents bought a car in 1901. What are the chances that their horseless carriage was powered by steam?   40 in 100
    by electric batteries   38 in 100
    by a gasoline engine   22 in 100
Gasoline, of course, finally won out. The gasoline engine, in fact, became so popular that today 50 percent of the crude oil consumed in the USA is used for transportation—25 percent by automobiles, and 25 percent by trucks, trains, buses, and airplanes.

Owner Hassles
Insurance Claims   An individual files a claim with his or her automobile insurance company. What are the chances that there will be some sort of problem in getting the claim settled?   1 in 5
    If he or she files a claim against
        another company   1 in 2

Recall Response   A person in the USA owns an automobile that is recalled for repairs by the manufacturer. What is the likelihood that the owner will actually take the car back to the dealer?   57.5 in 100
The more serious the safety problem, the more likely owners are to respond. Pollution-device recalls result in only about 50-percent compliance. Television set recalls, on the other hand, reach 75-percent return.

Theft
Risk   Pick a car at random anywhere in the USA. What are the odds that it will be stolen next year?   1 in 143

Professionalism   A car is stolen. What are the odds that it is taken by a professional thief?   35 in 100
At the time that they were stolen, 80 percent of stolen cars were unlocked, and 40 percent had keys left in the ignition.

Two cars travel the streets or highways in the USA. One has been stolen; the other has not. One will have an accident. What are the odds that it will be the stolen vehicle?   200 to 1

Disappearance   What are the odds that the owner of a stolen car will never see it again?   2 in 3

Highways
Bridge Age   What are the chances that a given highway bridge in the USA was built before 1935?   71 in 100

Paved Roads   Randomly select a stretch of roadway anywhere in the USA. What are the chances that it is paved?   81 in 100
In 1904, only 7 percent of public roads were paved.

Driving
Heedlessness   A motorist drives along a major U.S. highway. What are the chances that he or she is exceeding the legal speed limit?   70 in 100
  is not wearing a seat belt   86 in 100

Teenage Drivers   A teenager obtains a driver's license. What is the risk that he or she will have an accident while driving during the next year?   39 in 100
Teenage drivers have an 80-percent greater chance of accidents, and a 70-percent greater risk of a fatality, than motorists overall. Even so, teenagers are not the riskiest drivers. The twenty-to-twenty-four age group has the highest accident rate of all—slightly above that for teenage motorists.

Accidents
Risks   A person in the USA is involved in a motor vehicle accident. What are the chances that he or she will survive?   98.5 in 100
  will be injured   10 in 100
In 1958, the risk of death per automobile accident was 1 in 28; today it is

1 in 68. The 55-mile-per-hour speed limit, better restraint systems, and stronger auto construction have been identified as factors improving the chances of surviving automobile accidents.

Hospitalization   A patient is admitted to a hospital. What is the probability that an automobile accident, in some form, is to blame?   1 in 3

Child Risk and Restraint   A child less than six years old roams freely in a car. If the car is involved in an accident, what are the chances that the child will be killed?   1 in 208
If the child is appropriately restrained with seat belts, the risk falls dramatically. From 1970 to 1975, there were no deaths reported among 3,574 children appropriately restrained before car accidents.

Teenage Deaths   A teenager dies in the USA. What are the chances that he or she was killed in an auto accident?   38 in 100
This is more than five times the number who die from suicide (7.5%).

Fatality Risk   What are the odds that a given individual will die next year in an automobile accident as a driver or passenger?   1 in 4,000
    as a pedestrian   1 in 16,000

Mailbox Collision Fatalities   Pick a motorist driving anywhere in the USA. What are the chances that this driver will suffer a fatal collision with a mailbox?   7 in 10 million
Although this is less than one chance in a million, someone in the USA dies this way almost every year.

Bad Days   A person will die in an automobile accident next week. What are the chances that the fatal accident will happen on Saturday?
18 in 100
    on Tuesday   10 in 100

Suicides and Fatalities   A famous person commits suicide, the news of which is widely reported. How much does this raise the odds of one's being involved in a fatal traffic accident during the following week?   9.12 in 100
In other words, there are about 9 percent more traffic fatalities following a famous suicide than normally.

BUSES

Travel   A person travels more than 100 miles from home. What are the chances that the trip is made by bus?   1 in 50
Fully 97 percent of trips longer than 100 miles are made by car or airplane and only 0.4 percent by train.

Producers   Pick one of the sixteen firms that manufactured buses four decades ago. What are the chances that the firm still makes buses?   1 in 4
   makes city buses   1 in 8

CYCLES

Accident Risks   An individual at least occasionally drives or rides a motorcycle. What are the chances that he or she will be involved in an accident this year?   3 in 100
   in a fatal accident   3 in 2,000
At least 90 percent of all motorcycle accidents result either in injury or in death.

Accident Causes   A motorcyclist is about to have an accident. What are the chances that it will occur when an automobile makes a left turn into the path of the oncoming cycle?   45 in 100

A person is killed while riding a bicycle. What is the probability that the accident was caused by the cyclist's violation of a traffic law?
7 in 10

Cycle Fatalities   What are the chances that a given person will be killed next year on his or her motorcycle?   1 in 666   1.5 in 1,000
   on a moped   2 in 2,000   0.5 in 1,000
   on a bicycle   1 in 11,111   0.09 in 1,000
Of all reportable motorcycle accidents, 6 percent are fatal.

Helmet Laws   A state has a motorcycle helmet law. What are the chances that any given motorcyclist in that state is wearing a helmet?
94.5 in 100

In those states that once had a helmet law but later repealed it, about 60 percent of cyclists wear their protective headgear.

Heedlessness   A motorcyclist is killed. What are the chances that he or she was not wearing a helmet?   85 in 100
    had been drinking   53 in 100

TRAINS

Services
Freight Hauling   A railroad company earns a dollar. What are the chances that it comes from hauling freight?   95 in 100

Commuter Trains   A person in the USA purchases a railroad ticket. What are the chances that he or she will board a commuter train? 3 in 4
On average, each commuter train can carry as many passengers as 1,000 automobiles.

Mail Transport   A letter is mailed from one city to another. What are the chances that it will travel at least part of the way by railroad? 15 in 100
Most intercity mail today travels by air.

Passenger Travel
Intercity Travel   A person travels from one city to another in the USA. What are the chances that he or she is making the trip by train? less than 1 in 100
In the USSR, 1 in 2 intercity travelers goes by train.

Risk   A passenger embarking on a 500-mile railroad trip boards a train in the USA. What are the chances that he or she will be killed in a railroad accident?   1 in 1,200,000

Freight Trains
Length   What are the chances that any given freight train will have seventy cars or more?   1 in 2

Car Types   A railroad car is loaded with freight. What are the chances that the car is an unequipped boxcar?   12.5 in 100
    an equipped boxcar   8 in 100
    a type of hopper   43 in 100
    a flatcar   13 in 100

Cargo   Choose any car of a freight train at random. What are the chances that it carries coal?   22 in 100
    chemicals or allied products   8   in 100
    motor vehicles and equipment   6.5 in 100
    grain   6   in 100
There is a 43-percent chance that the car is empty.

TRUCKS

Cargo   Goods are moved from one U.S. location to another. What are the chances that they are carried by truck?   3 in 4
Trucks move 85 percent of our clothing, 80 percent of our meat and dairy products, and 76 percent of our furniture and fixtures. Fully 78 percent of U.S. freight transportation dollars go to the trucking industry.

Excess Weight   A loaded tractor-trailer truck moves down a U.S. highway. What are the chances that the vehicle exceeds the state's weight limit?   22 in 100

Accidents   A beer truck is loaded for its day's deliveries. What are the chances that it will be involved in an accident within the next 1,000 miles?   1 in 67

4   Crime and Punishment

Crime in our society continues to exist largely due to the unpredictability of any given instance of criminal activity. But in few other areas of our life is probability more seriously called into play. Criminals often know the odds of being caught. Would-be victims and crime prevention personnel consult odds on risks of assault, robbery, homicide, and other crimes. Insurance companies base their rates directly on probabilities. The odds of theft are important to home and auto owners and retail businesses. Odds relating to circumstances of criminal activity are useful to citizens, crime prevention personnel, and law enforcement officers.

If a criminal doesn't manage to beat the odds against apprehension, chance often plays a large part in the detection devices used in building a case, and often in the jury's verdict as well. And in sentencing, a judge must always make a decision based on the odds of a given sentence's having the desired effect on the guilty person's future behavior.

CRIME

Arson
Prevalence   An insurance company in the USA pays a dollar for fire damage. What are the chances that the dollar goes to cover damage caused by arson?   1 in 2

Assault and Petty Theft
Mugging Risks   What is the risk to a person in the USA of being assaulted or mugged for money or possessions next year?   3 in 100

Unreported Crime   In the USA, the risk of being victimized by crime is somewhat greater than FBI statistics indicate. This is because not all crime is reported to authorities. What are the chances that a victim will file a formal report for theft?   27 in 100
   for assault or mugging with theft   33 in 100
   for vandalism   50 in 100

School Crimes   A student walks into a public high school class in the USA. What are the chances that he or she will be robbed at school this year?   7 in 100
   will be attacked   1 in 100

Family Members   A person assaults a member of his or her own family. What are the chances that this occurs during an argument over a spouse's infidelity?   17 in 100

Injury   A person in the USA is robbed. What are his or her chances of being injured during the robbery if the thief is carrying a gun?
23 in 100
   is carrying some other weapon   40 in 100
   is carrying no weapon at all   70 in 100
Of all injuries, however, those inflicted by guns are twice as likely to be fatal as those from any other weapon.

Hotel Theft   A person enters a hotel in the USA. What are the chances that he or she will steal at least one item from the hotel? 1 in 3

Bank Robbery
Risk to Banks What is the risk that any given bank in the USA will be held up this year? 1 in 20

This is up slightly from just under 4 percent in 1973. The absolute number of bank holdups has almost doubled since 1973, but for any given bank, the risk has not been rising as rapidly because the actual number of banks increased nearly 50 percent between 1973 and 1978.

Bad Days There will be a bank holdup this week. What are the chances that it will take place on Friday? 1 in 2

Apprehensions Someone decides to rob a bank. What is the robber's risk of being caught with all his or her accomplices? 61 in 100

Risk of Prison A person holds up a bank. What are the chances that he or she will be caught and go to prison? 4 in 5

However, embezzling from the bank entails only a 20-percent risk.

Crimes Against Children
Child Abuse A child lives in the USA. What are the chances that he or she will be battered by a parent to an extent requiring medical treatment? 44 in 1 million

Some people argue that if all cases were actually known, this figure would be much higher.

Incest A child grows up in the USA. What are the chances that he or she will at some time be the victim of incest with a parent?
as high as 1 in 20

Sexual Molestation A man sexually molests a female child. What are the chances that he is at least mildly intoxicated? 77 in 100
  that he is an alcoholic 40 in 100

Crimes Against Property
Risks Here is a list of crimes against property. From FBI estimates, what is anyone's risk of having any one happen to him or her next year?

Having money or property stolen	10 in 100
Having property vandalized	10 in 100

Having a car stolen   1 in 100
Having his or her home burglarized   1 in 1,500

Murder and Homicide

Victim Gender   A person in the USA is murdered. What are the odds that the victim is male?   2 in 3

Relatives   What are the odds that any given murder victim in the USA was killed by a member of his or her own family?   1 in 4

Killer's Age   A person has been murdered. What are the odds that the killer is older than fifty?   less than 1 in 10

Annual Risk   Choose at random a person living in each of the following places. What is his or her risk of being murdered this year?
Nicaragua   1 in 333
New York City   1 in 7,162
USA   1 in 14,200
Tokyo   1 in 56,338
Spain   1 in 1,000,000

Shooting Death Risk   What are the chances that any one person chosen at random from among those living in the USA will be shot to death?   less than 1 in 20,000
This does not compare favorably with Japan, where the risk is about 1 in 2 million.

Black Males in NYC   A black male resides in New York City. What are the chances that he will be murdered?   1 in 20
In contrast, any given soldier in the U.S. Army during World War II had only 1 chance in 40 of being killed in combat.

Lovers' Quarrels   A person has been murdered. What are the chances that the victim died as the result of a lovers' quarrel?
1 in 14

Female Victims   There has been a murder. What are the chances that the victim is female and was killed by her spouse or "lover"?   1 in 5

Weapons   A person is murdered in the USA. What are the chances that a gun was the weapon?   7 in 10
   a knife   2 in 10

Double Crime   A murder is committed somewhere in the USA. What are the chances that this happens during the course of another crime, such as a rape or burglary?   3 in 10
Half of such murders happen during robberies, 1 in 10 occurs during sexual crimes, and 1 in 20 involves narcotics.

First Threat   A person is murdered. What are the chances that the victim produced a weapon before the murderer did?   38 in 100

Bad Days   A person will be murdered next week. What are the chances that the murder will take place on Saturday?   18 in 100
   on Wednesday   10 in 100

Gangland Murder   A gangland murder occurs in Chicago. What are the chances that the killer will be caught and convicted?   1.3 in 100
This is based on 1,000 such killings from 1919 through 1967.

Rape
Alcohol   A man uses force or threat of force to have sex with a woman. What are the chances that he is at least mildly intoxicated?
54 in 100

Defense Tactics   A rapist attacks. If the victim screams and tries to run away, what are her chances of avoiding the rape?   86 in 100
  If she *only* screams or *only* tries to
    run away   68 in 100

Repeat Victims   A woman is raped. What are the chances that this is at least the second time that she has been victimized by rape?
24 in 100
The researchers who found this statistic believe it to be the lowest probable estimate. The true incidence of repeated rape may be higher.

Apprehensions   A woman is raped. What are the chances that her attacker will be apprehended?   51 in 100

will be apprehended and prosecuted   38 in 100
will be apprehended, prosecuted,
    and sent to jail   18 in 100

Statutory   A man sits in a jail cell serving time for rape. What are the chances that his crime was not forcible rape but statutory rape (having sex with a girl under the age of consent)?   4 in 5

Shoplifting
General Profile   Project the image of a typical shoplifter in your mind. Note the person's age, sex, and *modus operandi*. Chances are that you pictured a teenage boy slipping a display item under his coat. In fact, what are the chances that the next act of shoplifting in the USA will be committed by a person over twenty?   74 in 100
    between twenty-one and thirty   38 in 100
    between thirty-one and sixty   31 in 100
    who is female   55 in 100
    who conceals an item in clothing   37 in 100
    who conceals an item in a
       shopping bag   36 in 100
    who conceals an item in a purse   19 in 100
    who conceals an item in a briefcase   7 in 100
    who switches price tags   1 in 100

Apprehensions   What are the chances that the next person to shoplift will be caught?   1 in 35
    will go to jail   1 in 1,200
A shoplifting attempt from a store that has declared all-out technological war against shoplifters faces a better than 50–50 risk of being discovered.

Violent Crime
Prevalence   Within the next 31 seconds, a violent crime will occur somewhere in the USA. What are the chances that it will be an aggravated assault?   50 in 100
    a murder   25 in 100
    a forcible rape   7 in 100
When all crimes in the USA, violent and nonviolent, are considered, one crime occurs on the average of every 3 seconds.

Repeat Victims   A person is the victim of a violent crime. What are the chances that this is at least the second time that he or she has been victimized?   28 in 100

Blacks   A black person in the USA is assaulted, robbed, or raped. What are the chances that the attacker is also black?   87 in 100
More blacks were killed by other blacks during 1977 than died during the Vietnam War.

Youth in Crime
Arraignments   What is the probability that any given child between the ages of ten and seventeen will go to court this year for illegal activities?   3 in 100

Special Youth Crimes   A teenage girl is an inmate of a youth deten-tion center, a correctional center, or a similar institution. What is the probability that she is there because of an act that would not be a crime for an adult (running away from home, for example)?
70 in 100
For boys, the probability is 23 in 100.

Types of Involvement   A child is between ten and seventeen years old. What are the chances that he or she will be involved this year in a homicide?   31 in 1 million
   in an aggravated assault   630 in 1 million
   in commiting rape   103 in 1 million

Age of Victims   An adolescent commits a crime. What are the chances that the victim is another adolescent?   41 in 100
   an elderly person   10 in 100
   a child under thirteen   10 in 100

Abuse of Parents   In a two-parent family with at least one child be-tween three and seventeen years old, what are the chances that a child will intentionally hurt (hit, stab, beat, or shoot) a parent at least once a year?   1 in 10
There is reason to believe that violence occurs more often in single-parent families than in two-parent families. Between 1,500 and 2,000 parents a year are killed by their children.

Gang Victims A teen gang member injures someone. What are the chances that the victim belongs to the same gang?   3 in 5
Even in the largest U.S. cities, less than 10 percent of teenage boys belong to gangs. In ghetto areas, however, the figure is much higher.

Fear An elderly citizen lives in a large U.S. city. What are the chances that he or she stays home after 3:00 p.m., when school lets out, because of a fear of teenagers?   1 in 5

CRIME DETECTION

Lineups Police in the USA and Great Britain organize a lineup to identify a suspect. What are the chances that a witness will identify *someone* in the lineup?   7 in 10

Hypnosis A person is the victim of a crime but cannot remember any details. What are the chances that hypnosis will yield valuable information?   3 in 5
   that the information will lead to
      an arrest   1 in 5

Voice Analysis. A voice analyzer is used to ascertain whether a criminal suspect is telling the truth or lying. What are the chances that the analyzer will correctly indicate the suspect's guilt or innocence? 55 in 100

Computer Crime Someone uses a computer to commit a crime. What are the chances that he or she will be found out?   1 in 100

JUSTICE SYSTEM

Pretrial
Unsolved Crimes A crime is committed and reported to the police. What are the chances that the culprit will never be known?   3 in 5

Dropped Charges A person faces felony charges from the Los Angeles Police. What are the chances that the charges will eventually be dropped?   1 in 2

Full Trials   A person in the USA will ultimately be convicted of a crime. What are the chances that he or she will receive a full trial?
1 in 10
The rest will plead Guilty, usually as the result of plea bargaining.

Jury Trials
Verdicts.   A person faces trial by jury. What are the chances that he or she will be acquitted?   33 in 100
   will be found guilty   63 in 100
Fewer than 5 in 100 trials result in hung juries.

Jury Workings   A twelve-person trial jury takes its first vote, and more than half the jurors vote Guilty. What are the chances that the defendant can still avoid a Guilty verdict?   14 in 100
In 5 percent of the cases, the defendant will ultimately be acquitted. In 9 percent, there will be a hung jury.

   If fewer than half the jurors initially
      vote Guilty   98 in 100
Of these instances, 91 percent will eventually result in acquittal, 7 percent in hung juries.

These are U.S. figures. In Germany, only a simple majority is required for a Guilty verdict, while in France, a two-thirds majority is needed. The jury must vote unanimously for a defendant to be convicted in the USA.

Judge-Jury Concurrence   A jury finds a defendant not guilty. What are the chances that the judge, had he or she made the decision, would have agreed with the jury's decision?   42 in 100
   If the jury had voted Guilty   96 in 100
Judges, on average, tend to be more strict with defendants than are juries.

Insanity Judgments   Choose at random one murder case currently being tried in the courts. What are the chances that the defendant will be judged insane?   1 in 25
Defendants who have been judged innocent by reason of insanity, however, are just as likely to repeat their crimes when released as are convicted criminals.

Two defendants in separate states face juries to hear the verdicts. The first is on trial in Oregon, the second in New York. One will be found not guilty by reason of insanity. What are the chances that the defendant who receives this verdict is in the Oregon courtroom?   9 in 10
Despite its smaller population, there were more successful insanity pleas in Oregon than in New York during the years 1971 through 1976.

Sentences
Recidivism   A judge sentences a person to prison, and the individual serves time. What are the chances that he or she will be imprisoned again?   27 in 100
In certain cases, alternative sentencing has shown promise as an effective substitute for imprisonment. When judges sentence guilty defendants to serve the public and/or the victim, the recidivism rate is sometimes as low as 2.7 percent.

NYC Felony Terms   A person is arrested for a felony in New York City. What are the chances that he or she will spend a year or more in jail?   1 in 20
Of those arrested in New York on felony charges, 80 percent are ex-convicts.

Short-term Sentences   A judge in the USA sentences a criminal to prison. What are the chances that the sentence will be less than one year?   1 in 50
In Denmark, 81 percent of sentences are less than one year. In Sweden, fully 91 percent are this light. (These are overall figures, not considering the type of crime involved.)

War Criminals   Select a person from the 85,802 people investigated for war crimes. What are the chances that he or she was convicted?
7 in 100
    was sentenced to life imprisonment   1 in 500

PRISON

Inhabitants   A person lives in the USA. What are the chances that he or she currently lives in a prison?   215 in 100,000   1 in 465

Figures in other nations are much lower:

Sweden	32 in 100,000	1 in 3,125
Denmark	28 in 100,000	1 in 3,571
Netherlands	18 in 100,000	1 in 5,555

Early Release   A convict enters a U.S. federal prison. What is the probability that the prisoner will be released within five years?
94 in 100

Homosexual Activity   A man goes to prison. What are the chances that he will experience homosexual activity there?   3 in 10
Estimates range from 15 to 50 percent.

Education   A convict is behind bars at a U.S. federal prison. What are the chances that he or she has never earned a high school diploma?
85 in 100
More than half of federal prison inmates (52%) have never attended high school at all.

Employment and Crime   It is often thought that people commit crimes out of the frustration of unemployment. What are the odds that any given convict had a job when he or she committed the crime that resulted in the sentence?   2 in 3

Capture of Escapees   A prisoner escapes from a U.S. federal prison. What are the chances that he or she will be caught and returned within six months?   4 in 5

5   Business and Money

There are many risks for those who work in or run businesses. To achieve success, the product or service must meet the public's needs, and the business affairs must be well managed. Few of those who are eager to go into business for themselves are aware of the probability that their business will fail. Nor are large corporations entirely free of this risk. The consumer must also face risks. Decisions are always being made on the basis of the probability that a given product or service is or is not what it seems to be. What are the chances that a label tells us all that we should know?

Money, of course, is of concern to all of us—how much we have, will make, will lose, can spend—and how we compare with others. The risk of a tax audit seems almost an obsession at times, even if we have nothing to fear. And, of course, investing—the "other" way to make (or lose) money—is in many ways a matter of chance.

This chapter provides odds on many areas of the financial world, both corporate and personal.

BUSINESS WORLD

Corporations

Largest Non-U.S.   A corporation is one of the ten largest non-U.S. industrial firms. What are the chances that it is a petroleum company? 1 in 2

an automotive firm   1 in 10

Largest U.S   A corporation is among the ten U.S. firms with the highest cash holdings in 1979. What are the chances that it is a petroleum company?   3 in 5

an automotive firm   1 in 5

Headquarters Locations   Someone wishes to locate the corporate headquarters of one of the 500 largest U.S. corporations. What are the chances that it is in New York City?   14 in 100

Chicago	5 in 100
Pittsburgh	3 in 100
Saint Louis	3 in 100
Stamford, Connecticut	3 in 100
Cleveland	2 in 100
Los Angeles	2 in 100

Bell Telephone Research   Imagine that you could catch one random dollar of the Bell Telephone System's revenue. What are the chances that your dollar is designated for research?   1 in 100

McDonald's   Select a McDonald's restaurant in the USA at random. What are the chances that this facility was purchased from the parent corporation by a franchisee?   3 in 4

Sears   What are the chances that any given dollar of the U.S. gross national product comes from Sears, Roebuck and Co.?   1 in 100

Government Safety Inspections   A facility in the USA is subject to inspection by the federal government's Occupational Safety and Health Administration (OSHA). What are the chances that this firm will be inspected this year?   1 in 40

For most small business establishments—those outside the most dangerous areas of manufacturing or processing—the odds are about 1 in 1,300.

Office Life

Executive Activities   A top executive of a major U.S. corporation is at work. What are the odds that the activity that he or she is now engaged in will last less than 9 minutes?   1 in 2

Filing   An employee in a typical office files a piece of paper. What are the chances that the paper will ever be removed from the file for reference?   less than 1 in 20

Paper-Clip Use   A person at work in Great Britain picks up a paper clip. What are the chances that it will be used to clip papers together? 20 in 100

will fall to the floor and be swept away	25 in 100
will be used as a chip in a card game	19 in 100
will be bent and twisted during a telephone conversation	14 in 100
will be used to hold a garment together	7 in 100
will be used as a toothpick or ear scratcher	5 in 100
will be used as a nail cleaner	5 in 100
will be used as a pipe cleaner	4 in 100

Grapevine   An executive hears a business-related rumor through the grapevine. What are the chances that this rumor is essentially correct? 3 in 4

Principles

Ethics   Millions of people in the USA are employed in business. What is the probability that any one of these persons feels that he or she must at least occasionally compromise personal principles and ethics to help the company or the boss?   7 in 10

Internal Theft   There has been a theft from a business firm. What is the probability that one of the company's own employees is responsible?   9 in 10
It is estimated that shoplifters steal only one ninth as much as employees.

Environmental Concern   The business manager of a typical company is asked, "Would you authorize spending $125,000 to prevent polluting a stream beside your operation or would you risk a $25,000 fine?" What is the probability that a manager in the USA would agree to spend the $125,000?   65 in 100

in Switzerland	61 in 100
in Denmark	49 in 100
in Italy	48 in 100
in the Netherlands	46 in 100
in West Germany	46 in 100
in Belgium	39 in 100
in Norway	38 in 100
in France	33 in 100
in Great Britain	33 in 100

Business Failures

General   A new business opens in the USA. What are the chances that it will not survive more than one year?   1 in 4

more than two years   1 in 2

Of the more than 5 million private businesses in the USA, only 1 in 50,000 was started before 1800. Fully 80 percent of all new businesses disappear within ten years.

Restaurants   Choose at random an eating and drinking establishment. What are the chances that the business will eventually fail? 20–25 in 100

Restaurant Fires   A restaurant burns to the ground. What are the chances that it will never reopen?   4 in 5

The odds are nearly 1 in 3 that the restaurant fire was caused by arson.

Camera Stores   A neighborhood camera store celebrates its second year in business. What are the chances that it will be able to survive at least one more year?   97 in 100

that it will remain a privately-owned

shop with no branch offices   95 in 100

The most common causes of retail camera store failures are inexperienced management and poor location.

Jewelry Stores   What are the chances that any given retail jewelry store will be in business a year from now?   better than 99 in 100 Jewelry stores rank among the top ten in business survival rate, and most are independently owned. According to Retail Jewelers of America, Inc., a retail jewelry store must have annual sales of a quarter of a million dollars to net a profit before taxes of $25,000.

ADVERTISING AND MARKETING

Advertising Expenditures   Each year, millions of dollars are spent in the USA to purchase advertising. What are the chances that any given dollar is spent to buy time on network TV?   32 in 100

on local TV	22 in 100
in magazines	21 in 100
in newspapers	15 in 100
on local radio	5 in 100
on network radio	1.5 in 100

Cigarette Advertising   One brand of cigarette outsells a rival brand. What are the chances that the manufacturer of the better-selling brand also spent more money to advertise it?   78 in 100 Some examples from 1978 sales and advertising figures:

Brand Name	Billions of Cigarettes Sold	Millions of Advertising Dollars Spent
Marlboro	101.25	43.7
Winston	84.7	41.9
Kool	59.0	37.3
Camel	26.4	36.0
Carlton	10.1	23.9

Comic-Book Advertisements   Randomly pick a page in a comic book sold on any newsstand. What are the chances that there is an advertisement on that page?   1 in 4

Drug Advertisements   A pharmaceutical firm prepares a drug advertisement for a medical journal or for a mailing to physicians. What are the chances that the advertisement contains warnings of side effects or special precautions?   4 in 100

mentions cost	6.3 in 100
gives recommended dosage	14 in 100
lists active ingredients	43 in 100

Coupons   A corporation prints a coupon for a price reduction on one of its products. What are the chances that the coupon will ever be redeemed?   15 in 100

Coupons may be one of the fastest growing industries in the USA. During the early 1970s, 58 percent of the nation's families reported actively using coupons. Today, 80 percent use coupons at least occasionally.

Mail Advertising   What are the chances that any given piece of U.S. mail is an advertisement?   26 in 100

a business transaction	40 in 100
a piece of correspondence	22 in 100

Mail Response   A person receives an advertisement in the mail for a mail-order product. What are the chances that he or she will order the product?   1 in 50

PRODUCTS

Consumer Reaction

New Product Failure   A new product is developed and marketed. What is the probability that it will fail in the marketplace?   4 in 5

Consumer Complaints   A consumer files a complaint with the Better Business Bureau. What are the chances that the complaint is in regard to the poor quality of a product?   9.2 in 100

to credit and billing	8.3 in 100
to selling practices	3.3 in 100
to advertising practices	3 in 100

Most BBB complaints (60%) concern unsatisfactory repair services or problems with product delivery. The BBB actually handles more consumer inquiries than complaints. The questions people ask most concern insurance plans and work-at-home schemes.

Characteristics

Breakfast Cereals   A person in the USA begins the day with a bowl of cereal. What are the chances that it comes from one of the Big Four cereal producers: Kellogg's, General Mills, General Foods, or Quaker Oats?   9 in 10

Christmas Trees   A tree is cut to be sold for Christmas in the USA. What is the probability that no one will buy it?   10–15 in 100
This is the usual figure. In 1975, only 3.5 percent of the available trees went unsold.

Clothespins   Pick a state of the USA at random. What are the chances that you selected a state with a clothespin manufacturing industry?   1 in 25
Only Maine and Vermont have clothespin manufacturers.

Coffee   What are the chances that the next cup of coffee served in the USA will be instant coffee?   1 in 3
When an instant brand is served, the chances are nearly 9 in 10 that one of three corporations produced it: General Foods (Brim, Maxim, Maxwell House, Mellow Roast, Sanka, Yuban), Proctor & Gamble (Folger's, High Point), or Nestlé (Nescafé, Nestlé Decaf, Sunrise, Taster's Choice). The chances are 1 in 3 that the instant coffee is decaffeinated.

A coffee bean finds itself behind a Folger's Mountain Grown Coffee label. What are the chances that the bean was not, strictly speaking, grown on a mountain but that it came from a plant raised at an elevation of less than 2,000 feet?   3 in 10

Diapers   A baby whose diaper needs changing cries somewhere in the USA. What are the chances that the person who changes the diaper will reach for a disposable product?   3 in 5
By 1982, 3 in 4 crying U.S. babies will be soothed with disposable diapers.

Meat   Someone in the USA eats beef or poultry for dinner. What are the chances that the animal from which the meat came was fed drugs with its food?   83 in 100

Pickles   A pickle is eaten in the USA. What are the odds that it is a dill pickle rather than a sweet pickle?   2 to 1   67 in 100

Razors   A man wakes and begins to shave. What are the odds that he will use a safety razor rather than an electric shaver?
4 to 1   80 in 100
This is true even though more than half of all U.S. men own electric shavers.

Rubber   A quantity of rubber is manufactured in the USA. What is the probability that it was derived from natural rubber from Malaysia or Indonesia?   3 in 10
The remainder is synthesized from petroleum products.

Smoke Detectors   A family has a smoke detector on every level of its home. A fire starts in the home. What are the family's chances of getting out safely within 3 minutes?   89 in 100
If the family has only one detector and that one is outside the sleeping area, the chances are 35 in 100.

Soft Drinks   Someone in the USA opens a soft drink. What are the chances that it is Coca Cola?   26 in 100
Pepsi Cola	18 in 100
7-Up	6 in 100
Dr. Pepper	5 in 100
Tab	3 in 100
Mountain Dew	2 in 100

Tires   A manufacturer in the USA orders a load of rubber to produce tires. What is the probability that the order is for natural rubber?
1 in 5
The remainder is synthesized from petroleum products. Radial tires use up to 40 percent natural rubber, while aircraft and machinery tires use even more.

A tire on a vehicle in the USA is showing wear. What are the chances that it will be retreaded?   1 in 5

THE MONEY SYSTEM

Inflation and Democracy Choose one of the forty democratic countries whose inflationary rate reached 15 percent during the ten years between 1963 and 1973. What are the chances that this country was forced to alter or abolish its democratic form of government?
95 in 100

Checks A U.S. citizen receives a bill. What are the chances that this person will pay it with a personal check?   4 in 5
It is estimated there is $80 billion of U.S. currency in actual circulation, compared to total checking deposits of more than $220 billion. Thus, if every American attempted to cash a check tomorrow for the total balance of his or her checking account, there would not be enough cash to go around.

Coins Select any one of the six coins minted in the USA—penny, nickel, dime, quarter, half-dollar, and dollar. What are the chances that the one that you chose has the head facing to the right?   1 in 3
    is made of 95 percent copper and
        5 percent zinc   1 in 6
The other coins are 75 percent copper and 25 percent nickel.

PERSONAL FINANCES

Income
Annual Income Pick a person at random somewhere in the world. What are the chances that this individual survives on less than $75 per year?   1 in 50

Poverty Level A child in the USA is of preschool age. What are the chances that he or she lives in a home with an income below the federally defined poverty level?   1 in 6

Taxable Income What are the chances that any one taxpayer in the USA had income of more than $1 million last year?   1.7 in 100,000
    $500,000 to $1,000,000   7 in 100,000
    $100,000 to $500,000   3 in 1,000

$50,000 to $100,000	15 in 1,000
$30,000 to $50,000	5 in 100
$20,000 to $30,000	16 in 100
$15,000 to $20,000	15 in 100
$10,000 to $15,000	19 in 100
$5,000 to $10,000	18 in 100
less than $5,000	25 in 100

By comparison, the top 5 percent of U.S. taxpayers made more than $12,000 a year in 1958 and more than $24,000 a year in 1977. Some professional estimators expect that 5 percent of U.S. taxpayers will have incomes of more than $50,000 a year in 1990.

Corporate Salaries   A person heads one of the 750 major U.S. corporations. What are the chances that he or she makes (including fringe benefits) more than $300,000 per year?   18 in 100
   between $200,000 and $300,000   29 in 100
   between $100,000 and $200,000   46 in 100
   less than $100,000   7 in 100

Social Security   An unmarried person over the age of sixty-five lives in the USA. What are the chances that this individual is dependent on Social Security for at least half of his or her income?   61 in 100
   for nearly all of his or her income   32 in 100
For married persons over sixty-five, the figures are somewhat lower—51 and 15 in 100, respectively.

Divorce Settlements   A couple is getting a divorce. What are the chances that the woman will be awarded $5,000 a year or more in support?   5 in 100
   will have an alimony settlement   14 in 100
   will be awarded child support   44 in 100

Child Support   A mother is awarded child support in a divorce. What are the chances that she will actually receive payments regularly? 47 in 100

Expenditures
Medical Services   A person in the USA spends a dollar. What are the chances that it is spent for some form of medical services?
11.5 in 100

| on a recreational activity | 6 in 100 |
| to view a spectator sport | 1 in 1,000 |

The spectator-sports dollar represents less than 2 percent of the average person's recreation expenditures.

Food A family spends a dollar on food. What are the chances that the dollar goes to a restaurant?   39 in 100
It is estimated that by 1990, nearly half of all food dollars will be spent in restaurants.

Charities A person in the USA donates money to charity. What are the chances that the gift is given to a religious organization?
44 in 100

to a health organization or hospital	15 in 100
to an educational institution	14 in 100
to a social welfare group	9 in 100
to the arts or humanities	7 in 100
to a civic or public association	3 in 100

Loans

Cosigned Loans A person is asked to cosign a finance company loan by someone that he or she knows. What are the chances that the borrower will be unable to meet the terms of the loan and that the cosigner will be asked to pay back all or part of it?   3 in 4

Repossessions Randomly select any car financed in the USA. What is the likelihood that the car will one day be repossessed?   1 in 50

Student Loan Repayments A college student obtains a government-backed loan to finance his or her education. What are the chances that the loan will be paid back on time?   83 in 100

TAXES

Sources

Personal Income A dollar from personal income taxes is deposited in the U.S. Treasury. What are the chances that the dollar comes from someone whose income is in the top 5 percent of the population?
39 in 100

in the top 1.5 percent	23 in 100
in the top 25 percent	70 in 100
in the bottom 5 percent	1 in 1,000

In 1978, 72 percent of all income tax dollars came from individuals reporting taxable incomes of $16,000 or more.

Unreported Income   Imagine a stack of approximately 215 billion one-dollar bills, representing the total amount owed in taxes to the U.S. government. What are the chances that any one of those bills represents a dollar not paid to the government because it was never reported as income by anyone?   15 in 100

This figure comes from the Internal Revenue Service (IRS), an organization that is probably biased in its estimates of unreported income.

Audits

Corporation Audit Risks   What are the chances that the federal tax return of any given corporation with assets of more than $250 million will be audited?   100 in 100

with assets of $100 million to $250 million	75 in 100
with assets of $1 million to $10 million	21 in 100
with assets under $100,000	4.2 in 100

Individual Audit Risks   What are the chances that any given individual's federal tax return will be audited if he or she reports taxable income of more than $50,000?   10.6 in 100

of between $15,000 and $50,000	3 in 100
of less than $10,000 (with itemized deductions)	2.5 in 100
of less than $10,000 (with standard deductions)	0.7 in 100

Outcome   A U.S. tax return is audited by the IRS. What are the chances that the taxpayer will wind up owing the federal government money?   2 in 3

Disputes

Out-of-Court Settlements   A taxpayer files a petition to have a U.S. federal tax court hear a dispute with the Internal Revenue Service. What are the chances that the government will settle out of court? nearly 4 in 5

Winners   A U.S. federal tax dispute goes to court. What are the chances that the taxpayer (corporation or individual) will win the decision?   11 in 100

    that there will be a split decision   27 in 100

    that the IRS will win   62 in 100

The IRS chooses its cases carefully. Only those in which its chances of winning (and covering legal expenses) seem high actually go all the way to court.

INVESTMENTS

Bonds

Municipal Bond Rating   A municipality issues a bond. What are the chances that Moody's or Standard & Poor's services will give it a rating?   less than 3 in 4

Bond Yields   What are the chances that bond yields will reach the year's high during the month of August?   4 in 5

This is largely due to a lack of buying during the summertime and to the increased number of government bond offerings that often occur during this month.

Stocks

NYSE Stocks   Pick a stock traded in the USA. What are the chances that the trade is handled by the New York Stock Exchange?   7 in 10

Stock Ownership   A share of stock on the New York or American stock exchange changes hands. What are the chances that it is owned by a pension fund?   20–25 in 100

Pension funds are increasing their stock market holdings by approximately 10 percent per year.

January Forecast   What is the probability that the movement, either up or down, of the Dow-Jones industrial averages during January will forecast the ultimate direction of the market for the entire year?
79 in 100
This is based on stock market performance since 1950.

Pre-Easter Movement   What are the chances that the Dow-Jones industrial averages will rise on the Wednesday and Thursday before Good Friday?   4 in 5
These odds are based on the years since 1960.

Midyear Movement   In any given year, what are the chances that the stock market will be lower on June 30 than it is on May 1?   87 in 100

Election Effects   In a presidential election year, what is the probability that the Dow-Jones industrial stock averages will hit the year's high during November or December?   68 in 100
     In other years   33 in 100

In a presidential election year, what are the chances that the stock market will be higher on the January 1 following the election than on the August 1 before the election?   69 in 100
This pattern has occurred since 1900.

Institutional Investors   The director of investments of a large financial institution begins the day buying some stocks and selling others. An individual decides today to begin a personal investment program. What are the chances that ten years from now the individual's program will show a bigger percentage gain (or smaller percentage loss) than that of the institutional investor?   1 in 2
On the average, institutions and individuals fare about the same over the long term. Because of tight laws forbidding the use of inside information in making investments, and because of the greater flexibility that most individuals have in shifting their funds from one investment to another, some authorities believe that large institutions may actually be at a slight disadvantage compared to the small investor.

Commodities
Monthly Volume   What are the chances that the month with the low-

est volume of all contracts traded on the Chicago Mercantile Exchange next year will be February?   29 in 100
April   27 in 100

What are the chances that the month with the highest trading volume for the year will be August?   22 in 100

Beef   What are the chances that live animal beef prices will hit their lows for next year during December or January?   55 in 100

Pork Bellies   A pork belly contract is traded on the Chicago Mercantile Exchange. What are the chances that the final closing price will be higher than the opening price?   64 in 100
    that pork belly prices will peak in
        September of any given year   1 in 5
    that the low prices for the year will
        be reached in December or
        January   1 in 2

Shell Eggs   Shell egg contracts begin trading on the Chicago Mercantile Exchange. What are the chances that the final closing price will be lower than the opening price?   51 in 100

Turkeys   What are the chances that a farmer can get the year's highest price for his turkeys in December or January?   3 in 5
    that turkey prices will be higher in
        January than in February   7 in 10
    that prices will be higher in
        November than in October   7 in 10

6   Work

No matter what your relationship to the world of work, the odds in this chapter will enhance your perspective. If you are considering a career change, knowing how the available jobs are distributed can improve your chances of making the best choice, and knowing the power of some of the obstacles along the way to your goal can help you avoid them. If you have a job, you may be interested in discovering the hazards and risks associated with various work situations. Some people choose to put their lives on the line each time they report for work. But there are other risks as well; how does your job stand in relation to divorce, suicide, and financial problems?

You can gain more perspective on your own work situation and on that of your fellow workers as you discover the odds on job and employee characteristics.

JOBS

Job Characteristics

Job Classification   What are the chances that any given worker in the USA is employed in a managerial or professional capacity?
less than 1 in 4
More than 40 percent of seventeen-year-olds, however, want such jobs.

Educational Requirements   A person has a job in the USA. What are the chances that the job requires less than a four-year college degree?   9 in 10

Nonprofit Sector   What are the chances that the next job opening in the USA will be in the not-for-profit sector (government, churches, colleges, social organizations, and so forth)?   1 in 3

Sears   What are the chances that any given high school student in the USA will someday work for Sears, Roebuck and Co.?   1 in 30

Flextime   What is the probability that any given worker in the USA is now allowed to work a flexible time schedule?   5 in 100
   in West Germany   10 in 100
   in Switzerland   28 in 100

Pensions   A person has a job in the USA. What are the chances that he or she is covered by a private pension?   44 in 100
Communications companies and public utilities generally provide pensions for the largest percentage of their employees. The lowest percentages tend to be in wholesale and retail trade, construction, and service industries.

Inherited Jobs (China)   A new employee reports to work at a factory in the People's Republic of China. What are the chances that this person inherited the new job from his or her parents?   4 in 5
In an effort to curb population growth, the government of China guarantees jobs only to the first two children in each family.

Compensation (China)   A person has a job in China. What are the chances that the worker receives a regular wage paid in money?
1 in 5
Most workers in China are paid in rice or other grains.

Obstacles

Failure A law school graduate takes the bar exam. What are the chances that he or she will fail?   35 in 100
In New Jersey, more than half the bar examinees (53%) failed in 1979.

Phony Credentials A job applicant claims to have a degree from UCLA. What are the odds that the applicant is lying?
approximately 1 in 100

Polygraph Results An applicant is interviewed for a job and submits to a polygraph (lie detector) examination. On the basis of the test's results, the prospective employer rejects the applicant. What are the odds that the polygraph was wrong and that the applicant was actually innocent?   1 in 3

Job Mobility

Professionals What are the chances that any given U.S. citizen with a professional job will leave that job this year?   1 in 5

Over-Forty Workers A male worker more than forty years old loses his job. What are the chances that his next job will be at a lower-level position?   4 in 5

College Faculty An individual is a full-time college faculty member. What are the chances that four years from now he or she will have tenured status?   53 in 100
    will have left the school before a
        decision on tenure was made   22 in 100
    will have been denied tenure   15 in 100
    will still be waiting for a tenure
        decision   10 in 100
These probabilities are based on a national survey of psychology faculty, but they are probably representative of other disciplines as well.

Basketball Coaches A college in the NCAA Division I appoints a head basketball coach. What are the chances that the coach will be at the school less than ten years?   92 in 100
    less than three years   50 in 100

Teachers   A college student majoring in education completes all course requirements and is certified to teach school. What are the chances that he or she will actually be teaching in a classroom three years later?   1 in 2

Congressional Representatives   A member of the U.S. House of Representatives faces an election. What are the chances that he or she will be reelected?   96 in 100
Representatives are more likely to be reelected than senators, but incumbents hold a distinct edge over their political opponents at the polls.

Presidents   When an incumbent president seeks a second term, what are the chances that he will be renominated by his own party?
94 in 100
    that he will be reelected   70 in 100
Franklin Pierce was the only president who failed to be renominated by his own party.

WORKERS

General Characteristics   A person is at work in the USA. What are the chances that this person provides a service?   65 in 100

holds a white-collar job	50 in 100
has some college education	50 in 100
is female	42 in 100
is a high school graduate	42 in 100
is less than twenty-five years old	23 in 100
belongs to a labor union	20 in 100
has a higher occupational or social status than his or her parents	20 in 100
works part time	20 in 100
works for a government agency	17 in 100
has a college degree	17 in 100
is self-employed	7 in 100

The USA has traditionally been a manufacturing and farming nation, but that has changed drastically during this century. In 1900, for example, 70 percent of U.S. workers helped produce goods. Today, the relationship between goods and services has been almost totally reversed.

College Graduates   Choose at random one person who graduated from college in the years between 1962 and 1969. What are the chances that he or she got a professional, technical, or managerial job?   90 in 100

a clerical job	3 in 100
a sales job	3 in 100
a blue-collar job	3 in 100
no job	1 in 100

From 1969 through 1976, the percentage of graduates getting professional, technical, and managerial jobs dropped to 64. Here are the percentages for the other categories.

Clerical	10
Sales	8.4
Blue-collar	7.3
Unemployed	4.7

Smokers   An employee is absent from work today. What are the chances that he or she is a smoker?   56 in 100

Ethnic Professionals   A Chinese-American is employed in the USA. What are the chances that he or she holds a professional position? 23 in 100

Overall, 14 percent of all U.S. workers hold professional positions. Certain ethnic groups—people from the West Indies, Japan, and the Philippines, for example, in addition to Chinese-Americans—consistently break into the professions at a higher rate than the U.S. average.

Postal Employees (Rome)   Select at random a postal employee in Rome. What are the chances that he or she will not report to work on any given summer day?   1 in 2

Women

Professionals   Four professions are listed below. If you were to randomly choose one professional from each of them, what are the odds that the person whom you chose would be a woman?

Accounting	1 in 4	25 in 100
Social sciences	1 in 4	25 in 100
Law	1 in 10	10 in 100
Medicine	1 in 10	10 in 100

Women are moving out of the traditional "female professions." In 1960, more than half of all women who worked in professional occupations (54%) were teachers or nurses. By 1980, only 44 percent of women professionals chose those fields.

Advancement   A woman between the ages of thirty and forty-four reenters the work force. What are the odds that she will be unable to advance beyond the level of the job that she held when younger? nearly 1 in 3

Unemployed Scientists   A woman has a Ph.D. degree in a scientific or engineering field. What are the chances that she is currently unemployed?   3.9 in 100
Among comparably trained men, the chances are less than 1 in 100.

A woman is trained as a physicist. What are the chances that she is currently unemployed?   5 in 100
Only 1.9 percent of male physicists are unemployed.

Marital Status   A woman works outside the home. What are the chances that she is married?   65 in 100

Medical Professionals
Nurses   A professional works as a registered nurse. What are the chances that he or she is married?   72 in 100
works in a hospital	61 in 100
is less than forty years old	50 in 100
works in a doctor's office	8 in 100
works in a nursing home	8 in 100
is in nursing education	4 in 100
is male	2 in 100

RNs   An individual graduates from nursing school and becomes a hospital nurse. What are the chances that he or she will work in a cardiac intensive-care unit within a year?   12 in 100

LPNs   A licensed practical nurse enters a patient's room somewhere in the USA. What are the chances that the nurse is male?   3 in 100

Physicians   What are the chances that any given physician practicing in the USA is female?   10 in 100
  is black   2.2 in 100
Today, 25 percent of U.S. medical students are female, and 6 percent are black. In the Soviet Union, fully 3 in 4 physicians are women.

Specialists   A physician practices medicine in the USA. What are the chances that he or she is a specialist?   1 in 2

Chiropractors   Choose at random one chiropractor from among all those in the world. What are the chances that the one that you selected practices in the USA?   81 in 100

Occupational Therapists   An occupational therapist is employed in the USA. What are the chances that his or her job involves work with the physically disabled?   60 in 100
  with the emotionally disabled   39 in 100

Veterinarians   A person becomes a licensed veterinarian in the USA. What are the chances that he or she will enter private practice?
4 in 5
  will deal only with pets   2 in 5

Politicians
Presidents   Choose at random one president of the United States. What are the chances that he was a lawyer?   24 in 39   62 in 100
  won a presidential election with less

than half the popular vote	13 in 39	33 in 100
never went to college	10 in 39	26 in 100
had a name ending in "son"	8 in 39	20 in 100

These presidents were Thomas Jefferson, James Madison, Andrew Jackson, William Henry Harrison, Andrew Johnson, Benjamin Harrison, Woodrow Wilson, and Lyndon Johnson.

  graduated from Harvard   5 in 39   13 in 100
John Adams, John Quincy Adams, Theodore Roosevelt, Franklin D. Roosevelt, and John F. Kennedy were all Harvard graduates.

died on the fourth of July   3 in 39   8 in 100
Both Thomas Jefferson and John Adams died on July 4, 1826. Five years later James Monroe also died on the fourth of July.

was a university president   2 in 39   5 in 100
Woodrow Wilson served as president of Princeton University. Dwight D. Eisenhower once served as president of Columbia University.

had fifteen children   1 in 39   3 in 100
John Tyler holds the current record for most children.

was arrested and fined while in
    office for breaking the speed limit
    on his horse   1 in 39   3 in 100
This fate befell Ulysses S. Grant.

was a draft dodger   1 in 39   3 in 100
Grover Cleveland was the only U.S. president with this dubious distinction.

was born in a hospital   1 in 39   3 in 100
Jimmy Carter is the only U.S. president to have been born in a hospital.

Congressional Representatives   What are the chances that any given member of the U.S. Congress is a lawyer?   51 in 100
    a businessperson or banker   30 in 100
    a farmer   5 in 100
    a member of the clergy   1 in 100

Choose a member of Congress at random. What are the chances that he or she is Roman Catholic?   24 in 100
    Methodist   14 in 100
    Episcopalian   12 in 100
    Baptist   11 in 100
    Jewish   6 in 100
This is based on the composition of the U.S. Congress in 1979.

Senators   A U.S. senator rises to speak. What are the chances that he or she has an outside income of more than $20,000 a year?
67 in 100

is a lawyer	55 in 100
is a millionaire	40 in 100

Supreme Court Justices A new justice is appointed to the Supreme Court of the United States. What are the chances that he or she will serve for ten years or more?   65 in 100
   for twenty years or more   31 in 100
Supreme Court justices are appointed for life. William O. Douglas, who retired in 1975, served longer than any other justice—thirty-six years.

Elected Officials Of all the federal, state, and local elected positions, what is the probability that any given one is held by a woman? 1 in 12

Military
Army Recruits A new recruit is accepted by the U.S. Army. What are the chances that he or she does not have a high school diploma? 46 in 100

Marine Recruits A young marine recruit participates in practice combat maneuvers. What are the chances that he or she has a high school diploma?   75 in 100
  will reenlist when his or her tour of

duty ends	25 in 100
is black	18 in 100

Religious
Seminarians A man enrolls in a Roman Catholic seminary. What are the chances that he will ever be ordained as a priest?   1 in 8

Priests A seminary graduate becomes an ordained Roman Catholic priest. What are the odds against the priest's ever becoming a cardinal?   2,931 to 1

Popes The cardinals of the Roman Catholic Church elect one of their number to be the next pope. What are the pope's chances of someday being canonized a saint?   5–6 in 100

Scientists

Specialties   A person is a full-time scientist. What are the chances that he or she works in the life sciences?   50 in 100

the social sciences	16 in 100
engineering	11 in 100
the physical sciences	10 in 100
the mathematical sciences	6 in 100
psychology	5 in 100
the environmental sciences	3 in 100

Weapons Researchers   A scientist works in the USA or the USSR. What are the chances that he or she is engaged in some kind of weapons research?   1 in 4

Only a small fraction of 1 percent are directly engaged in arms control.

Other Workers

Accountants   A person in the USA works as an accountant. What are the chances that he or she is a certified public accountant (CPA)? 1 in 5

Astrologers   A person in the USA makes a living either as an astronomer or as an astrologer. What are the chances that he or she is an astrologer?   91 in 100

Astronauts   Pick one of the first twenty-three U.S. astronauts to go on a space mission. What are the chances that he was an only child or the oldest child in a family?   91 in 100

Chemical Engineers   A person receives a bachelor's degree in chemical engineering. What are the chances that he or she will eventually earn a master's degree?   24 in 100
   a doctoral degree   6 in 100

Comedians   A person works as a professional comedian in the USA. What are the chances that he or she is Jewish?   4 in 5

Economists   A person is an economist. What are the chances that he or she is employed by the U.S. government?   5–6 in 100

Foresters   A person works as a forester in the USA. What are the chances that his or her job is in one of the national forests?   2 in 3

Landscape Architects   A landscape architect designs the setting for a new home. What are the odds that he or she earns $100,000 or more a year?   1 in 50

Lawyers   A person is a U.S. citizen. What is the probability that he or she is a lawyer?   1 in 530
In 1900, the probability was 1 in 1,100; in 1951, it was 1 in 700. Approximately 1 in 200 employed persons in the USA works as a lawyer.

Managers   A person is a management employee for the Bell Telephone System. What are the chances that he or she works as a lower-level manager or supervisor?   91 in 100
    as a district or division manager   8 in 100
    as a general manager   1 in 100

Police Officers   A police officer prepares to face another day of duty somewhere in the USA. What are the chances that the officer is black? 8 in 100
    female   5 in 100
    black and female   4 in 1,000

Principals   Walk into a public school in the USA anytime during school hours. What are the chances that the principal is at that moment working in a classroom with a teacher and students?
less than 1 in 10

Railroad Engineers   A railroad engineer works in the USA. What are the chances that the engineer makes more than $30,000 a year?
1 in 2

Stenographers   A stenographer is hired. What are the chances that he or she will hold the position two years or less?   1 in 2

Taxidermists   What are the chances that any given taxidermist in the USA graduated from the Northwestern School of Taxidermy?
9 in 10

Teachers   What are the chances that any given public school teacher plans to stay at his or her job until retirement?   3 in 5
This number is steadily decreasing.

OCCUPATIONAL HAZARDS

Assault
Police   A U.S. police officer reports for duty. What are the chances that he or she will be assaulted at least once in the next year?
1 in 10
At least 40 percent of all police injuries occur while officers are intervening in interpersonal disputes.

IRS Officers   A U.S. government employee is assaulted. What are the chances that the victim works for the Internal Revenue Service (IRS)?
41 in 100
Employees of the IRS receive 74 percent of all threats to government workers. The IRS employs only about 2.9 percent of federal civilian employees.

Teachers   A person is a public school teacher. What are his or her risks of being physically attacked at school by students this year?
1 in 20

High School Teachers   A teacher works in an urban high school. What are the chances that he or she will be attacked this month?
1 in 55
The chances are only 1 in 500 if the teacher works in a rural high school.

Injury
Firefighters   The alarm sounds at the fire station. A firefighter grabs the appropriate gear and climbs onto the truck. What risk does he or she face of being injured in fighting this fire?   2.8 in 100
Each year more than 100,000 U.S. firefighters are injured. Nearly 90 percent of the fires causing injuries could have been arrested by the quick use of a fire extinguisher.

Drillriggers   A person is employed as a drillrigger. What are the chances that this worker will suffer an on-the-job injury this year?
37 in 100

Most of these accidents (43%) involve hands or fingers. The drilling industry has an accident rate more than double the accident rate for all industries (16%).

Jockeys   A professional jockey is about to begin another racing season. What are his or her chances of being severely hurt—requiring hospitalization for at least two weeks—this year?   1 in 10

Mail Carriers   What are the odds that any given mail carrier will be bitten by a dog this year?   1 in 16

Financial Problems
Actors   What are the odds that any given union actor can make more than $2,000 a year as an actor?   less than 1 in 4
In fact, only 23 percent of Screen Actor's Guild members earned more than this amount in 1977.

Farmers   A farmer struggles to balance his financial books in the late night hours. What are the chances that he will someday lose the land through foreclosure or bankruptcy?   3 in 100

Corn Growers   A U.S. farmer loses a corn crop. What are the chances that the loss is primarily due to drought?   68.4 in 100
    excess moisture   11.9 in 100
    wind   6.7 in 100
    hail   4.2 in 100
    disease   1.8 in 100
    flood   1   in 100
    insects   0.7 in 100

Divorce
Executives   A married man is chairman or president of one of the largest U.S. corporations. What are the chances that he is still married to his first wife?   95 in 100
Top male corporate executives have one of the highest marital stability rates in the USA. Middle-management and upper-level female executives, however, face a 40-percent risk of having a first marriage end in divorce.

Police   A police officer is married. What are the chances that the marriage will end in divorce?   42 in 100

Police officers have the highest divorce rate of any occupational group.

Rejection

Circus Performers (USSR)   A person applies to circus training school in the Soviet Union. What are the chances that the applicant will be rejected?   39 in 40

Medical Students   An individual applies to become a student at a medical school. What are his or her chances of being rejected?
64 in 100
There are approximately 15,100 openings each year. If these increase, or if the number of applicants decreases, the odds for acceptance improve.

Merchant Marine Officers   A person applies to the U.S. Merchant Marine Academy at Kings Point, N.Y. What are the chances that his or her application will be rejected?   93 in 100
A graduate of the academy has a 94-percent chance of obtaining a job as an officer aboard a ship.

Veterinarians   A qualified college graduate applies to a school of veterinary medicine. What are the chances that he or she will be rejected?   85 in 100
More than 35 percent of recent veterinary school graduates are female.

Writers   Material for a book is submitted to an editor at a nonsubsidy publishing house. What are the chances that it will be rejected?
9 in 10

Suicide

Female Physicians   Two women of equal age live in the USA. One is a physician, and the other is not. One will someday take her own life. What are the chances that it will be the doctor?   4 in 5
It is a popular myth that among physicians only psychiatrists are at high risk to kill themselves. Actually, physicians as a group have a high suicide rate, and female physicians are more likely to end their own lives than are their male colleagues. The risk of suicide is particularly high among all medical specialists who treat chronic diseases for which there is little hope for cure.

Other Professionals   A person works as a professional in the USA. What are the chances that this person will commit suicide this year if he or she works as a chemist?   120 in 100,000
    as a dentist   83 in 100,000
    as a physician   79 in 100,000
    as a lawyer   54 in 100,000
    as an engineer   45 in 100,000
In the general population, about 40 in 100,000 persons take their own lives each year.

Death
Coal Miners   A coal miner, a construction worker, and a farmer go to work. One of them will be killed on the job today. What are the chances that the victim will be the coal miner?   35 in 100
Coal miners (6.3 deaths per 10,000 workers per year), construction workers (6.1 per 10,000), and farmers (5.8 per 10,000) all have dangerous jobs that pose similiar risks for on-the-job fatal injury. The most dangerous jobs, however, are those of astronauts, race-car drivers, professional fighters, electric power line workers, and steeplejacks.

Matadors   What are the chances that any given Spanish matador will die this year in the ring?   less than 1 in 1,000

Jockeys   It is horse racing season again. What are the chances that two or more professional jockeys will be killed while racing this year? 1 in 2

FBI Agents   What is the risk that any given FBI agent will be killed on duty next year?   1 in 10,000
Only twenty-six FBI agents have been killed since 1908.

Soldiers   Choose at random a U. S. soldier who was sent to Vietnam between 1965 and 1974. What are the chances that this soldier was killed?   2 in 100
    was wounded   11 in 100

Navy Pilots   A randomly selected navy pilot is never involved in combat action. What are his chances of dying in a job-related accident during a twenty-year career?   23 in 100

Police   When the next police officer loses his or her life on duty, what are the chances that it will be while enforcing traffic laws?   17 in 100
    while making arrests for crimes
        other than robbery and burglary   22 in 100
    while intervening in a robbery or
        chasing and catching a robbery
        suspect   18 in 100
    in an unprovoked or ambush attack   13 in 100
    while handling a disturbance call   11 in 100
    while investigating suspicious
        persons   9 in 100
    in dealing with prisoners   7 in 100
    in dealing with mentally deranged
        people   3 in 100
Any officer's risk of being killed on the job in a year's time is 1 in 5,000.

Other Hazards

Kidnapping   An American businessman is kidnapped in another country. What are the chances that he will be killed by his captors? 1 in 17

Cancer   One individual works as a beautician. Another person of the same age and sex works in another field. One develops bladder cancer. What are the chances that the beautician is the victim?   3 in 4
A similar risk (71%) exists for lung cancer.

Unfair Treatment   A U.S. government employee feels that he or she has been treated unfairly by a superior. A complaint is filed with the federal appeals system. What are the employee's risks of losing? 7 in 10

Personal Problems   A person has job responsibilities related to U.S. nuclear weapons. What are the chances that he or she will at some time be disqualified because of drug abuse, alcoholism, mental illness, or discipline problems?   1 in 33

Height   Two men, equally qualified, apply for a sales position. One man stands six feet one inch tall, the other, five feet five. What are the chances that the taller of the two will be offered the job?   72 in 100

7   Games of Chance

Maximizing your chances of winning in games of chance—be they friendly bridge or poker games or casino games—requires familiarity with the odds, and entire—and very detailed—books have been written on this subject. The odds presented here provide some insight into these fascinating games—that are up to a point very orderly.

There may be surprises in store as you discover the odds in various casino games and how they relate to payoffs. These should help you choose your game—if they don't make you stay at home—and probably make the occasional victory even sweeter.

There is also an introduction to the intricacies of sports betting, and whether you do it legally or in a small office pool, the possibilities will be intriguing. (Some of the odds to help you win your wagers are presented in the next chapter.) Winning may be a matter of chance, but it doesn't have to be blind luck.

Winners

Payouts   A player bets a dollar in craps. What are the chances that it will be paid out to a winner?   98 in 100

in casino roulette	95 in 100
in horse racing	82 in 100
in a state lottery	67 in 100

Slot machines pay out from 75 to 95 percent, and keno can return from less than 1 percent to 75 percent.

Casinos   What are the chances that any given casino, over a year's time, will lose money from its casino games?   1 in 50 billion

Dice   Choose any number on a die. What are the chances that this number and the number on the opposite side add up to seven? 100 in 100

BACCARAT

Casino's Edge   A baccarat dealer (the banker) sits at the table with two other players. A nonparticipating player can bet on whether the dealer will win with a two-card total of 8 or 9. What are the chances that the dealer will win with a correct count of 8 or 9 within two cards? 18.75 in 100

Casinos pay four times the wager on this event. Because it occurs only once in 5¼ times, however, the casinos—as usual—have an advantage. The largest casino advantage in baccarat is for "side," or nonparticipating, bets like this one. Participants, banker, and players work with a much narrower casino advantage. The casino's edge against a participant player is only 1.34 percent, and against the banker it is 1.19 percent.

BACKGAMMON

One Man   The man on the bar is aiming for a particular space. What are the chances that he will hit a blot one point away?   11 in 36

two points away	12 in 36
three points away	14 in 36
four points away	15 in 36

five points away	15 in 36
six points away	17 in 36
seven points away	6 in 36
eight points away	6 in 36
nine points away	5 in 36
ten points away	3 in 36
eleven points away	2 in 36
twelve points away	3 in 36
twenty-four points away	1 in 36

This is assuming that there are no enemy points between the player and the blot.

Entry   What are the chances of entering a man from the bar with only one point covered?   35 in 36

with two points covered	32 in 36
with three points covered	27 in 36
with four points covered	20 in 36
with five points covered	11 in 36

With two men on the bar and only one point covered, what are the chances of reentering both men at once?   25 in 36

with two points covered	16 in 36
with three points covered	9 in 36
with four points covered	4 in 36
with five points covered	1 in 36

BINGO

Winning   Imagine that you enter a bingo hall and purchase one card. There are 150 players for this game, using a total of 450 cards. What are the chances that you will win this game?   1 in 450
Every bingo card has an equal chance of winning.

Full-Card   There are twenty-four bingo numbers on each card. What are the chances that all of the numbers on any given card will be covered within the first twenty-four calls?
1 in 25,778,669,578,994,555,700

in 50 or fewer calls	1 in 212,085
in 55 or fewer calls	1 in 10,359
in 60 or fewer calls	1 in 715
in 65 or fewer calls	1 in 65
in 70 or fewer calls	1 in 7

BLACKJACK

Losers   The worst blackjack hands that a player can receive—those with the lowest chance of winning—are those that total from 12 to 17. What are the chances that any given blackjack hand will be one of these "losers"?   43.4 in 100

Double or Nothing   A blackjack normally pays 1.5 times the bet. A player can choose not to take this money and try instead to double the original bet by taking one more card and hoping for a 10 or a face card. Someone decides to try for this double-or-nothing. What are his or her chances of winning?   3 in 10

Blackjack Frequency   What are the chances that any given blackjack hand will, in fact, contain a blackjack if the dealer uses one deck of cards?   1 in 20.7
   four decks   1 in 21

Dealer's Strategy   In casinos, the blackjack dealer's strategy is to hit up to 17 and stand thereafter. If a player follows the same strategy as the dealer, what are the chances that the player will win the next bet? 47 in 100
Many people believe that the player has a 50–50 chance when playing according to dealer's strategy. Here is where the player loses, however: When the player breaks 21, he or she loses the game even though the dealer may also break.

   Actually, both dealer and player will break 8 percent of the time. If these instances were considered ties instead of losses for the player, the player would have an advantage. The player's real advantage (getting 1.5 times his or her bet on blackjacks) occurs just enough to reduce the 8-percent loss on breaks to an overall 6 percent.

Outcomes   A blackjack hand contains an ace and a 6. What are the chances that by taking another card the player will hurt the hand?
38 in 100
    If the hand contains an ace and a 5   32 in 100
The chances of improving the hand or staying the same are 62 in 100 if the player holds the ace–6 combination and 68 in 100 if he or she holds the ace–5.

A player holds two cards less than 10, totaling 14 points, with no aces. If he or she chooses to take another card, what are the chances of breaking 21?   48 in 100
If one card in the hand is a 10 or above, the chances of breaking are 46 in 100. The chances of improving the hand or staying the same are 54 in 100.

A player holds two cards less than 10, totaling 15 points, with no aces. If he or she chooses to take another card, what are the chances of breaking 21?   54 in 100
If one card in the hand is a 10 or above, the chances decrease slightly, to 52 in 100. The chances of improving the hand or staying the same are 48 in 100.

Win–Lose   Two players have 16-count blackjack hands. The dealer's open card is any card from a 2 through a 6. One player stands; the other requests another card. If one player wins and one loses, what are the chances that the player who stands will win?   61 in 100
    If the dealer's open card is a high
    card   83 in 100

Strategy   Three people play blackjack at separate tables in a casino. Imagine that they all receive the same hand: two 8's, with the dealer showing a 10 card. One player stands, hoping that the dealer will break 21; the second asks for another card; and the third splits the two 8's, doubling his or her bet. What are the chances that the player who stands will be bettered by the player who takes another card?
53 in 100
    by the player who splits   56 in 100

Card-Counting   Imagine that you have mastered a card-counting system for blackjack. You play in several casinos until the best possible situation that your system recognizes develops. What are the chances that you will win the next hand?   55 in 100

Card-counters rely on extremely narrow statistical advantages and must play hundreds of games to win money from the casinos. The "best" situation happens very rarely. Counters often play during spells, or "streaks," when the odds are against them. Their probabilities of winning range from 48 (assuming that they never make an error) to 55 in 100. Because the odds are so slightly in their favor (when they favor card-counters at all), counters also use intricate betting strategies, adjusting their bets to the probabilities facing them at any given moment.

Lawrence Revere, author of *Playing Blackjack as a Business,* who plays under ideal conditions, reports that he expects to lose money once in every nine casino visits.

Probable Gains   Imagine that you could play blackjack in a statistically perfect fashion, making every decision without a mistake—not using any card-counting system, but simply using mathematically precise rules for every hand. You bet $1 each time. After 100 hands, what are the chances that you will have won between $10 and $15?
2.1 in 100

lost between $10 and $15	2 in 100
won more than $20	1 in 10,000

BRIDGE

Hands   What are the chances that any given bridge hand will contain a singleton?   1 in 2

a void	1 in 19
four aces	1 in 378
five honors in one suit	1 in 500
a singleton and a void	1 in 2,211
all cards in one suit	1 in 158,753,389,899
a perfect no-trump (AKQ, AKQ, AKQ, AKQJ)	1 in 158,753,389,899
all spades	1 in 365,013,559,599

Here is a bridge oddity: The seven-no-trump contract is awarded the most points and can overbid any other hand; yet a hand of all one suit is just as rare.

Here is how rare a perfect no-trump hand is: If 20,000 people gathered to play bridge, and each person played 500 hands each day, one person would receive the hand in about forty-four years—and would deserve it!

High-Card Points   What are the chances that any given bridge hand will contain twelve or more high-card points?   35 in 100
An average bridge hand will contain ten high-card points.

Outstanding Trumps   The opposition holds six trump cards. What are the chances that one partner holds four and the other two?
49 in 100
    that each player holds three   36 in 100

The opposition holds four trump cards. What are the chances that they are split 3–1?   50 in 100
    that each player holds two   41 in 100

What are the chances that three trumps are split 2–1?   78 in 100

Finesses   The chances of winning one finesse are 1 in 2. A player attempts two finesses. What are the chances that at least one finesse will be successful?   3 in 4
    that both finesses will succeed   1 in 4

COIN FLIPPING

Four of Six   In six tosses of a coin, what are the chances of getting four heads?   15 in 64
Here is how a mathematician would figure this one:

$$\frac{6!}{4!2!} \times \left(\frac{1}{2}\right)^4 = \frac{6\times5\times4\times3\times2\times1}{(4\times3\times2\times1)\,(2\times1)} \times \frac{1}{64} = \frac{15}{64} = .234$$

Breakdown of possibilities in 6 coin flips:
6 heads	0 tails	1 in 64
5 heads	1 tail	6 in 64
4 heads	2 tails	15 in 64
3 heads	3 tails	20 in 64

2 heads	4 tails	15 in 64
1 head	5 tails	6 in 64
0 heads	6 tails	1 in 64

Eleven Heads   A person has beat the odds of 1,023 to 1 and flipped ten straight heads. What are the chances that the eleventh flip will come up heads?   1 in 2

But the odds are still 1 in 2,048 that anyone could produce heads on eleven straight flips on any other attempt.

CRAPS

Winning   A person plays craps at a gambling house. What are the chances that he or she will win the next game?   49.3 in 100

two consecutive games	24 in 100
three consecutive games	12 in 100
four consecutive games	5.9 in 100
five consecutive games	2.9 in 100
twenty-seven consecutive games	1 in 12,467,890

This is the former world record, established at the Desert Inn, Las Vegas, in 1950.

thirty-four consecutive games	1 in 28,000,000,000

This is the current world record, established at the Horseshoe Inn, Las Vegas, in 1979.

First Roll   Someone rolls the dice in a crap game. What are his or her chances of winning (rolling a 7 or 11) on the first roll?
8 in 36   22 in 100

of losing (rolling a 2, 3, or 12)   4 in 36   11 in 100

The chances, therefore, are 2 in 3 that more than one roll of the dice will be required to decide the bet.

Any Roll   What are the chances of rolling any of these numbers on the next roll of two dice?

Number	Chances in 100	Odds Against
2	2.8	35 to 1
3	5.6	17 to 1
4	8.3	11 to 1
5	11	8 to 1
6	14	31 to 5
7	16.7	5 to 1
8	14	31 to 5
9	11	8 to 1
10	8.3	11 to 1
11	5.6	17 to 1
12	2.8	35 to 1

Making the Point   After the first roll, what are a player's overall chances of making his or her point?   about 1 in 4   27 in 100

    of making a 4 or a 10   1 in 3   33 in 100

    of making a 5 or a 9   2 in 5   40 in 100

    of making a 6 or an 8   5 in 11   45 in 100

Pass Line Bet   The pass line bet is the most commonly known craps bet. The numbers 7 and 11 win for the bettor on the first roll, while 2, 3, and 12 are first-roll losers. When any other number is thrown on the first roll, it becomes the "shooter's number" and must be thrown on any subsequent roll before a 7 is rolled. If the bettor's number appears before a 7, the pass line bettor wins. If the 7 shows up first, the bettor loses. The pass line bet is one of the best risks in casino gambling. The odds for winning are 49.293 in 100.

Don't-Pass Line Bet   As good as the pass line bet is for the bettor, the don't-pass line bet has a slight statistical edge. A don't-pass bet loses when the first roll is 7 or 11, wins on 2 or 3, and has no bet on a 12. Thereafter, the don't-pass bettor roots for a 7 and against the shooter's number. If the 7 shows up first, the don't-pass bettor wins. The chances of winning the don't pass? At 49.299 in 100, it is still not an even wager, but for every 50,000 bets, the don't-pass player wins six more times than the pass-line bettor.

Hard Way Casino crap players can bet that the shooter will make his or her number "the hard way"—a hard-way 6, for example, is made by rolling two 3's (not a 1 and a 5, or a 4 and a 2). A player bets for a hard 4 or a hard 10. What are his or her chances of winning? 1 in 9 The usual casino payoff is 7 to 1, providing an 11 percent edge for the casino.

for a hard 6 or a hard 8 1 in 11

Here the usual payoff is 9 to 1—a house edge of 9.09 percent.

Any Craps Bet The shooter prepares to roll. Someone bets "any craps" (betting that the shooter will roll 2, 3, or 12). What are the chances of winning? 1 in 10

Since the odds against winning are 9 to 1 and most casinos pay 8 to 1, the casino's edge is 11.1 percent.

KENO

Regular An individual marks ten numbers on a keno ticket containing eighty numbers. What are his or her chances of having all ten numbers drawn? 1 in 9 million

The usual casino payoff is 25,000 to 1. Therefore, if 9 million people each bought a $1 ten-spot ticket, one person would win $25,000—a profit for the casino of $8,975,000.

The odds and maximum payoffs for other keno tickets are given in the chart.

Ticket	Odds Against Maximum Payoff	Usual Casino Maximum Payoff	Odds of Winning Anything	Total Return per $100,000 Bet
one-spot	3 to 1	2 to 1	1 in 4	$75,000
five-spot	1,551 to 1	820 to 1	1 in 20	$15,000
six-spot	7,753 to 1	1,800 to 1	1 in 88	$20,454
seven-spot	40,779 to 1	8,100 to 1	1 in 620	$29,032
eight-spot	230,000 to 1	18,000 to 1	1 in 1,400	$18,945
nine-spot	1,380,688 to 1	18,500 to 1	1 in 160,000	$1,750

LOTTERIES

Numbers Game   Someone places a bet in a numbers game. What are his or her chances of winning?   1 in 1,000
The usual payoff is 540 to 1.

Massachusetts   A 50¢ Massachusetts State Lottery ticket is sold to a hopeful buyer. What are his or her chances of winning the $1-million top prize?   1 in 11,000,000

New York   An individual buys a $1 ticket in the New York State Lottery "slot machine" instant game. What are the chances that he or she will win the $10,000 top prize?   1 in 504,000
    will win the $1 minimum   1 in 4

Great Britain   Someone places a bet in the Great Britain National Lottery. What are the player's chances of winning if his or her bet is for a 3-to-1 payoff?   1 in 16
    for a 100-to-1 payoff   1 in 300

Reader's Digest   What are the chances that any given entrant in a Reader's Digest sweepstakes will win the grand prize?
1 in 17,500,000
    will win the minimum $5 prize   1 in 450

Consecutive Wins   What are one player's chances of scoring back-to-back wins in a 250,000-to-1 chance lottery?   62,500,000,000 to 1
Incredibly, Walter Hogan of New Haven, Connecticut, overcame these odds in 1978.

MONOPOLY

Go to Jail   A roll of the dice begins a game of Monopoly. What are the chances that any player will go to jail at least once before his or her twenty-first turn?   59.7 in 100

Out of Jail   To get out of jail, a player must roll a double (two 1's, two 2's, and so on). What are the chances that he or she can get out of jail on the first roll of the dice?   16.6 in 100

within two rolls   30.6 in 100

First Twenty Turns   What are the chances that in his or her first twenty turns a player will land on any Chance or Community Chest? 89.5 in 100

on the B&O Railroad	50.5 in 100
on Boardwalk	44.8 in 100
on Mediterranean Avenue	38 in 100
on both Boardwalk and Park Place	17 in 100
on all four railroads	5 in 100

POKER

Straight

Hands   A game of straight poker is under way. What are the chances that any given hand will contain one pair?   1 in 2.4

two pair	1 in 20
three of a kind	1 in 46
a straight	1 in 255
a flush	1 in 509
a full house	1 in 694
four of a kind	1 in 4,165
a straight flush	1 in 72,193
a royal flush	1 in 649,740

The chances of being dealt five consecutive straight flushes is one in 700 quintillion.

Winning Hands   In two-handed straight poker a player holds two jacks. What are the chances that he or she will win the pot?
47 in 100

If the player holds two queens   51 in 100

A pair of aces stands a 55-percent chance to win a two-handed straight poker pot, but the same pair has only a 14-percent chance in a four-handed game.

Seven-Card Stud

Winning Hands In a four-handed seven-card stud (or draw poker, joker wild) game, a player has three 10's in hand. What are the chances that he or she can win the pot?   49 in 100

In a two-handed game, three 10's have an 86-percent chance to win.

Draw

Hands In draw poker, what are the chances of improving two pair? 1 in 12

    of drawing to an inside straight (for
        example, 3, 4, –, 6, 7)   1 in 12
    of hitting an open straight (for
        example, 3, 4, 5, 6)   1 in 6

What are the chances of making a straight, a flush, or a straight flush by drawing to a hand containing four cards in one suit, missing one card from being consecutive?   1 in 4

What are the chances of making a straight, a flush, or a straight flush by drawing to a hand containing four consecutive cards of one suit? 1 in 3

Improving Hands In five-card draw poker, one player is dealt the 4, 5, 8, and 10 of hearts, and the 10 of diamonds. The player tries for a flush by discarding the diamond. What are the chances that he or she will get the flush?   1 in 4

Another strategy would be to keep the 10's and draw three cards. What would be the chances of making two pair?   1 in 5

    three of a kind   1 in 8
    a full house   1 in 97
    four of a kind   1 in 360

ROULETTE

What are the chances that a roulette player will "hit" if he or she bets red, black, odd, even, high, or low?   9 in 19   47 in 100

The odds against winning are 10 to 9, and most casinos pay 1 to 1.

Here are the odds and the payoffs for other bets:

Bet	Chances of Winning		Odds Against	Usual Casino Pay
any single number	1 in 38	2.6 in 100	37 to 1	36 to 1
any two numbers	1 in 19	5.26 in 100	18 to 1	17.5 to 1
any four numbers	2 in 19	10.5 in 100	17 to 2	8 to 1
any six numbers	3 in 19	15.8 in 100	16 to 3	5 to 1
column bet (twelve numbers)	6 in 19	31.6 in 100	13 to 6	2 to 1

Casinos pay each bet as if there were thirty-six numbers on the board, but actually there are thirty-eight numbers. The two extra numbers (0 and 00) give the house its edge of 5.26 percent on every bet.

SPORTS BETTING

Booking Odds   While in Nevada a person decides to place a bet on team sports (specifically, football and basketball). His or her chances of winning are given in the chart.

One bet on	Chances of winning	Bet	Bettor can win	For every 100 bets, bookmaker pockets	To consistently win money, single-team choices must be correct
one team	1 in 2	$11	$10	$100	53 in 100
a two-team parlay	1 in 4	$10	$24	$400	65 in 100
a three-team parlay	1 in 8	$10	$50	$375	59 in 100
a four-team parlay	1 in 16	$10	$90	$437.50	58 in 100

Baseball Bets

For many people, baseball has the most difficult sports-betting system to understand. It is also the least profitable for bookmakers, whose profit margin on baseball betting is lower than for virtually any other gambling attraction. The best bargains for the bettor are the 15-cent and 20-cent lines offered where gambling is legal. Both systems are constructed to equalize all teams' chances as much as possible. This makes the bettor's chances of winning or losing money in the long run virtually equal, regardless of his or her choices. The bettor pays a higher price to bet on a team expected to win, but betting on an underdog provides a chance to win more than the original wager.

Look over the baseball odds board at a Nevada casino. For each amount, what do the bookmakers believe are the "real" chances for a team to win?

15-Cent Line

Book-makers' quote	A bet on the favorite costs	A bet on the under-dog costs $1 and can win	Book-makers believe the favorite's chances are less than	Book-makers believe the underdog's chances are less than	Book-maker's commission is
Pick	$1.10	—	50%	50%	10.0%
120–105	1.20	$1.05	55	49	6.8
125–110	1.25	1.10	56	48	6.4
130–115	1.30	1.15	57	47	6.1
135–120	1.35	1.20	57	45	5.9
140–125	1.40	1.25	58	44	5.7
145–130	1.45	1.30	59	43	5.5
150–135	1.50	1.35	60	43	5.3
155–140	1.55	1.40	61	42	5.1
160–145	1.60	1.45	62	41	4.9
165–150	1.65	1.50	62	40	4.8
170–155	1.70	1.55	63	39	4.6
175–160	1.75	1.60	64	38	4.5
180–165	1.80	1.65	64	38	4.3
185–170	1.85	1.70	65	37	4.2
190–175	1.90	1.75	66	36	4.1
195–180	1.95	1.80	66	36	4.0
200–185	2.00	1.85	67	35	3.9

20-Cent Line

Book-makers' quote	A bet on the favorite costs	A bet on the under-dog costs $1 and can win	Book-makers believe the favorite's chances are less than	Book-makers believe the underdog's chances are less than	Book-maker's commission is
Pick	$1.10	—	50%	50%	10.0%
125–105	1.25	$1.05	56	49	8.7
130–110	1.30	1.10	57	48	8.3
135–115	1.35	1.15	57	47	8.0
140–120	1.40	1.20	58	45	7.7
145–125	1.45	1.25	59	44	7.4
150–130	1.50	1.30	60	43	7.1
155–135	1.55	1.35	61	43	6.9
160–140	1.60	1.40	62	42	6.7
165–145	1.65	1.45	62	41	6.5
170–150	1.70	1.50	63	40	6.25
175–155	1.75	1.55	64	39	6.1
180–160	1.80	1.60	64	38	5.9
185–165	1.85	1.65	65	38	5.7
190–170	1.90	1.70	66	37	5.5
195–175	1.95	1.75	66	36	5.4
200–180	2.00	1.80	67	36	5.3

Basketball Bets

Accuracy   In Las Vegas, the oddsmakers set the betting point-spread "line" for a professional basketball game. What are the chances that the game's outcome will be exactly as the line predicts?   5.8 in 100

within 1 point	12.6 in 100
within 2 points	20.2 in 100
within 3 points	26.8 in 100
within 4 points	34 in 100

Football Bets

"Over-Under" Bet   In Las Vegas and other places where gambling is legal, there is a professional football bet that goes by various names, most simply, the "over-under" play. The bookmaker states the total points expected to be scored in an NFL game. The bettor may choose to wager that the actual total will be over, or under, the bookmaker's estimate.

Here is the likelihood of various point totals for all NFL games:

11 points or fewer	2 in 100	38 points or fewer	57 in 100
16 _"_ _"_ _"_	5 in 100	39 _"_ _"_ _"_	58 in 100
20 _"_ _"_ _"_	11 in 100	40 _"_ _"_ _"_	61 in 100
22 _"_ _"_ _"_	14 in 100	41 _"_ _"_ _"_	63 in 100
24 _"_ _"_ _"_	20 in 100	42 _"_ _"_ _"_	64 in 100
27 _"_ _"_ _"_	26 in 100	43 _"_ _"_ _"_	66 in 100
30 _"_ _"_ _"_	32 in 100	44 _"_ _"_ _"_	69 in 100
31 _"_ _"_ _"_	36 in 100	47 _"_ _"_ _"_	76 in 100
32 _"_ _"_ _"_	38 in 100	49 _"_ _"_ _"_	80 in 100
33 _"_ _"_ _"_	39 in 100	53 _"_ _"_ _"_	85 in 100
34 _"_ _"_ _"_	45 in 100	57 _"_ _"_ _"_	91 in 100
35 _"_ _"_ _"_	46 in 100	65 _"_ _"_ _"_	95 in 100
36 _"_ _"_ _"_	48 in 100	69 _"_ _"_ _"_	98 in 100
37 _"_ _"_ _"_	53 in 100		

The most common point total is 34. It occurs about 5 percent of the time, or once in every twenty games.

Parlays

Most gambling facilities, and one or two state lotteries, offer parlays—systems that allow a bettor to win higher payoffs by combining bets on more than one game. When the bettor makes each bet against the line (the predicted point spread between each pair of teams), he or she had best assume that his or her accuracy in choosing winners will be approximately 50 percent. This is because the purpose of the point spread is to equalize the teams and bring the actual odds close to 50 percent, regardless of which team the bettor chooses.

Some lotteries, newspaper promotions, and other sports-prediction pools pay off simply for predicting the winners, regardless of the final margin between teams. The participant wins for correctly predicting the winners of seven, ten, or fourteen (the number of weekly contests in the National Football League) games. When this sort of lottery concerns baseball, most bettors achieve little better than 50-percent accuracy; seldom do even the most knowledgeable professional sports handicappers surpass 55- or 60-percent accuracy levels in baseball.

It is possible to be more accurate in predicting football winners. The average bettor accurately chooses winners of NFL games 60 to 70 percent of the time. (This is down from the consistent 70 percent routinely achieved during the years before 1978, when rule and schedule changes produced much closer—and more difficult to predict—contests.)

It might not be terribly difficult to make money on sports bets if a bettor needed only to correctly predict the winning team in order to win. Bets on these sports, however, are not placed on the winning team, but on the team that will win by more—or lose by less—than the number of points that the bookmakers believe should separate the teams. This means that the actual chance for any given bettor to correctly identify the team that beats the line in any game is 50 percent. Yet to consistently win money on single-team wagers, the bettor must pick the line-beaters at a 53-percent rate—and be even more accurate on parlay wagers.

A small mathematical surprise occurs when the bookmaker's profit is compared to the bettor's break-even percentage. On single bets, the bookmaker has a 10-percent profit margin. He takes in $11 in wagers, and pays $10 in winnings—giving a $1 (or 10 percent) profit. Strangely enough, the bettor can pay this 10-percent commission and still make money simply by maintaining a 54-percent accuracy rate.

College football may be the most predictable of all major sports events. Even a novice can usually pick the winners of 2 in 3 college games. More knowledgeable persons often exceed 70-percent accuracy, and sharpies consistently hit winners at an 80-percent rate.

The chances of correctly picking winners in various parlays depend on the general accuracy rate for the sport being predicted.

Fifty Percent A bettor's average accuracy rate is approximately 50 percent. (That is, he or she correctly predicts the winners about half the time.) What are his or her chances of correctly predicting all winners of two games?   1 in 4   25 in 100

three games	1 in 8	12.5 in 100
four games	1 in 16	6.25 in 100
five games	1 in 32	3.1 in 100
six games	1 in 64	1.6 in 100
seven games	1 in 128	
eight games	1 in 256	
nine games	1 in 512	
ten games	1 in 1,024	

Fifty-five Percent At 55-percent average accuracy, what are the chances of correctly predicting all winners of two games?
1 in 3.3   30.3 in 100

three games	1 in 6	16.6 in 100
four games	1 in 11	9.1 in 100
five games	1 in 20	5 in 100
six games	1 in 36	2.8 in 100
seven games	1 in 66	1.5 in 100
eight games	1 in 119	
nine games	1 in 217	
ten games	1 in 395	

Sixty Percent   At 60-percent average accuracy, what are the chances of correctly predicting all winners of two games?
1 in 2.8   35.7 in 100

three games	1 in 4.6	21.7 in 100
four games	1 in 7.7	13 in 100
five games	1 in 13	7.7 in 100
six games	1 in 21	4.7 in 100
seven games	1 in 36	2.8 in 100
eight games	1 in 60	1.7 in 100
nine games	1 in 99	1 in 100
ten games	1 in 165	
eleven games	1 in 273	
twelve games	1 in 459	
thirteen games	1 in 766	
fourteen games	1 in 1,276	

Racing Bets

Daily Double   At the racetrack, ten horses are scheduled to run in each of the two Daily Double races. A bettor takes the two digits in his or her age (for instance, 2 and 5) and uses them for a Daily Double bet. What chance does he or she have to win?   1 in 100

Exacta Bets   Exacta bettors win by picking the two fastest horses in a specified race and their exact order of finish. If a bettor were to choose two digits at random as his or her exacta bet, what would be the chances of winning in a ten-horse race?   1 in 90

| in a nine-horse race | 1 in 72 |
| in an eight-horse race | 1 in 56 |

Trifecta Bets   To place a trifecta bet, the bettor selects the horses that he or she expects to be the top three finishers and the exact order in which they will finish. In an eight-horse race, if a bettor does not assess each horse's chances, but instead chooses three numbers at random, what would be his or her chances of winning?   1 in 336

Pick Six   Computerized betting has made the newest racing wager possible. Called "Pick Six," the game, which began at certain California racetracks in 1980, requires the bettor to choose the winners of six consecutive races. The payoffs can be enormous. One "Pick Six" $2 bet can win more than $100,000, and at least one person has returned home with $300,000 in winnings from one perfect bet.

The odds of selecting six consecutive winning horses depends, of course, on the bettor's normal accuracy in predicting winners of individual races. What is the bettor's chance of collecting on a "Pick Six" wager if the bettor chose six horses randomly?   1 in 531,441
This assumes that each race has nine horses running.

If the bettor normally identifies the winner no more than once in every four races	1 in 4,096
If every selection the bettor made became the favorite horse in the race	1 in 729

Favorites win on an average of 1 in 3 races.

If the bettor can normally select the winner about half the time	1 in 64

OTHER GAMES

Bolita   A person plays Bolita, a popular Latin American game of chance. What are his or her chances of winning?   1 in 100
The usual payoff is 70 to 1.

Gin Rummy   A player receives ten cards in gin rummy. What are the chances that he or she will have a meld?   2 in 5
   after the first draw   nearly 1 in 2

Pinochle   What are the chances that the right card will be found in the widow of three cards with only one space open?
1 in 6   17 in 100

with two spaces open	1 in 3	33 in 100
with three spaces open	1 in 2	50 in 100
with four spaces open	3 in 5	60 in 100
with five spaces open	2 in 3	67 in 100

Scrabble   A player draws seven tiles to begin a game of Scrabble. What are the chances that his or her opening set of letters will include an *E?*   87 in 100

an *O*	58 in 100
a *G*	22 in 100

Solitaire   A player deals one card up and six down, to set up a traditional seven-pile Klondike solitaire game. What are the chances that the player will win, getting all cards into four equal stacks?   1 in 30
Although Klondike is by far the most well-known solitaire game, it is among the most difficult to win. It is possible to win certain other solitaire games more than half the time.

Tarok   A person calls for a king in a four-handed game of Tarok, a popular Czechoslovakian card game. What are the odds that this person will find the called king in the talon (six cards dealt face down on the table)?   1 in 8
In Tarok, the bidder never knows whether or not he or she will have a partner. Whoever has the called king will be the partner of the bidder. If the called king is in the talon, the bidder faces the stiff competition of three opponents.

Birthday Lottery   Twenty-four people are gathered together. What are the chances that any two of the twenty-four share a birthday?
52 in 100
If thirty people are gathered together, the chances increase to 68 in 100; and if forty people are gathered together, to 85 in 100.

8   Sports

Whether you are making a friendly wager or a professional gambling bet, your chances of predicting a winner can probably be improved by consulting statistics as well as your hunches. And sports statistics abound. As presented in this chapter, you may find many new ways to consider the odds.

In addition to the odds of the occurrence of a specific score or winning margin and the odds that a team with certain characteristics will win, you will find information on many factors related to winning and scoring. Some historical perspective is often found as the odds reflect rules changes and scoring trends over time. There are also odds related to the various characteristics of players, their chances of making it to the top of their field, and the probable length of their career. High school and collegiate sports are covered in many cases as well as professional ones. The championship games—baseball's World Series, tennis's Wimbledon, and horse racing's Triple Crown, for example—are sampled as well.

AUTO RACING

Starting Position   A driver begins the Indianapolis 500 from the pole position. What are his or her chances of winning?   11 in 64
   from the number 2 position   10 in 64

Average Speed   Select any winner of the Indianapolis 500 from the 1970s. What are the chances that he averaged more than 150 miles per hour?   8 in 10
   more than 160 miles per hour   3 in 10
Of the Indy's first ten winners, none averaged more than 100 miles per hour, and one actually won with an average speed of less than 75. Over the years, fewer than half the drivers who started the race have actually completed the full 500 miles.

BASEBALL (COLLEGIATE)

Game Characteristics   An NCAA Championship College World Series game is under way. What are the chances that it will be a shutout?
10 in 100
   an extra-inning game   8 in 100
   a game decided by one run   22 in 100
   a game decided by ten runs   7 in 100

Final Game Characteristics   What are the chances that the final game of the College World Series will be a shutout?   12 in 100
   an extra-inning game   12 in 100
   a game decided by one run   45 in 100

BASEBALL (PROFESSIONAL)

Players
Prospects   An individual wants to become a major league baseball star. He signs with a club and begins competing with other players to make it to the top. What are the chances that he will someday play in the major leagues?   1 in 20
   will play ten years or more in the majors   1 in 140

| will reach the Baseball Hall of Fame | 1 in 1,500 |
| will win baseball's triple crown of batting | 1 in 23,000 |

Only eleven players have won the triple crown: Rogers Hornsby (twice), Ted Williams (twice), Ty Cobb, Lou Gehrig, Heinie Zimmerman, Jimmy Foxx, Chuck Klein, Joe Medwick, Mickey Mantle, Frank Robinson, and Carl Yastrzemski. Yastrzemski was the most recent winner, in 1967.

Rules   A major league baseball player takes the field to begin another game. What are the chances that he has never read the rules of baseball?   4 in 5

Twenty-Game Winners   A major league pitcher will win twenty games for his team next year. What are the chances that he is less than thirty years old?   72 in 100

Some of baseball's greatest pitchers did not hit their prime until after thirty, and others, great in their twenties, seemed to go on and on. But, on the average, the game belongs to the young. The most common age for twenty-game winners is twenty-seven.

American League MVP   Randomly select a winner of the American League's Most Valuable Player award from 1931 to 1979. What are the chances that he won the honor playing for the New York Yankees? 35 in 100

| for New York or Boston | 49 in 100 |
| for New York, Boston, or Detroit | 63 in 100 |

National League MVP   What are the chances that the winner of the National League's Most Valuable Player award for any given year played for the St. Louis Cardinals?   27 in 100

| for St. Louis or Cincinnati | 47 in 100 |
| for St. Louis, Cincinnati, or the Dodgers (L.A. or Brooklyn) | 65 in 100 |

The Game

Pitchers   A major league baseball game is about to begin. What are the chances that one of the starting pitchers will complete the game? 1 in 2

In 1928, one or both pitchers went all the way in nearly every game (96%). With the advent of the strong relief pitcher, this proportion has dropped in every decade. American League pitchers, because the designated-hitter rule does not allow them to be removed for pinch hitters, are slightly more likely to pitch complete games than are their colleagues in the National League.

No-Hitters   A fan attends a major league baseball game. What are the chances that he or she will witness a no-hitter by one of the pitchers? 1 in 1,347

   a no-hitter by both pitchers (for nine
      innings)   1 in 1,814,409

A pitcher setting out to pitch two consecutive no-hit games would face these same odds. Johnny Vander Meer is the only major league pitcher ever to have thrown back-to-back no-hitters.

   a perfect game (no walks, no hits,
      no errors, no runs) by one pitcher   1 in 20,000

Base Hits   What are the chances that the next base hit in a major league game will be a single?   71 in 100

   a double   18 in 100
   a triple   3 in 100
   a home run   8 in 100

Walks   A batter walks during a major league baseball game. What are the chances that he will score?   37 in 100

Base Stealing   A runner tries to steal a base in a major league game. What are the chances that he will make the steal safely?   63.5 in 100
This does not include instances when runners are picked off base.

Fielding Errors   A player has a fielding chance in a major league game. What are the chances that he will make an error?   3 in 100

Extra Innings   What are the chances that any given major league baseball game will go into extra innings?   1 in 8

Out-of-the-Park Hits   What are the chances that a batter will hit a baseball out of Comiskey Park, home of the Chicago White Sox, during any given season?   42 in 100
Babe Ruth, Lou Gehrig, Jimmy Foxx, Ted Williams, Mickey Mantle, and Harmon Killebrew are among the players who have hit a ball onto or over the Comiskey Park roof. No batter yet has hit a fair ball completely out of Yankee Stadium. Babe Ruth, Mickey Mantle, and Reggie Jackson have come closest.

Home Runs
Season   What is the probability that someone in the major leagues will hit more than fifty home runs in any given season?   31 in 100
This was accomplished only seventeen times between 1920 and 1975.

League Champion   A player hits thirty-five home runs one year in the major leagues. What are the chances that he will be the home-run champion of his league for that season?   28 in 100
   If he hits forty home runs   48 in 100

Repeat Champion   A major league player wins his league's home-run championship this year. What are his chances of winning it again next year?   3 in 10

Leader's Chances   The leading home-run hitter in the major leagues steps up to the plate. What are the chances that he will hit a home run this time?   6–8 in 100
This figure includes walks and is equivalent to 1 home run for every 12 to 16.5 times at bat. The best performance in this regard was in 1920, when Babe Ruth hit 1 home run for every 11.33 times at bat.

Individual Season Home Runs   Choose at random a baseball player who competes in the major leagues. What are the chances that he will hit at least forty home runs this year?   1.3 in 100
This is based on records for the 162-game schedule only.

Rookie Expectations   A baseball player begins his rookie season in the major leagues. What are the chances that before his career is over he will have hit at least forty home runs in each of three or more seasons?   1.7 in 1,000

Scoring

Home Team Advantage   What is the probability that the home team will win any given major league baseball game?   53 in 100
This is based on the results of nearly 12,000 games.

A first division major league baseball team is playing another first division team, or a second division team is playing another second division team. What are the chances that the home team will win?
52 in 100
    if a first division team is at home
        against a second division team   60 in 100
    if a second division team is at home
        against a first division team   48 in 100

Each Inning   Choose one team in any major league baseball game. What are the chances that this team will score in the next inning?
    a National League
      team   1 in 4
    an American League
      team   1 in 3
In any given inning, it is more difficult for a National League team to score than for an American League team. Some experts argue that the designated-hitter rule is responsible for this difference. For several years, American League teams have scored about 10 percent more runs than teams in the National League. This is an average of nearly one extra run per game.

For both leagues, these odds hold for every inning, although the first inning has a very slight statistical edge in producing runs. The ninth inning is a very special case. Read on.

Ninth Inning   A major league team comes to bat trailing in the ninth inning. What are the chances that the team will be able to score? 1 in 4
Many followers of baseball believe that it becomes tough to "get 'em out" in the ninth. Actually, the odds are about the same in the ninth inning as in any other.

In the American League, the overall chances of scoring in the ninth are somewhat less than in other innings because something unusual seems to happen. The home team, if it comes to bat, continues to have about a 1-in-3 chance of scoring, but the visitors' chances at bat drop to about 1 in 5. This does not seem to happen in the National League, and there seems to be no explanation for why things get so tough for American League visitors or why the two leagues differ in this respect.

If the game is tied in the ninth inning, each team faces a 1-in-5 chance of scoring.

First Run   A major league team scores first in a game. What are the chances that this team will go on to win the game?   64 in 100

Team Record   Two major league baseball teams take the field. What are the chances that the game will be won by the team with the higher overall batting average so far this season?   54 in 100
   by the team that has scored the
      most runs so far in the season   54 in 100
   by the team that has allowed the
      fewest runs to be scored against
      it to date   53 in 100
   by the team whose starting pitcher
      has the lower earned-run average
      to date   55 in 100

Lead Advantage   What are the chances that a major league team will win its game if at some point before the last inning it has a one-run lead?   64 in 100

a two-run lead	73 in 100
a three-run lead	77 in 100
a four-run lead	89 in 100
a five-run lead	95 in 100

Winning Margins   What is the probability that the winning team in a major league baseball game will have only one more run than the loser?   32 in 100

two runs	24 in 100
three runs	13 in 100
four runs	8 in 100
five runs	7 in 100
six runs	5 in 100
seven runs	4 in 100
eight runs	3 in 100
nine runs	2 in 100
ten or more runs	2 in 100

This is based on more than 28,000 games.

General   What are the chances that a major league baseball team will win the next game that it plays if it has just won a game?   50 in 100

has won two consecutive games	52 in 100
has won three consecutive games	51 in 100
has won four consecutive games	45 in 100
has won five consecutive games	54 in 100
has won six consecutive games	52 in 100

These tabulations are based not on probability statistics but on actual observation of winning streaks during the 1976 season.

Winning Streaks   What are the chances that a major league baseball team will win its next five games? An accurate answer, of course, depends on how good the team is. Some basic odds are given in the chart below.

Team Winning Percentage	Chances of Winning Its Next	
	Five Games	Ten Games
40	1 in 100	1 in 10,000
50	3 in 100	1 in 1,000
60	8 in 100	1 in 400

Losing Streaks   What are the chances that a major league baseball team will lose the next game that it plays if it has just lost a game? 49 in 100

has lost two consecutive games	52 in 100
has lost three consecutive games	56 in 100
has lost four consecutive games	55 in 100
has lost five consecutive games	54 in 100
has lost six consecutive games	43 in 100

These tabulations are based not on probability statistics but on actual observation of losing streaks during the 1976 season.

The Race

Player Age   The average age of the players on a major league team is twenty-five. What are the chances that the team will have a better season this year than last?   75 in 100

will suffer a serious decline, losing at least ten games more than last year	13 in 100

If the average age of the team is thirty years or more, the chances of a better season are only 39 in 100.

Win-Loss Record   The baseball season begins. What are the chances that the best team in either league will win more than 60 percent of its games?   84 in 100

What are the chances that the worst team in the league will win less than 40 percent of its games?   86 in 100
     less than 30 percent   12.5 in 100

Playoff Chances   Pick a National League baseball team at random. What are the chances that this team will qualify for the playoffs?
1 in 6
For American League teams, the chances are 1 in 7.

Pennant Wins   A major league team begins the season. To win the league championship, what are the chances that this team will need to win at least 100 games this year?   32.5 in 100
     at least ninety games   97 in 100

A major league baseball adage holds that the team in first place on July 4 will win the league championship. What are the chaces that this will hold true?   63 in 100
The chances that a July 4 leader will win its division are virtually the same as the chances that the midseason leader would have captured the league championship in the years before divisional play, 1901–1968.

Close Races   What are the chances that any major league baseball team that wins a divisional title next season will win it by four or fewer games?   1 in 3
During the sixty-eight years in which each league stood as an entity without divisions, "close" (by four games or fewer) races occurred 40 percent of the time. The lower rate since the creation of divisions does not necessarily mean less excitement for the fan. With the old system, there were only two races each year. Now there are four—virtually assuring at least one close major league race a season.

Best Season Record   A major league baseball championship playoff game is under way. What is the probability that the team with the best overall season record will win the game?   69 in 100
     will win the league championship
          playoff   81 in 100

Playoff Repeats   A major league team wins the league playoff series this year. What are the chances that this team will participate in the playoffs again next year?   1 in 2

The losing team has only a 40-percent chance of reaching the playoffs again next year.

World Series

Team Participation   What are the chances that any given major league baseball team will go more than five years without playing in a World Series?   67 in 100

   a decade or more   40 in 100

Number of Games   What are the chances that this year's World Series will end in four games?   19 in 100

   in five games   25 in 100
   in six games   20 in 100
   in seven games   36 in 100

Win Patterns   A team wins the first game of the World Series. What are the chances that this team will go on to win the Series?
60 in 100

The chances, however, that this team will win the second game are only 42.5 in 100.

A team wins the first two games of the World Series. What are the chances that this team will win the Series?   66.7 in 100

The two teams in the World Series split the first two games. What are the chances that the team that wins the third game will win the Series? 62 in 100

If the teams are tied two apiece, what are the odds that the fifth-game winner will win the Series?   68.2 in 100

Home Team Win   It is the seventh game of the World Series. Based on previous seven-game series, what are the chances that the home team will win?   38 in 100

Las Vegas Odds   What is the probability that the team favored by the Las Vegas oddsmakers at the beginning of the World Series will actually win it?   44 in 100

World Series Opponents   The baseball season begins. What are the chances that it will end with a World Series played by Yankees and Dodgers?   13 in 100

by Yankees and Giants   9 in 100
by Yankees and Cardinals   7 in 100

Other pairings have been rare. These probabilities are, of course, based on actual World Series data. Statisticians, giving each team an equal chance of appearing in the Series, would tell us that the "real" chances for any given pairing are 1 in 168.

Proximity Series   What are the chances that the World Series in any given year will be played entirely in one city?   3.6 in 100

This is roughly equivalent to about once in twenty-eight years. If one counts San Francisco–Oakland as a one-city rivalry, the odds rise to approximately 5 in 100, or once every twenty years.

will be played entirely in one state   1 in 10
will be played entirely outside the
  USA   1 in 168
will be played entirely indoors   1 in 168

BASKETBALL (HIGH SCHOOL)

Players   Choose at random a young male athlete who will play high school basketball next season. What are the chances that he will eventually play NCAA basketball?   2 in 100

NBA professional basketball   1 in 2,600

High school football players have nearly twice the chance of making a collegiate team in their sport as do high school basketball players.

Winner's Total Points   A high school plays a basketball game. What are the chances that the winning team will score at least 45 points? 96 in 100

53 points or more	80 in 100
55 " " "	75 in 100
64 " " "	49 in 100
71 " " "	25 in 100
81 " " "	10 in 100
85 " " "	5 in 100
95 " " "	1 in 100

Winning Margin   When a given high school basketball game ends, what are the chances that the winning margin will be only 1 point? 3 in 100

2 points or less	6 in 100
6 " " "	24 in 100
12 " " "	51 in 100
21 " " "	75 in 100
30 " " "	91 in 100
43 " " "	99 in 100

BASKETBALL (COLLEGIATE)

Scores

Winner's Total Points   Two college basketball teams take the floor. What are the chances that the team that wins will score more than 60 points?   95 in 100

63 points or more	93 in 100
64 " " "	94 in 100
67 " " "	85 in 100
70 " " "	75 in 100
76 " " "	60 in 100
78 " " "	50 in 100
80 " " "	46 in 100
82 " " "	40 in 100
84 " " "	35 in 100
85 " " "	33 in 100
87 " " "	30 in 100
89 " " "	25 in 100
92 " " "	20 in 100
100 " " "	10 in 100
106 " " "	5 in 100
116 " " "	1 in 100

Winning Margin   The clock ticks away the final seconds of a college basketball game. What are the chances that the final margin separating the two teams will be only 1 point?   3 in 100

2 points or less	7 in 100
3 " " "	15 in 100
5 " " "	25 in 100
7 " " "	33 in 100
9 " " "	40 in 100
10 " " "	47 in 100
11 " " "	51 in 100
14 " " "	60 in 100
16 " " "	67 in 100
17 " " "	70 in 100
19 " " "	75 in 100
21 " " "	80 in 100
31 " " "	90 in 100
38 " " "	95 in 100
48 " " "	99 in 100

Championships

Overtime   What are the chances that any given NCAA championship basketball game will go into overtime?   1 in 10

Winning Margin   What are the chances that the winning margin in next year's NCAA championship basketball game will be only 1 point? 7.5 in 100

2 points or less	12.5 in 100
3 " " "	17.5 in 100
4 " " "	22.5 in 100
5 " " "	30 in 100
6 " " "	32.5 in 100
7 " " "	37.5 in 100
8 " " "	40 in 100
9 " " "	40 in 100
10 " " "	45 in 100
11 " " "	52.5 in 100
12 " " "	66 in 100
19 " " "	90 in 100

Champion's Outlook   A team wins the NCAA championship this year. What are the chances that the team will fail to win half its games next year?   1 in 42

Only one team has ever lost more games than it has won in the year following a national championship: Stanford, in 1943, won ten games and lost eleven.

BASKETBALL (PROFESSIONAL)

Players

Height   A player walks onto the court in the NBA today. What are the chances that he stands at least 6 feet 2 inches tall?   92 in 100

6 feet 3 inches or more	84 in 100
6 feet 4 inches or more	74 in 100
6 feet 5 inches or more	65 in 100
6 feet 6 inches or more	56 in 100
6 feet 7 inches or more	46 in 100
6 feet 8 inches or more	34 in 100
6 feet 9 inches or more	25 in 100
6 feet 10 inches or more	15 in 100
6 feet 11 inches or more	9 in 100
7 feet or more	4 in 100

This is the way it was in the 1979–1980 season—the first year with the three-point rule. Some observers believe that this new rule will help more "short" players gain entry into the NBA.

In the 1945–1946 season, only 1 in 2 NBA players was taller than 6 feet 2 inches.

NBA Draft Choices   A new professional basketball player trots onto the court. What are the chances that he was chosen in the first round of the draft?   49 in 100

in the first two rounds	71 in 100
in the first three rounds	84 in 100
in the first seven rounds	94 in 100

Basketball skills are easily assessed, so almost all the players who become NBA stars and those who establish long careers are drafted early.

Career Expectations   A college basketball star lands a position on an NBA team roster. What are the chances that his professional basketball career will last only 1 year?   30 in 100

2 years or less	42 in 100
3 " " "	53 in 100
4 " " "	62 in 100
5 " " "	69 in 100
6 " " "	76 in 100
7 " " "	81 in 100
8 " " "	86 in 100
9 " " "	91 in 100
10 " " "	95 in 100

A player stands an even chance of looking for a new job within three years.

Scoring

Field Goal Accuracy   What are the chances that the next two-point field goal attempt in an NBA game will score?   48 in 100

This is the league average. To illustrate how the game has changed over the years, the best individual field goal success rate between 1946 and 1959 was 49 percent, by Ken Sears of the New York Knickerbockers in the 1958–1959 season. Today the average NBA player scores with nearly the same accuracy as the top players of twenty or thirty years ago.

Assists   What are the chances that the next goal scored in the National Basketball Association will come from an "assist" (a teammate's pass allowing a player to score)?   55 in 100

Three-Point Goals   A player in the NBA lofts a shot from beyond the three-point line. What are the chances that the shot will score?
26 in 100

Players in the now defunct American Basketball Association were slightly more accurate, succeeding in 29.7 percent of their three-point attempts.

What are the chances that in any given NBA game there will be at least one three-point goal?   72 in 100

two or more three-point goals	42 in 100
three or more three-point goals	12 in 100

Some authorities make this analysis of the impact of the three-point field goal rule instituted in 1979. Under this rule, very long shots can score three points. Currently, these are successful about 30 percent of the time (this should increase as more outside shooters enter the league). With two-point attempts nearing a 50-percent rate, strategies seeking two-point baskets and those trying for three-point scores will be virtually equal in effectiveness; under either strategy, 100 shots will produce approximately 100 points.

Free Throws   What are the chances that the next NBA player who steps up to the free-throw line will make the shot?   **3 in 4**
On average, players are slightly more accurate during the middle portions of the game than during the very first minutes or near the end.

Turnovers   A National Basketball Association team loses the ball (because of a foul, a traveling violation, an intercepted pass, or an out-of-bounds play). What are the chances that the opposing team will capitalize on this turnover by scoring a basket?   **1 in 2**

Overtime   What are the chances that a given NBA game will be tied at the end of the regulation time and will go into overtime?   **1 in 22**
When a game does go into overtime, the chances are 1 in 10 that it will require at least a second overtime to reach a decision.

First Quarter Lead   A team leads after the first quarter of an NBA game. What are the chances that it will go on to win?   **63 in 100**
    if the team leads at halftime   **69 in 100**
    if the team leads after the third
      quarter   **79 in 100**

Home Team Advantage   Two NBA teams compete. What are the chances that the home team will win?   **63.4 in 100**
This probability is based on 12,402 games from 1947 through 1977. The range has been from a low home team advantage of 55.7 percent in 1948 to a high of 74.9 percent in 1951. The home team won 65.2 percent of the games in 1980.

The Boston Celtics hold the all-time standard for home team dominance during an entire season. When a visiting team walked onto the Celtics' home court in Boston during the 1959–1960 season, what risk of defeat did they face?   **93 in 100**

In that season, only two teams were able to overcome the Celtics' home court advantage in twenty-seven tries.

Scores

Team Scoring   Two teams struggled in a 1937–1938 National Basketball League game. What are the chances that one of the teams emerged with fewer than 36 points?   1 in 2

Modern teams of the newer NBA have averaged more than 100 points per game since 1957. Wilt Chamberlain of the Philadelphia '76ers alone averaged 50.4 points per game—more than most entire teams scored two decades earlier. In one game against the New York Knicks in 1962, Chamberlain scored a record 100 points.

Winner's Total Points   Two NBA teams take the floor. What are the chances that the winning team will score more than 87 points?
99 in 100

90 points or more	98 in 100
95 " " "	97 in 100
100 " " "	91 in 100
101 " " "	90 in 100
105 " " "	81 in 100
107 " " "	75 in 100
110 " " "	65 in 100
114 " " "	50 in 100
115 " " "	47 in 100
120 " " "	30 in 100
122 " " "	25 in 100
129 " " "	10 in 100
135 " " "	5 in 100
145 " " "	1 in 100

The most common score for a winning team in a professional basketball game is 112, even though this is the winner's score in only 4 percent of the games.

Winning Margin   What are the chances that a given NBA contest will be decided by just 1 point?   6 in 100

2 points or fewer	15 in 100
3 " " "	22 in 100
4 " " "	29 in 100

5 points or fewer	36 in 100
6 ″ ″ ″	43 in 100
7 ″ ″ ″	49 in 100
8 ″ ″ ″	53 in 100
9 ″ ″ ″	57 in 100
10 ″ ″ ″	62 in 100
11 ″ ″ ″	68 in 100
12 ″ ″ ″	71 in 100
13 ″ ″ ″	74 in 100
14 ″ ″ ″	77 in 100
20 ″ ″ ″	90 in 100
25 ″ ″ ″	95 in 100
37 ″ ″ ″	99 in 100
40 points or more	1 in 120

Two pro basketball teams will usually score at least 150 points in a game and may score as many as 280. Yet it is not uncommon for one basket—only 1 percent of the total—to separate the two teams at the end of the game. Half the games are decided by 7 points or fewer.

A 2-point spread separates the winner from the loser in 9 percent of the games—the most common point spread in pro basketball.

Home-Visitor Point Margins   Simple point spreads do not tell the entire story in pro basketball. In this sport, the home team advantage is a very real factor. What are the chances that the winner in any given NBA game will claim victory by only 1 point?

If the home team wins	6 in 100
If the visiting team wins	8 in 100

The chances of other point spreads are given in the chart.

Margin	Chances of This Margin	
	When Home Team Wins	When Visiting Team Wins
2 points or less	14 in 100	21 in 100
3 ″ ″ ″	19 in 100	29 in 100
4 ″ ″ ″	24 in 100	40 in 100
5 ″ ″ ″	31 in 100	46 in 100
6 ″ ″ ″	38 in 100	54 in 100
7 ″ ″ ″	43 in 100	62 in 100
8 ″ ″ ″	47 in 100	67 in 100

9 points or less	51 in 100	71 in 100
10 ″ ″ ″	54 in 100	77 in 100
13 ″ ″ ″	67 in 100	86 in 100
15 ″ ″ ″	74 in 100	91 in 100
17 ″ ″ ″	80 in 100	94 in 100
23 ″ ″ ″	90 in 100	99 in 100
41 ″ ″ ″	99 in 100	

Because the home team wins most games, the average point spread shifts to the home side.

Half of all NBA point spreads fall within this range: visitors by 5, home team by 11. In other words, the visiting team wins by more than 15 points in only 1 in 40 NBA games; the home team wins by 15 points or more in 1 out of 3 games.

Playoffs

Team Chances   An NBA team begins a new season. What are the chances that the team will reach the postseason playoffs?   55 in 100
Of the NBA's twenty-two teams, twelve will qualify for the playoffs. These are the average chances, of course. Some teams have a better chance of reaching the playoffs, while other teams have virtually no chance at all.

Home Team Advantage   Two teams compete in the NBA playoffs. What are the chances that the home team will win?   2 in 3
Because playoff teams are very evenly matched, it would seem that the home team advantage would be less than that in regular season games. This does not happen, however. If anything, the home team edge increases during the important playoff games.

Rallies   A team is down three games to one in the NBA championship playoffs. What are the chances that the team can rally to win the series?   1 in 256
This is a theoretical probability because no team has yet come back from a three-games-to-one deficit to capture the championship.

BOWLING

U.S. Bowlers   According to the *Guinness Book of World Records*, there are 65 million bowlers in the USA. Imagine that every bowler decided to bowl at the same time on a given day. Assuming that every lane in the country could hold four bowlers, what would be the odds against finding a lane to bowl on?   114 to 1

Organizations   A bowler lives in the USA. What are the chances that he or she belongs to one of the two largest bowling associations, the American Bowling Congress or the Women's International Bowling Congress?   11.5 in 100

Spares   A professional bowler studies the pin arrangement before rolling the second ball of the frame. What are the chances that he or she will successfully convert the situation into a spare?   95 in 100
This is an overall average and includes those seemingly—and sometimes actually—impossible splits.

4–7–10 Splits   A professional bowler faces a 4–7–10 split. What are the odds against making a spare?   10 to 1

Men's Averages   A man is a member of the American Bowling Congress. What are the chances that his average exceeds 200?
4 in 1,000

exceeds 190	2 in 100
exceeds 180	9 in 100
exceeds 170	26 in 100
exceeds 160	49 in 100
exceeds 150	71 in 100
exceeds 140	84 in 100
exceeds 130	93 in 100
exceeds 120	97 in 100
exceeds 110	98 in 100

Perfect Games   A male bowler rolls the first ball in sanctioned play. What are the chances that he will achieve a perfect 300 score for this line?   1 in 490,000
    A female bowler   1 in 18 million
Elvin Mesger of Sullivan, Missouri, leads all bowlers in this department, with twenty-seven sanctioned 300-games to his credit.

Bowler of the Year   An individual wins the women's Bowler of the Year award of the American Bowling Congress. What are the chances that she will win the award again next year?   2 in 5
    that the men's award winner will win
        again next year   1 in 6
    that either winner will capture his or
        her title again at some time   1 in 2

BOXING

Championship Rounds   A championship boxing match can end at any time. What are the chances that any given heavyweight match will last more than one round?   93 in 100
    more than five rounds   67 in 100
    more than ten rounds   40 in 100
For light-heavyweight contests, the comparable figures are 98, 75, and 60 in 100, respectively. The chances of a middleweight bout's lasting more than ten rounds are even greater—67 in 100.
    Joe Louis holds the current record (5) for the most one-round knockouts in heavyweight championship fights. His most famous first-round knockout was of Germany's Max Schmeling just before World War II.

Championship Knockouts   The boxers touch gloves in the center of the ring and return to their corners. The heavyweight championship is on the line. The bell rings. They come at each other. What are the chances that one of them will win by a knockout?   75 in 100
    in a light-heavyweight championship   45 in 100
    in a middleweight championship   40 in 100

Challenger's Chances   Everyone knows that the champion is usually favored when he enters the ring. What are the challenger's chances of winning in any given heavyweight bout?   1 in 5   20 in 100
    light-heavyweight bout   1 in 6   16 in 100
    middleweight bout   1 in 3   33 in 100

Undefeated Heavyweight Champions   What are the chances that the next world's heavyweight champion will win every match as champion?   15 in 100

Rocky Marciano, Joe Louis, Gene Tunney, and James Jeffries never lost a fight as heavyweight champions. Louis and Jeffries both retired and then were defeated in attempts to regain their titles. Rocky Marciano is the only champion who never lost a pro fight.

FOOTBALL (HIGH SCHOOL)

Ties   What are the chances that any given high school football game will end in a tie?   1 in 40
   in a scoreless tie   1 in 500

Shutouts   When two high school football teams meet, what are the chances that the loser will fail to score at all?   31 in 100

High Scores   A high school team scores 50 points or more in a game. What are the chances that the team will win by at least 50 points? 52 in 100
A 50-point offense with a 50-point margin happens about once in every twenty high school football games—or about twice as often as tie games.

Winner's Total Points   Two high school teams take the field for a football contest. What are the chances that the team that wins will score fewer than 6 points?   1 in 120

6 points or fewer			5 in 100	
7	"	"	"	7 in 100
10	"	"	"	9 in 100
12	"	"	"	11 in 100
13	"	"	"	14 in 100
14	"	"	"	23 in 100
20	"	"	"	29 in 100
26	"	"	"	50 in 100
34	"	"	"	69 in 100
37	"	"	"	75 in 100
49	"	"	"	90 in 100

Since field goals are rare in high school football, most scores are touchdowns. About 9 percent of winning teams score exactly 14 points. This is the most common of all winning or tie scores.

Despite the short playing time of high school games, football at this level is a high-scoring sport. Winning high school teams, on average, outscore both college and professional teams. These statistics are based on nation-wide playing records, but there are a few regional differences. Rainy areas with natural turf, particularly the extreme Northwest and Mississippi's bayou region, often have slightly lower scores.

Winning Margin   Two high school football teams begin a game. What are the chances that the game will end in a tie?   1 in 40   2.5 in 100

What are the chances that the winning margin will be only 1 point? 5 in 100

2 points or less	12 in 100
3 " " "	13 in 100
4 " " "	15 in 100
5 " " "	16 in 100
6 " " "	22 in 100
7 " " "	24 in 100
8 " " "	27 in 100
9 " " "	28 in 100
10 " " "	30 in 100
12 " " "	34 in 100
13 " " "	36 in 100
14 " " "	43 in 100
18 " " "	50 in 100
26 " " "	69 in 100
29 " " "	75 in 100
49 " " "	94 in 100

Approximately 7 percent of all high school football games are decided by exactly 14 points—the most frequent of all outcomes.

FOOTBALL (COLLEGIATE)

Home Team Advantage   In any given college football game, what are the chances that the home team will win?   51 in 100
This is based on the outcomes of more than 3,300 games.

Field Position   An NCAA college football team takes the ball on its own 20-yard line. What are the chances that the team will score on this possession?   12 in 100

If the ball is taken on the 50-yard line, the chances of scoring increase to 48 in 100.

Shutouts   What are the chances that the loser of a college football game will fail to score any points at all?   16 in 100

   that both teams will fail to score   1 in 400

High Scores   What are the chances that the winner of the next college football game played in the USA will score more than 50 points and win by this margin as well?   1 in 100

When a team does score more than 50 points, the chances that the winning margin will also exceed 50 points are 1 in 5.

Winner's Total Points   What are the chances that the winning team in any given college football contest will score fewer than 7 points?
2 in 100

7 points or fewer	3 in 100
10 ″ ″ ″	7 in 100
12 ″ ″ ″	8 in 100
13 ″ ″ ″	11 in 100
14 ″ ″ ″	16 in 100
16 ″ ″ ″	17 in 100
17 ″ ″ ″	21 in 100
18 ″ ″ ″	23 in 100
19 ″ ″ ″	25 in 100
20 ″ ″ ″	28 in 100
21 ″ ″ ″	36 in 100
22 ″ ″ ″	38 in 100
23 ″ ″ ″	41 in 100
24 ″ ″ ″	47 in 100
26 ″ ″ ″	52 in 100
28 ″ ″ ″	67 in 100
34 ″ ″ ″	75 in 100
49 ″ ″ ″	96 in 100

The most common score by a winning team is 21 points, even though only 8 percent of winners make exactly that number.

Winning Margin A college receiver prepares to run back the opening kickoff. What are the chances that the game will be decided by 1 point?   3 in 100

2 points or fewer			8 in 100
3	"	"	"	15 in 100
4	"	"	"	18 in 100
5	"	"	"	22 in 100
6	"	"	"	24 in 100
7	"	"	"	31 in 100
8	"	"	"	35 in 100
9	"	"	"	36 in 100
10	"	"	"	40 in 100
11	"	"	"	43 in 100
12	"	"	"	46 in 100
13	"	"	"	49 in 100
14	"	"	"	55 in 100
18	"	"	"	60 in 100
21	"	"	"	70 in 100
24	"	"	"	77 in 100
49	"	"	"	99 in 100

Winning margins of 3 and 7 points are the most common in college football; each occurs about 7 percent of the time. Ties occur in only 2 percent of all games.

Championships

Big Eight Pick a year between 1944 and 1980 at random. What are the chances that Nebraska or Oklahoma won or tied for the Big Eight Conference championship that year?   94 in 100

Championship Polls A team wins the AP or UPI poll for the NCAA football championship. What are the chances that this team will be named the champion by either poll in the following year?   18 in 100

Heisman Trophy

Conferences The Heisman Trophy is awarded annually to the outstanding collegiate football player in the USA. Based on past winners, what are the chances that the next Heisman winner will belong to an Ivy League Conference team?   7 in 100

Southeastern   9 in 100

Southwestern	9 in 100
Big Eight	9 in 100
Pac Ten	11 in 100
Big Ten	20 in 100
independent	33 in 100

The Atlantic Coast Conference, in forty-five years, has failed to produce even one Heisman winner.

Winners   A college football star wins the Heisman Trophy. What are the chances that he will make the starting lineup of an NFL team? 1 in 4

FOOTBALL (PROFESSIONAL)

Players
Professional Draft Choices   NFL teams draft the best players among college seniors each year. When each team has drafted one player, a new round begins. What are the chances that a player will survive the early season squad cuts and begin a career as an NFL player if he was drafted in the first round?   99 in 100

in the second round	90 in 100
in the third or fourth rounds	84 in 100
in the fifth through seventh rounds	56 in 100
in the eighth through fourteenth rounds	35 in 100
in the fifteenth or a later round	25 in 100

Injuries   An athlete has landed a job as a starting player in the NFL. What are the chances that, before the season's end, he will be on the disabled list due to an injury?   19 in 100

that he will miss at least one game because of an injury	39 in 100

Running Greats   A running back in the NFL will ultimately rank among the few great players who gain more than 6,000 yards in their careers. What are the chances that in his rookie year he will gain fewer than 400 yards?   33 in 100

fewer than 600 yards	50 in 100
more than 1,000 yards	8 in 100

To date, Pittsburgh's Franco Harris is the only member of the exclusive 6,000-career-yards club to break 1,000 yards in his first NFL season (1972). Earl Campbell of the Houston Oilers and the St. Louis Cardinals' Otis Anderson both rushed for more than 1,200 yards in their rookie years, and most observers expect each of them to hit the 6,000-yard mark before they end their careers.

The all-time career rushing leader is Jim Brown of Cleveland, who totaled 12,312 yards. O. J. Simpson of Buffalo and San Francisco is second, with 11,236 yards at the end of the 1979 season.

Scoring

Home Team Advantage   What are the chances that the home team will win any given NFL game?   58 in 100

Field Goals   A team in the NFL attempts a field goal. What are the chances that it will be successful?   61 in 100
When the goalposts were on the goal line, the odds in favor of success were 63 in 100. The two statistics are essentially identical, because when the NFL moved the goalposts 10 yards away from the goal line, the consequences of a failed attempt also changed. Under the new rule, the opposing team takes the ball at the line of scrimmage from which the field goal was missed. Previously the ball was placed on the 20-yard line in every instance. As a result, the average field goal attempt is made from closer to the goal line than before.

Extra Points   A team in the NFL scores a touchdown. What are the chances that the extra-point attempt will be successful?   90.3 in 100

Third-Down Conversions   An NFL team lines up for a third-down play. What are the chances that the team will make a first down on this play?   39 in 100

Punt Returns   What are the chances that one team in the next NFL game will return a punt for a touchdown?   1 in 28
This is equivalent to approximately 1 touchdown run back in every 161 punts. The average team scores a touchdown on a punt return only once every two seasons.

Quarter Scoring   What are the chances that one of the teams in any given NFL game will score in the first quarter?   58 in 100
Here are the chances (in 100) that one or both teams will score in each quarter:

Scoring Outcome	Quarter			
	1st	2nd	3rd	4th
one or both teams score	58	67	66	65
both teams score	26	44	38	46
neither team scores	10	6	4	14

High-Scoring Quarter   What are the chances that in any NFL game more points will be scored by the two teams in the first quarter than in any other quarter?   9 in 100

in the second quarter	37 in 100
in the third quarter	17 in 100
in the fourth quarter	37 in 100

Lead Advantage   In any given NFL game, what are the chances that the team that ultimately wins the game will be the one that leads at the end of the first quarter?   75 in 100

end of the second quarter	78 in 100
end of the third quarter	86 in 100

Winning Margin   Two teams play an NFL regular season game. What are the chances that the game will be decided by a margin of 1 point? 4 in 100

2 points or less	9 in 100
3 " " "	22 in 100
4 " " "	29 in 100
5 " " "	33 in 100
6 " " "	40 in 100
7 " " "	48 in 100
8 " " "	50 in 100
9 " " "	53 in 100
10 " " "	58 in 100
11 " " "	62 in 100
12 " " "	64 in 100
13 " " "	66 in 100
14 " " "	69 in 100

17 points or less	77 in 100
20 ″ ″ ″	83 in 100
21 ″ ″ ″	88 in 100
25 ″ ″ ″	93 in 100
28 ″ ″ ″	95 in 100

Game Characteristics   In any given NFL game, what are the chances that one team will fail in an extra-point attempt?   26 in 100

that there will be no fumble turnovers	15	in 100
that one team will score a safety	6	in 100
that there will be no intercepted passes	5	in 100
that both teams will fail in extra-point attempts	3	in 100
that there will be no "sacks" (quarterback thrown for a loss while trying to pass)	3	in 100
that there will be no touchdowns	2	in 100
that there will be no turnovers	1.5	in 100
that there will be no yards lost through penalties	1	in 48,000
that there will be no punts	1	in 78,000

Perfect Record   What are the chances that the NFL will have an undefeated team in regular season games next year?   1 in 25
Only the Chicago Bears (1934 and 1942) and the Miami Dolphins (1972) have won all their regular season games in one year. The Bears won with thirteen- and eleven-game schedules, and Miami played fourteen season games. The 4-percent probability may be an overoptimistic estimate for the future, however, because to have an undefeated season now, a team would have to win sixteen games.

Season Forecast   Two NFL teams prepare for the first kickoff of the season. Last season one team won more games than the other. What are the chances that the team that did better last year will win more games again this year?   70 in 100

will win fewer games	24 in 100
will win the same number	6 in 100

Grey Cup Games

Total Points   Despite the weather and tough defenses, the Grey Cup game for the Canadian Football League championship traditionally is a wide-open, high-scoring affair. What are the chances that in the next Grey Cup contest the two teams together will score more than 50 points?   17 in 100

40 points or more	37 in 100
35 " " "	50 in 100
30 " " "	63 in 100
22 " " "	85 in 100

Winner's Total Points   What are the chances that the team that wins the Grey Cup will score more than 10 points in the championship game?   97 in 100

16 points or more	75 in 100
22 " " "	50 in 100
28 " " "	25 in 100
40 " " "	6 in 100

Winning Margin   What are the chances that any given Grey Cup game will be decided by only 1 point?   6 in 100

3 points or fewer	20 in 100
6 " " "	33 in 100
10 " " "	54 in 100
13 " " "	75 in 100

Perhaps the greatest string of thoroughly exciting Grey Cup games occurred between 1971 and 1976. The winning margin in four of those years was less than 5 points. Then, in 1977, the Montreal Alouettes engineered the first rout of the 1970s, pounding the Edmonton Eskimos 41–6.

GOLF

U.S. Golfers   What are the chances that any given person in the USA plays golf?   1 in 20

Holes-in-One   A golfer tees off, beginning play on an eighteen-hole golf course with three par-three holes. What are the chances that this is his or her game for a hole-in-one?   1 in 10,000

For a professional male golfer, the chances increase to 1 in 920; for a female professional, to 1 in 1,160.

The longest recorded hole-in-one was by Robert Mitera, whose drive found the hole 444 yards away on the tenth green of the Miracle Hills Golf Course, Omaha, Nebraska, in 1965. The most prolific hole-in-one marksman is Art Wall, Jr., a former Masters champion, who has aced more than forty holes.

Consecutive Holes-in-One   What are the odds against two players' making consecutive holes-in-one?   about 2 billion to 1
Ron Peterson and Barry Abraham of Vancouver, British Columbia, accomplished this feat in 1978. The same odds hold for two successive holes-in-one by a single player.

against three consecutive holes-in-one   90,071,134,505,408 to 1

Winning Strokes   Based on performances since 1950, what are the chances that a golfer will need to finish with fewer than 280 strokes to win the Masters Tournament?   42 in 100
the PGA Tournament   59 in 100
the British Open   48 in 100
the U.S. Open   26 in 100

Tournament Playoffs   The contestants tee off for the start of a PGA tournament. What is the likelihood that the contest will end in a play-off?   1 in 5

PGA Holes-in-One   What are the chances that one of the players in a PGA tournament will score a hole-in-one before the tournament ends? 54 in 100

Ryder Cup   What are the chances that the USA will win the Ryder Cup next year?   86 in 100
Ryder Cup matches are played biennially between the USA and Great Britain. The USA has not lost a Ryder Cup since 1957 and has lost only three times in the history of Cup play. In 1980, the series stood at USA 19, Great Britain 3.

GYMNASTICS

1980 Male Olympic Champion   Select a gymnast, place him among the top three finishers in any of the six individual male gymnastic events of the 1980 Moscow Olympics. What are the chances that he is Soviet?   11 in 18

East German or Soviet   15 in 18

Aleksandr Dityatin, a Soviet gymnast, won medals in all of the individual events. Including team events, Dityatin won eight medals—3 golds, 4 silvers, and a bronze—the most won by any individual during any single Olympics.

HOCKEY

Collegiate Champs   Pick a year between 1951 and 1981. What are the chances that in that year the NCAA hockey championship was won by Michigan?   20 in 100

by Denver   17 in 100

by Rensselaer Polytechnic Institute   3 in 100

Average Goals Allowed   A man plays goaltender in the NHL. What are the chances that he will allow an average of fewer than three goals per game over the season?   17 in 100

four or more goals per game   11 in 100

Of those goalies who play in ten or more games, roughly 1 in 6 holds the opposition to fewer than three goals per game.

Shutouts   A goaltender skates onto the ice to begin an NHL game. What are the chances that he will shut out the other team?
3.8 in 100

Successful Goals   There is a shot on goal in an NHL game. What are the chances that it will score?   1 in 9

Penalty Scores   An NHL player leaves the ice to spend time in the penalty box. What are the chances that his team will score without him?   1 in 40

Home Team Advantage   What are the chances that the home team will win any given NHL game?   64 in 100

Ties   What are the chances that any given NHL game will end in a tie?
1 in 6
   in a scoreless tie   1 in 684

Offense-Defense   In all team sports, people argue endlessly about whether offense or defense is the more important. One way to look at this is to determine which one produces more victories. When any two pro hockey teams are compared, what are the chances that the team that ends the season with more standings points (the combination of wins and ties) will be the one that during the season has scored more goals?   85 in 100
   that has allowed fewer goals   81 in 100
In other words, offense in hockey has a very slight advantage over defense in determining the year's final standings.

Playoffs   The face-off begins another NHL season. What chance does each team have to qualify for the postseason playoffs?
76 in 100
This is almost certain to change within the next few years. The NHL has been criticized for eliminating only five of its twenty-one teams from championship contention in the eighty-game regular season.

Stanley Cup   Based on past performance, what are the chances that a Canadian team will win the NHL championship, the Stanley Cup, next year?   3 in 5

What are the chances that the Stanley Cup winner next year will sweep the championship series four games to none?   31 in 100
   will win four games to one   26 in 100
   will win four games to two   31 in 100
   will win four games to three   11 in 100

HORSE RACING

Betting Favorites   And . . . they're off! The horses bolt from the starting gate. What are the chances that the favored horse will win?
1 in 3
   will finish in the money (first,
      second, or third)   2 in 3

Betting Odds   The horses line up for the start of a race. What are the chances that the winner will be among those leaving the gate at 4-to-1 odds or less?   4 in 5   80 in 100

Specifically, here are the chances that each horse has at each odds level:

Odds at Start of Race	Wins Necessary for Bettor to Profit	Actual Likelihood that the Horse Will Win
Even	more than 50%	47 in 100
2 to 1	more than 33%	29 in 100
3 to 1	more than 25%	21 in 100
4 to 1	more than 20%	16 in 100
25 to 1	more than 4%	1.2 in 100

Leaders   Ten horses run a 6-furlong race. One horse leads after the first quarter mile. What are the chances that it will win?   33 in 100
will be among the first three
finishers   50 in 100

If the horse leads at the half mile, what are the chances that it will win?   45 in 100
will be among the first three
finishers   60 in 100

If the horse leads at the stretch, what are the chances that it will win?   67 in 100
will be among the first three
finishers   95 in 100

Winning Margins   The tote board at the racetrack flickers as it maintains a continuous record of the bets placed on the horses entered in the next race. The odds are often very close because the races tend to be close. What are the chances that the two fastest horses in the next race will be separated at the finish by no more than 1 second? 88 in 100

A second is only a small amount of time, but a horse that wins a race by that margin is five lengths ahead of the competition.

Incidentally, horse races do not officially begin when the bell rings and the announcer shouts "They're off!" The official timing device starts after the starting gates open and the first horse reaches the starting pole.

Dead Heats   The horses round the final turn and pound toward the finish line. What are the chances that the race will end in a dead heat (tie) for first?   1 in 768

Derby Fillies   A filly runs in the Kentucky Derby. Based on previous Derby results, what are the chances that she will win?   6 in 100
Of the thirty-one fillies racing in the Kentucky Derby through May 1980, only two have crossed the finish line in first place, Regret (1915) and Genuine Risk (1980).

Disqualifications   Choose any of the official Kentucky Derby or Preakness winners. What are the chances that this champion won because of disqualification of another horse?   0
Winning horses can be disqualified because of foul claims or evidence of drugs in blood or urine. Such disqualifications are extremely rare, however, in prestigious horse racing events.

Triple Crown   A horse has won the Kentucky Derby and the Preakness. It is time for the Belmont Stakes. What are the chances that this horse will win the Belmont, taking the Triple Crown of horse racing? 55 in 100

Based on historical data from the past sixty years, what are the chances that there will be a Triple Crown winner next year?   1 in 5

Kincsem's Winning Streak   If you had been around between 1876 and 1879 and had had a chance to bet on the horse Kincsem in any of the fifty-four races that he entered, what are the chances that you would have won?   100 in 100
This is the best streak in the history of horse racing.

Willy Shoemaker   As of May 22, 1980, Willy Shoemaker, the jockey with more wins than any other, had ridden 7,841 horses to victory. Whenever Willy mounts a horse, what are the chances that he will ride it to the winner's circle?   23.3 in 100

Winning Jockeys   There are 1,500 jockeys registered in the USA. Choose any one at random. What are the chances that your choice failed to win a single race last year?   1 in 3

Races Entered   What are the chances that the winner of any given horse race in the USA was entered in at least one other race within the previous twenty-five days?   84 in 100

Travers Stakes Fillies   What are the chances that a filly will win the Travers Stakes next year?   less than 1 in 20

Race Horse Investing   Assume that you have enough money to purchase any thoroughbred you like. You raise the horse with care; you hire competent groomers and trainers. What are the chances that your horse will ever run in a money race?   41 in 100
    will win enough to earn its keep   14 in 100
    will win the Kentucky Derby   1 in 30,000
Investing in a Derby winner gets more competitive every year. In 1919, Sir Barton was one of 1,665 registered foals. In 1948, Citation was one of 8,434. By 1979, Spectacular Bid emerged as the best of the registered crop of 30,000.

Horse Color   A thoroughbred horse is registered in the USA. What are the chances that the horse is white?   1 in 187,500

Gelding   A male thoroughbred horse faces a risk that threatens few human males. Many quality horses are gelded (castrated) at some time during their lives. What are the chances that any given male thoroughbred horse will be gelded?   1 in 4

Hambletonian's Progeny   Select at random a thoroughbred entered in a harness race. What are the chances that this horse's lineage can be traced back to one forebear, Hambletonian, foaled in 1849?
95 in 100

OLYMPIC GAMES

Perhaps more than in any other sporting event, it may be dangerous to predict future performance by past results in the Olympics. Here are a number of Olympic Games events that U.S. contestants have entered over the years. If U.S. athletes repeat their successes in the future, what are their chances of winning each of these events? These figures do not include the 1980 Moscow Olympics.

Men's Events
Basketball   90 in 100

Track and Field
   pole vault   89 in 100
   long jump   89 in 100
   shotput   78 in 100
   high jump   67 in 100
   400-meter relays   86 in 100
   110-meter hurdles   83 in 100
   400-meter hurdles   75 in 100
   100 meters   67 in 100
   200 meters   71 in 100
   400 meters   67 in 100
   800 meters   44 in 100
   1,500 meters   11 in 100
   5,000 meters   7 in 100
   10,000 meters   7 in 100
   marathon   17 in 100

Swimming and Diving
   springboard diving   81 in 100
   platform diving   64 in 100
   100-meter freestyle   59 in 100
   400-meter freestyle   56 in 100
   1,500-meter freestyle   40 in 100

Boxing
   flyweight   36 in 100
   bantamweight   7 in 100
   featherweight   13 in 100
   lightweight   27 in 100
   middleweight   33 in 100
   heavyweight   36 in 100

Gymnastics (all around)   6 in 100

Male U.S. athletes have never won a gold medal in fencing, cycling, canoeing, or the modern pentathlon.

Women's Events
Swimming and Diving

springboard diving	85 in 100
platform diving	64 in 100
400-meter freestyle	58 in 100
100-meter backstroke	50 in 100
100-meter freestyle	43 in 100
200-meter breast-stroke	8 in 100

Track and Field

100 meters	45 in 100
200 meters	25 in 100
high jump	27 in 100
javelin throw	10 in 100
discus throw	9 in 100

Female U.S. athletes have never won a gold medal in the 400 meters, 1,500 meters, shotput, long jump, or gymnastics.

SOCCER

Fans   What are the chances that any given person attending a North American Soccer League game is female?   47 in 100

Players   A North American Soccer League contest is under way. What are the chances that the next player to touch the ball was born outside the USA?   55 in 100

Olympic Soccer   Based on past performance, what chance does each of these countries have of producing the championship soccer team in the next Olympic Games?

Great Britain	3 in 17	18 in 100
Hungary	3 in 17	18 in 100
Uruguay	2 in 17	12 in 100
Belgium	1 in 17	6 in 100
Canada	1 in 17	6 in 100
Czechoslovakia	1 in 17	6 in 100
East Germany	1 in 17	6 in 100

Italy	1 in 17	6 in 100
Poland	1 in 17	6 in 100
Sweden	1 in 17	6 in 100
USSR	1 in 17	6 in 100
Yugoslavia	1 in 17	6 in 100

World Cup   The World Cup finals began in 1930 and continue every four years as a world soccer championship series. Because of World War II, no tournaments were held in 1942 and 1946. If each country's team performs in the future as it has in the past, what chance does each country have of winning the next World Cup?

Brazil	3 in 11	27 in 100
Italy	2 in 11	18 in 100
Uruguay	2 in 11	18 in 100
West Germany	2 in 11	18 in 100
Argentina	1 in 11	9 in 100
Great Britain	1 in 11	9 in 100

TENNIS

First-Set Advantage   A player in any of the world's major tennis tournaments opens play. What are the chances that the player who wins the first set will win the match?   82 in 100

will win in straight sets   42 in 100

In spite of the probabilities, however, in the 1979 Wimbledon tournament, both Bjorn Borg and Martina Navratilova, who went on to become the singles champions, lost their first sets.

Straight Sets   During the first Wimbledon tournament, in 1877, S. W. Gore defeated W. C. Marshall in straight sets for the championship (6–1, 6–2, 6–4). What are the chances that next year's men's singles champion will win the final match in straight sets?   62 in 100

Champions   Based on past performance, what are the chances that a competitor from the USA will become the Wimbledon men's singles champion next year?   41 in 100

Australians have won 28 percent of the men's singles championships, and the French, 13 percent.

women's singles champion   58 in 100

Davis Cup   Based on past performance, what are the chances that the Davis Cup will be won next year by the team from the USA? 38 in 100

Australia	34 in 100
Great Britain	14 in 100
France	9 in 100
Italy	1.5 in 100
South Africa	1.5 in 100
Sweden	1.5 in 100

The USA won the 1979 Davis Cup by shutting out Italy, 5–0. Nearly one third of Davis Cup finals (31%) have ended in shutouts.

TRACK AND FIELD

Women's 200 Meters   Pick a number from 1 to 10. Now find your number on a list of the ten fastest women running the 200-meter run as of January 1, 1979. What are the chances that the woman in that position on the list is from East Germany?   2 in 5
  from the USA   1 in 5

Women's 400 Meters   Based on the twenty records set by women in the 400-meter race since 1957, what are the chances that the next record-setter will be from East Germany?   1 in 4   25 in 100
  from the USSR   1 in 5   20 in 100

Men's Mile   Based on mile records from Walter George's 4:18.4 in 1884 to Steve Ovett's 3:48.8 on July 1, 1980, when this record is broken, what are the chances that the man who does it will be from the USA?   23 in 100
  from Kansas   10 in 100
  Glenn Cunningham and Jim Ryan, both former world record holders for the mile, grew up in Kansas.

  from Great Britain   19 in 100
  from New Zealand   13 in 100

OTHER SPORTING ACTIVITIES

USA   A person lives in the USA. What are the chances that this individual regularly swims?   47 in 100

bicycles	35 in 100
fishes	30 in 100
camps out	27 in 100
bowls	21 in 100
plays tennis	14 in 100

Bobsledding   A two-person team wins the national AAU bobsledding championship. What are the chances that this team will win again next year?   26 in 100

that the team leader will someday sled again on a championship team   1 in 2

Horseshoe Pitching   The finals of a state horseshoe pitching contest are under way. What are the chances that the next horseshoe thrown will be a ringer?   65 in 100

will be a double ringer   42 in 100

Jai Alai   A player is registered for professional jai alai matches. What are the chances that he is a Basque?   9 in 10

Jogging   A person will be injured while jogging today. What are the chances that the jogging surface will be responsible?   3 in 5
Concrete is too hard for most joggers. Asphalt is only somewhat better. Most softer surfaces have holes and other irregularities.

Mountain Climbing   A mountain climber begins an ascent toward a peak in the Karakorams or Himalayas. What are the chances that he or she will not return alive?   1 in 20

Pocket Billiards   A man wins the World Pocket Billiards Championship. What chance does he have of successfully defending his championship next year?   22 in 100

Scuba Diving   A scuba diver explored U.S. waters in 1971. What are the chances that this diver was a woman?   1 in 20

The popularity of scuba diving increased dramatically among women during the 1970s. By 1975, 1 in 5 divers (20%) was female, and by 1980, women comprised nearly one third (30%) of the scuba-diving population.

Skateboarding   A person receives medical treatment for a skateboard injury. What are the chances that the injury includes a broken arm or leg?   30 in 100

cuts and/or bruises	24 in 100
strains and/or sprains	18 in 100

Yachting   Based on America's Cup yacht racing history, what are the chances that the USA will win the next America's Cup race? 91 in 100

9 Nature

The odds in this chapter primarily provide insights into the occurrence of natural phenomena, the wealth of the world—its minerals, plants, land, and energy—and the diversity of climate and weather. The odds relating to weather and land use are of constant practical use to the farmer—and often to the vacationer. The odds concerning mineral wealth are the material upon which multibillion-dollar efforts to mine or drill are based—and favorable odds often make both corporations and nations rich. Many of these same odds are important to energy consultants, and they guide the direction for seeking alternatives for the future. And the odds of there being intelligent beings in outer space help us keep ourselves in proper perspective, while they guide efforts by astronomers to reach ever farther into the universe.

This sample of odds will help draw attention to the interactions of our lives, our society, and our culture with natural phenomena and the world's natural resources.

NATURAL PHENOMENA

Earthquakes

Effects   Today a detectable earthquake occurs somewhere in the world. What are the chances that the quake will damage someone's property?   1 in 500
  that humans will feel it   1 in 100
There are almost 2,000 earthquakes in the world every day.

Insurance   A California home is destroyed by an earthquake. What are the odds that the homeowner has earthquake insurance?
1 in 20

Fatalities   A person is injured in an earthquake. What is the risk that this injury is fatal?   1 in 31

Geysers

Old Faithful   Pick any hour of the day. What are the chances that Old Faithful in Yellowstone National Park will not erupt during that 60-minute period?   8 in 100
While Old Faithful does not erupt hourly, it does shoot forth twenty-one to twenty-three times during each 24-hour period.

Hurricanes

Intensity   A hurricane hits the USA. What are the chances that it is classified as a minor hurricane?   59 in 100
  as a major hurricane   41 in 100
Nearly 30 percent of U.S. hurricanes are moderate in intensity.

Target Areas   A major hurricane makes a direct hit on the USA. What are the chances that at least part of its target area is in Florida?
39 in 100
  in Florida or Texas   67 in 100

Historic   Randomly choose a person who was living in Galveston, Texas, a few hours before the hurricane of 1900 struck the city. What are the chances that this person's home was completely destroyed?
68 in 100

that his or her home escaped
   damage   0
that the person was killed   16   in 100
that the person was left naked   2.6 in 100

The Galveston hurricane of 1900 killed more than 6,000 people and was the worst natural disaster in U.S. history.

Season   If a hurricane strikes the USA next year, what are the chances that it will strike in September?   57 in 100
  in August   21 in 100
  in August, September, or October   90 in 100

Tidal Waves   A person somewhere in the world is killed in a hurricane. What are the chances that it was the surging waters of a tidal wave, rather than the winds or rains directly, that caused the death? 9 in 10

Lightning

Superbolts   A lightning bolt strikes. What are the chances that it is a superbolt (at least 10 trillion watts)?   1 in 2 million
The odds are great that you will never see a superbolt, but if you are determined to try, the best time is during a winter storm over the Pacific, north of Japan.

Victim Gender   What are the odds that the next person struck by lightning will be a man?   6 in 7
As more women move into outdoor work and play, the risks to them are likely to increase.

Urban-Rural Risks   One person lives in a city; another lives in a rural area. One of the two is injured by lightning. What are the odds that the victim is the country dweller?   9 in 10
Large city buildings carry most lightning away without damage.

Survival   What are the chances that a person who is struck by lightning will survive?   65 in 100
Quick mouth-to-mouth resuscitation and heart massage can improve a lightning victim's chances of survival.

Fatality Risks   What are the chances of any one individual's being killed by lightning this year?   1 in 2 million

Relative Risks   A person dies either from being hit by lightning or from being bitten by a shark. Of the two, what are the odds that the death is caused by lightning?   3 to 1   75 in 100
　　by lightning rather than by bites or
　　　stings of venomous animals or
　　　insects   2 to 1   67 in 100
　　by lightning rather than by either a
　　　hurricane or a tornado   52 in 100

Tornadoes

Downbursts   A mobile home is damaged during a storm that includes a tornado. What are the chances that the damage was caused by a "downburst" (a rapidly moving downward air current that accompanies about half of all tornadoes) rather than by the tornado?   3 in 4

Fatalities   A tornado touches ground. What are the chances that it will take a human life?   1 in 25
Although relatively few tornadoes cause human death, those that are lethal usually take more than one life.

Months   What are the chances that any given tornado reported by the U.S. Weather Service is sighted in May?   22 in 100

June	20 in 100	December	3 in 100
July	11 in 100	January	2 in 100
August	7 in 100	February	2 in 100
September	5 in 100	March	6 in 100
October	3 in 100	April	15 in 100
November	3 in 100		

Volcanoes

Indonesia   Molten lava bubbles inside a volcano somewhere on the earth. What are the chances that this volcanic activity is taking place in Indonesia?   1 in 5
Counting inactive as well as active ones, 37 percent of the world's volcanoes are in Indonesia.

MINERAL RESOURCES

Aluminum
World Production   A ton of aluminum is mined somewhere in the world. What are the chances that this occurs in the USA?   38 in 100
  in Canada   15 in 100
  in the USSR   15 in 100
Australia will someday lead the world in aluminium (as it is spelled in Australia) production. That country now owns 26 percent of the earth's known aluminum reserves.

Use   A gram of aluminum is used in the USA. What are the chances that it is used in construction?   22 in 100
  in making a container or package   22 in 100
  in the transportation industry   21 in 100

Coal
Occurrence   Choose any square meter of West Virginia at random. What are the chances that there is coal beneath the surface?
69 in 100
Here are the chances (in 100) for the other thirty-four states that have coal reserves.

Illinois	67	Tennessee	11
North Dakota	45	South Dakota	10
Wyoming	41	Alaska	6
Iowa	36	Texas	6
Kentucky	36	Virginia	5
Missouri	35	Maryland	4
Montana	35	Arizona	3
Pennsylvania	33	Arkansas	3
Colorado	28	Louisiana	3
Ohio	24	North Carolina	3
Kansas	23	Mississippi	2
Oklahoma	21	Washington	2
Michigan	20	Nebraska	1.3
Alabama	19	Idaho	0.6
Indiana	18	Oregon	0.6
Utah	18	Georgia	0.2
New Mexico	12	California	0.1

For the country as a whole, coal can be found beneath 13 percent of the surface area. The USA has one third of the world's recoverable coal reserves; the USSR, one fourth; China, one fifth.

Copper

Recycling   What are the chances that the next copper product manufactured in the USA will be produced from recycled copper?   2 in 5
As the probabilities indicate, copper is one of the most recycled materials. This compares favorably with the 25-percent recycle rate for aluminum and 20 percent for new paper products.

Diamonds

Source/Purpose   A diamond is discovered somewhere in the world. What are the chances that it is found in Zaire?   32 in 100
   that it will be used for industrial
       purposes   20 in 100
More than half of all diamonds used for industrial purposes are imported by the USA.

Gold

Source   An ounce of gold is known to be recoverable. What are the chances that it is in the Republic of South Africa?   1 in 2
More than 60 percent of the gold mined in 1979 came from South Africa. In addition, South Africa owns 74 percent of the chromium, 71 percent of the platinum, and 45 percent of the manganese reserves in the world.

Use   An ounce of gold has been mined and refined. What are the chances that it now lies in government or central banks?   3 in 5

Iron

Source   What are the chances that any given kilogram of the world's supply of iron lies beneath soil in the USSR?   31 in 100

Nickel

Source   Somewhere on the earth a kilogram of the world's known nickel reserves lies below the ground. What are the chances that it is in New Caledonia?   44 in 100

Mercury
Source   What are the chances that any given gram of mercury is produced in Spain?   41 in 100

Oil
Recoverable   A drop of oil lies in a reservoir under U.S. soil. What are the chances that workers can bring it up?   32 in 100
This is an almost 30-percent improvement over the 1940s, when only 25 percent of the oil could be recovered. However, most oil still cannot be retrieved using state-of-the-art technology.

World Production   A barrel of crude oil is pumped out of the ground somewhere in the world. What are the chances that this oil comes from the USSR?   18 in 100
    from Saudi Arabia   17   in 100
    from the USA   16   in 100
    from Kuwait   3.5 in 100
In 1900, the USA and the USSR produced 94 percent of the world's oil.

Use   A barrel of crude oil travels to a refinery for U.S. consumption. What are the chances that it will be made into gasoline?   40 in 100
    into material used in clothing   1 in 100
    The materials from which clothes are made account for only 2–8 percent of the eventual retail price.

Oil and Gas Lottery   A person pays a ten-dollar fee to enter the U.S. government lottery for tracts of land for oil and gas exploration. What are the chances that this individual will win the drawing?   1 in 2,778
If the individual wins one of these lotteries, there is only a 10-percent chance that anyone will ever drill on his or her land tract.

Salt
Flavoring   A kilogram of salt is mined in the USA. What are the chances that it will be used to flavor food eaten by humans?
1 in 100

Silver
Use   A gram of silver is used in manufacturing a product in the USA.

What are the chances that it will end up in film or other photographic materials?   38 in 100
  in electrical appliances   25 in 100

Sterling   Imagine that a random molecule could be isolated from an object of sterling silver. What are the chances that the molecule would actually be copper?   7.5 in 100
Since pure silver is too soft for most applications, copper is mixed with it for strength.

Sources   An ounce of silver is produced. What is the likelihood that this ounce was recovered from ore containing primarily lead, lead and zinc, copper, copper and nickel, or gold?   3 in 4
Since silver is rarely mined in its pure form, its production depends largely upon factors related to these other metals.

Tin
Use   A U.S. manufacturer uses a gram of tin in a product. What are the chances that it is used to tin plate a part of the product?
43 in 100
  in solder   25 in 100
  in chemicals   10 in 100

Uranium
Ownership   What are the chances that a U.S. oil company owns the rights to any given uranium reserves in the USA?   47 in 100
Oil companies also own 12 percent of the USA's coal reserves.

Imports and Use
Manufacturing   Choose at random one kilogram of material used by a manufacturer in the USA. What are the chances that this material was imported from another country?

diamonds	100 in 100	nickel	77 in 100
natural rubber	100 in 100	zinc	62 in 100
manganese	98 in 100	potash	61 in 100
cobalt	97 in 100	mercury	57 in 100
bauxite	93 in 100	gold	54 in 100
chrome	92 in 100	petroleum	44 in 100

platinum	91 in 100	silver	41 in 100
asbestos	84 in 100	gypsum	34 in 100
tin	81 in 100	tungsten	25 in 100

The USA depends on other countries of the world for far more than oil.

Auto Industry What is the probability that automobile manufacturing utilizes any given kilogram of steel used in the USA?   21 in 100

aluminum	10 in 100
lead	55 in 100
zinc	37 in 100
rubber	65 in 100

ENERGY

Consumption
Sources A person in the USA uses a BTU of energy (BTU stands for British Thermal Unit, the international measure of all forms of energy). What are the chances that it comes from oil?   48.5 in 100

natural gas	25.4 in 100
coal	18.1 in 100
hydro (water) power	4 in 100
nuclear power	4 in 100
solar power	1 in 100
geothermal power	1 in 1,000
wood or waste power	1 in 1,000

Electric utility companies consume 30 percent of the nation's annual energy supply, while transportation accounts for another 25 percent. In 1978, the USA used 78 quadrillion BTUs.

Efficiency A particle of fuel enters a home furnace. What are the chances that it will produce usable heat?   1 in 2
Almost half the heat produced in most furnaces goes up the flue.

Sources
Dung A cow produces dung in India. What are the chances that the dung will be used as fuel for cooking food?   55 in 100
Cow dung is India's most important energy resource. More than 31 percent of India's energy is provided by dung, while only 6 percent comes from oil.

Geothermal   A person lives in Iceland. What are the odds that he or she lives in a building heated by natural hot water from below the surface of the earth?   1 in 2
Virtually everyone in Reykjavik uses this free geothermal heat.

Peach Pits   A BTU of energy is used for producing steam in canning at the Tri-Valley Growers Plant in Modesto, California. What are the chances that the energy comes from burning peach pits?   4 in 5

Peat   Certain energy officials believe that peat (partly decayed plant matter) will be one of the fuels of the future. When the next ton of peat is taken out of the ground, what are the chances that it will be in the USSR?   56 in 100
There are seventy-six electrical power plants fueled by peat in the USSR. The USA has the second largest peat supply in the world (13%), equivalent to 240 billion barrels of oil. The bulk of U.S. peat lies in Alaska, Minnesota, Michigan, Florida, and Wisconsin.

Wood   Somewhere in the world, a person cuts a piece of timber. What are the chances that it will be burned as fuel for warmth or cooking rather than being made into some sort of product?   1 in 2

A human being lives somewhere on this planet. What is the probability that this person works each day finding firewood to cook with?
37 in 100

Characteristics
Gamma Rays   A gamma ray particle strikes a 1-foot-thick slab of rock or soil. What are the chances that the particle will pass through the material?   1 in 1,000

Hydrogen   A particle of energy lies in a portion of hydrogen that will be exploded in a hydrogen bomb. What are the chances that this particular particle will be released as part of the explosive force?
1 in 100
Even though scientists can release enormous amounts of energy through nuclear reactions, they still are able to extract only a tiny portion of hydrogen's theoretical capacity in a thermonuclear explosion.

Nuclear Fuel   A single energy-releasing fission reaction takes place within a nuclear reactor. What is the probability that the reaction takes place in uranium 235?   60 in 100

in plutonium 239 (a product
produced by the fission process)   31 in 100
in uranium 238   5 in 100
in plutonium 241   4 in 100

Solar Energy Reflection   A calorie of sunlight strikes the earth. What are the chances that it will be reflected back into space?   29 in 100

will be absorbed by green plants   3.3 in 100

A calorie of sunlight falls on a hardwood forest. What is the probability that the energy will bounce back into space?   15 in 100

will be converted through
photosynthesis into plant tissue   1 in 250

AIR AND WATER

Air
Oxygen Generation   A green plant produces a molecule of oxygen. What are the chances that this plant is growing in the Amazon Basin? 1 in 2

Pollution   What are the chances that any given particle of air pollution in the USA comes from the emission of a combustion engine? 4 in 5

Blocked Energy   A particle of solar energy heads for a major U.S. city on a meteorologically clear day. What are the chances that it will actually reach the city without being blocked by smoke or other pollution? 4 in 5

Water
Distribution   What are the chances that any given liter of the earth's water is located in an ocean?   97 in 100

exists as ice   2 in 100

is located in a lake or river   1 in 10,000
is currently in the form of rain   less than 1 in 100,000

Fresh Water   What are the chances that any given drop of the earth's water is fresh water rather than ocean water?   2.6 in 100
Half the earth's freshwater supply lies in the Amazon Basin and the five Great Lakes.

Access   What are the chances that an individual selected randomly from anywhere on Earth is without access to safe drinking water?
1 in 3

A person lives in a rural area somewhere in the world. What are the chances that he or she has no ready access to drinkable water?
3 in 4
For people who live in urban areas, the chances drop to 1 in 5.

Snowflakes   What are the chances that any single undamaged snowflake is hexagonal (six-sided)?   98 in 100
The vast majority of snowflakes are hexagonal unless they collide with other flakes or melt. Due to the molecular structure of water (which consists of three atoms: one of oxygen and two of hydrogen), all undamaged snowflakes have points equal to a multiple of three.

LAND, PLANTS, AND AGRICULTURE

Land
Use   Randomly choose a square meter of land in the USA. What are the chances that this area is pastureland?   34 in 100

forestland	25 in 100
cropland	21 in 100
desert, tundra, or swamp	13 in 100
parkland (federal, state, or city)	4 in 100
within the limits of a city	3 in 100
under a highway	6.4 in 1,000
covered by a roof	1 in 2,000

Arable   Choose an acre of land anywhere in the world. What are the chances that it is suitable for growing food?   3 in 10
The rest is too steep, too cold, too dry, or too rocky.

U.S. Cropland   What are the chances that a particular acre of Alaska's total area is currently being used to grow crops?   5 in 100
Here are the chances (in 100) for the remaining states.

Alabama	10	Nebraska	40
Arizona	2	Nevada	1
Arkansas	22	New Hampshire	2
California	9	New Jersey	12
Colorado	14	New Mexico	2
Connecticut	5	New York	15
Delaware	40	North Carolina	16
Florida	8	North Dakota	61
Georgia	13	Ohio	39
Hawaii	4	Oklahoma	23
Idaho	10	Oregon	7
Illinois	64	Pennsylvania	14
Indiana	59	Rhode Island	3
Iowa	67	South Carolina	13
Kansas	51	South Dakota	33
Kentucky	17	Tennessee	15
Louisiana	14	Texas	14
Maine	2	Utah	2
Maryland	25	Vermont	9
Massachusetts	4	Virginia	44
Michigan	18	Washington	18
Minnesota	40	West Virginia	5
Mississippi	18	Wisconsin	27
Missouri	27	Wyoming	3
Montana	15		

Erosion   A particle of farm soil is swept up by heavy winds and settles in a U.S. waterway. What are the chances that it will be carried all the way to the ocean?   1 in 4
Most topsoil and other particles sink to the bottom as sediment. This sediment, useful on farms and rangeland, is actually harmful to rivers, lakes, and reservoirs.

Irrigation   A farmer irrigates a crop in the usual manner, letting water flow through the furrows. What are the chances that any given molecule of this water will actually be absorbed by a plant for moisture? 45 in 100
Depending on conditions, the range is from 30 to 60 percent.

Livestock Food   Choose at random an acre of arable land in the USA. What are the chances that the food grown on it goes to feed livestock? 3 in 4

Plants
Named   A plant species is growing somewhere on Earth. What are the chances that scientists know (have named and described) this species?   31 in 100

Extinction   A plant grows somewhere in the world. What are the chances that it will become extinct next year?   1 in 175
The world loses 200 plant species each year. With them go all their genetic material, their nutritional and medicinal possibilities, and special abilities to adapt to difficult living conditions. When these are lost, they are lost forever.

Grass   A type of land vegetation grows somewhere in the world. What are the chances that the vegetation is a type of grass?   3 in 10

Bamboo   Choose at random any year in the history of the world. What are the chances that the Madake bamboo plants of the world blossomed that year?   1 in 120
It makes no difference when this unique tree (actually a grass) is planted, nor where. During the same year in roughly every 120 years, every Madake throughout the world blossoms.

Food Plants   From a list of every known plant in the world, choose one name at random. What are the chances that you have chosen an edible plant that stands between survival and famine for the human population of the world?   13 in 800,000

Agriculture
Worldwide Food Production   A kilogram of food is produced some-

where in the world. What are the chances that its source is Europe?
36 in 100

Asia	30 in 100
USA	16 in 100
Latin America	7 in 100
Africa	6 in 100
Oceania	2 in 100

The USA produces a relatively small percentage of the world's food. However, compared to its population size, the USA is a super food producer.
While Asia and Europe together produce 66 percent of the world's food,
they account for 72 percent of the world's population. In contrast, the USA,
with less than 6 percent of the world's population, provides one sixth of the
world's food.

Soviet Agriculture   What are the chances that any given farm in the
USSR will have a drought this year?   2 in 3

A citizen of the USSR consumes a serving of produce grown in that
country. What are the chances that it was grown on a privately cultivated 1-acre plot of land?   37 in 100
Such plots cover only 3 percent of the USSR's tillable land; yet they account for a fair percentage of the Soviet food supply.

Plant Products   What are the chances that any given banana in the
world was grown in Ecuador?   33 in 100
Of all the bananas in the world last year, 1 in 3 grew in Ecuador. Leading
producers of other plant products are presented below.

Product	Leading Producer	Average Percent of Total World Production from 1975–1979
Barley	USSR	29
Cloves	Tanzania	66
Coffee	Brazil	38
Corn	USA	50
Cotton	USA	16
Grapefruit	USA	85
Grapes	Italy	28
Lemons	USA	43

Millet	China	50
Oranges	USA	90
Peppers	India	38
Potatoes	USSR	31
Rice	China	20
Rubber	Malaysia	44
Sorghum	USA	37
Sugar beets	USSR	31
Sugarcane	India	22
Sweet potatoes	China	29
Wheat	USSR	23

Corn   An ear of corn ripens in a U.S. field. What are the chances that it will be fed to livestock?   85 in 100
About half of all livestock corn is fed to pigs.

Cotton   A bale of cotton is produced in the USA. What are the chances that it was grown in California rather than Alabama?   4 to 1
80 in 100
California produces more cotton annually than Alabama and Georgia combined.

Olives   An olive tree grows somewhere on Earth. What are the chances that it stands in Europe?   3 in 4
Only 3 percent of the world's olive trees grow in the USA.

Peanuts   A peanut grows on a farm in the USA. What are the chances that it ultimately will be used for peanut butter?   1 in 2

Potatoes   A U.S. farmer digs a potato during the harvest. What are the chances that it will end up as potato chips?   14 in 100

Rice   A stalk of rice stretches upward in the summer sun. What are the chances that it is growing in Asia?   9 in 10

CLIMATE AND WEATHER

Cloud Cover
Daily   What are the chances that any given day in Yuma, Arizona, will

be classified as clear by the U.S. Weather Service?   68 in 100
    as partly cloudy   19 in 100
    as cloudy   13 in 100

Here are the probabilities (chances in 100) for various other U.S. locations:

Location	Clear	Partly Cloudy	Cloudy
Fresno, California	55	19	26
San Diego, California	41	32	27
Oklahoma City	38	27	35
Lincoln, Nebraska	32	26	42
Atlanta, Georgia	30	30	40
Houston, Texas	26	31	43
Billings, Montana	24	32	44
Portland, Oregon	19	19	62
Miami, Florida	20	33	47
Charleston, West Virginia	16	32	52
Hilo, Hawaii	9	34	57

Precipitation

Annual   What are the chances that Des Moines, Iowa, will receive 31 inches of precipitation or more this year?   1 in 2

Here is the average annual precipitation (in inches) for several other U.S. locations:

Yuma, Arizona	2.67
Las Vegas, Nevada	3.76
Bakersfield, California	5.72
Albuquerque, New Mexico	7.77
San Diego, California	9.45
Havre, Montana	11.55
Denver, Colorado	15.51
Minneapolis, Minnesota	25.94
Omaha, Nebraska	30.18
Atlanta, Georgia	48.34
Jacksonville, Florida	54.47
New Orleans, Louisiana	56.77
Quillayute, Washington	104.99

Daily   What are the chances that measurable precipitation will occur today in Hilo, Hawaii?   77 in 100

Here are the chances for other selected U.S. locations:

Juneau, Alaska	61 in 100
Quillayute, Washington	59 in 100
Sault Ste. Marie, Michigan	45 in 100
South Bend, Indiana	39 in 100
Miami, Florida	36 in 100
Birmingham, Alabama	32 in 100
Sheridan, Wyoming	30 in 100
Des Moines, Iowa	29 in 100
Denver, Colorado	24 in 100
Yakima, Washington	19 in 100
Los Angeles, California	10 in 100
Las Vegas, Nevada	7 in 100

Drought   **What are the chances that a severe drought will strike the western USA in the mid-1990s?   4 in 5**
This region experiences a drought approximately every twenty-two years; the last was in the mid-1970s.

Annual Snowfall   **What are the chances that 32 inches of snow or more will fall in Omaha, Nebraska, during the next snow season? 1 in 2**
Here is the average snowfall (in inches) for selected U.S. locations:

Birmingham, Alabama	1.1
Fort Smith, Arkansas	6.1
New York, New York (Central Park)	29.3
Chicago, Illinois	40.0
Youngstown, Ohio	57.6
South Bend, Indiana	70.4
Erie, Pennsylvania	83.6
Mount Shasta, California	108.3
Syracuse, New York	112.3
Valdez, Alaska	294.2
Stampede Pass, Washington	442.4

Christmas Snow   **Bing Crosby dreamed of a white Christmas, and many Hollywood stars each year profess a yearning for one. What is the chance that this year will bring a white Christmas to Los Angeles? 1.6 in 100**
   to Omaha, Nebraska   37 in 100

Temperature

Freezing Days   Pick one day of the year at random. What are the chances that Barrow, Alaska, will have a minimum temperature of 0° C or lower on this day?   89 in 100

Here are the probabilities for other selected U.S. locations:

International Falls, Minnesota	54 in 100
Fargo, North Dakota	49 in 100
Winslow, Arizona	39 in 100
Buffalo, New York	37 in 100
Chicago, Illinois	33 in 100
Annette, Alaska	22 in 100
Little Rock, Arkansas	22 in 100
Portland, Oregon	12 in 100
Tallahassee, Florida	10 in 100
Oakland, California	3 in 1,000

Weather Forecasts

Long-range Accuracy   The U.S. Weather Service issues a long-range precipitation outlook for the next three months. What are the chances that this forecast will be essentially correct?   55 in 100

Long-range weather forecasting beyond two weeks is still an inexact art. The U.S. Weather Service bases its long-term forecasts on computerized studies of weather patterns over the last thirty years. *The Old Farmer's Almanac* relies largely on solar activity for its long-term predictions. Both methods produce forecasts just slightly better than chance.

Short-range Accuracy   The U.S. Weather Service reports a precipitation probability of 85 percent for an area for tomorrow. What are the real odds that it will rain or snow during the coming 24 hours?   4 in 5

At certain probability levels, the Weather Service routinely overstates the real precipitation chances. Weather Service forecasts, however, are about 50 percent more accurate than guesswork.

OUTER SPACE

Planets   Look overhead on a clear night and choose a star. What are the odds that the star has planets orbiting it?   1 in 3

Other Civilizations   Scientists are currently using high-powered radio beams in attempts to contact other civilizations in our universe. But when the radio astronomer focuses on a star, no one knows whether or not there are living beings there to pick up the transmission. Scientists therefore are guided only by probabilities. What are the chances that the star we focus on tonight has a planet inhabited by a civilization advanced enough to receive our signals?   1 in 200,000

Supernovas   Scientists tell us that it is possible that a supernova explosion could destroy all life on Earth. What are the chances that this will happen next year?   1 in 100 million

Meteors   Two people go outdoors to search the skies for meteors. One of them watches before midnight and the other one after. One spots a meteor; the other does not. What are the chances that the post-midnight person was the lucky one?   83 in 100

Asteroid Names   Astronomers have discovered more than 2,000 asteroids. Think of a number from 1 to 2,000. What are the chances that the asteroid assigned that number in astronomy texts carries the name of a university spelled backwards?   1 in 2,000
The asteroid is number 694, Ekard, named for Drake University of Des Moines, Iowa. If you choose a low number, you are likely to get an asteroid named after a Greek or Roman god: number 1 is Ceres; 2, Pallas; and 3, Juno. Had you chosen number 710, your asteroid would be Gertrud.

Martian Atmosphere   One random molecule of the atmosphere of Mars is isolated. What are the chances that the molecule is carbon dioxide?   96 in 100

nitrogen	2.5 in 100
argon 40	1.5 in 100
oxygen	1 in 1,000

Solar System Matter   Imagine that all the matter in our solar system collapses into a ball of seething, random matter. Then from the ball one molecule is extracted. What are the chances that the molecule originally belonged to the sun?   999 in 1,000

to asteroids, comets, or the planets and their moons	1 in 1,000

10   Animals

The odds in this chapter can do no more than hint at the incredible variety in the animal kingdom. They represent a sampling of the fascinating world of animals, their distribution, habits, diet, reproduction, longevity, and threats to survival—or extinction. Considering some of the odds against their survival, you may find it amazing that they make it at all.

The selection of odds reflects the many risks in the animal's life cycle—for instance, that it will mate, that it will lay an egg, that the egg will hatch, that the offspring will survive to adulthood. Threats from the environment and predators are also included.

The odds of a human's being bitten by various types of animals, of dying from animal bites, or of contracting rabies are also presented. Many of these odds should dispel some old wives' tales.

Of most use perhaps will be the odds on being bitten by a mosquito. By choosing the color of your clothing wisely, you may be able to avoid this unwelcome contact with the world of animals.

SURVIVAL

Extinction   An animal was alive at the time when dinosaurs roamed the earth. What are the odds that it and all members of its species died when the dinosaurs did?   3 in 4

An animal species became extinct sometime during the last 2,000 years. What are the chances that it did not become extinct until the twentieth century?   1 in 2

Surviving Species   Of all the species of animals that have ever inhabited the earth, what are the chances that any given one still survives today?   7.5 in 100

AMPHIBIANS

Frogs
Live Food   A frog catches a fly. What are the chances that the insect was alive when it entered the frog's mouth?   100 in 100
A frog's eyes respond only to light and movement. If a creature does not move, the frog literally cannot see it. Thus, frogs eat only living (and moving) organisms.

Toads
Warts   A human touches a toad. What are the chances that the toad will cause warts to develop?   0
The bumps on the toad's body do, however, contain poison that can kill, but usually only sickens, an attacking animal.

BIRDS

Species in USA   Select at random one species of bird from the 9,000 in the world. What are the chances that the species is found in the USA?   7 in 100
Of all bird species found in the USA, 67 percent migrate.

Nectar Diet   Randomly select a bird anywhere in the world. What are the chances that it drinks nectar (liquid from flowering plants) every day?   1 in 5

Seafood Diet   Select at random any bird species in the world. What are the chances that this species gets its food from the ocean?
3 in 100

Coastal   What are the chances that any given species of bird lives its life within a few miles of a coast?   42 in 100

Island-dwelling   A species of bird became extinct sometime during the last 300 years. What are the chances that it was an island-dwelling bird?   91 in 100
Island-dwelling birds are extremely vulnerable to predators.

Banding   A bird is banded for scientific study. What are the chances that scientists will ever recover this particular bird?   7.5 in 100

Chickens
Numbers   If all the chickens and all the human beings were entered in a huge lottery, what are the chances that the winner would be a chicken?   1 in 2
One fifth of all the chickens in the world live in the USA.

Cranes
Reproduction   A whooping crane lays an egg. What are the chances that this egg will hatch a chick that will ultimately reach maturity?
1 in 2
Since whooping cranes usually lay only two eggs each year, their population increases slowly.

Wild   In mid-1979 the whooping crane population numbered 109. What are the chances that a randomly selected whooping crane lives in the wild?   76 in 100

Ducks
Eggs   A wild duck lays an egg in a nest on the ground. What are the chances that the egg will actually hatch?   15–40 in 100
Duck eggs are a common food for many mammals.

Hazards   A duck, along with 100 million other waterfowl, migrates south in the fall. What are the chances that the duck will return to its breeding ground the following spring?   2 in 5

will be killed by predators,
   accidents, disease, or
   environmental hazards   2 in 5
will be killed by a hunter   1 in 5

Virus Carriers   A mallard duck lives in the wild. What are the chances
that it carries influenza virus?   1 in 4

Eagles
Human Fatality   What are the chances that any given person will die
from being hit on the head by a tortoise dropped by an eagle?
1 in 74 billion
It happened to the great Greek playwright Aeschylus, but so far as we
know, he is the only person ever to have died this way.

Falcons
Missed Prey   A merlin falcon attempts to snatch a bird in midflight.
What are the chances that the falcon will miss on its first try?
95 in 100
The miss rate is higher for young falcons than for older falcons. All young
birds of prey seem to suffer similar accuracy problems. The great horned
owl at age six months, for example, misses its prey 90 percent of the time,
but by one year, it makes one catch in every four tries. Young predatory
birds have little food reserve (try missing nineteen of twenty meals if you
doubt this), and many die of starvation.

Gulls
Murders   What are the chances that any given herring gull chick will
be pecked to death by the adults of the colony?   23 in 100

Homosexuality   A female sea gull lives in the vicinity of Santa Barbara
Island, California. What are the chances that she is homosexual?
12 in 100

Hummingbirds
Weight   What are the chances that any given hummingbird weighs
less than a penny?   greater than 1 in 2
Hummingbirds are also the only species that can fly backwards.

Ospreys

Diet An osprey has a meal. What are the chances that it eats an insect?   5 in 100

a small bird	15 in 100
a rodent	80 in 100

Penguins

"Divorces" Two penguins mate. What are the chances that they will eventually "divorce" for new mates?   18 in 100
The penguin divorce rate is, therefore, far lower than the human rate, and the "remarriage" rate is much higher—nearly 100 percent.

Pheasants

Hatchings A pheasant hen tries to hatch a clutch of eggs. If she is not succcessful, she will try repeatedly throughout the nesting season (three nests per hen is average). What are the chances that her persistence will be rewarded with one successful hatch this year?
52 in 100

Nesting Habits What are the chances that any given cock pheasant was hatched along a roadside?   1 in 4   25 in 100
   was hatched during the first three
      weeks of June   3 in 5   60 in 100

Life Expectancy A pheasant chick is hatched. What are the chances that it will not reach its first birthday?   3 in 10

Pigeons

Doves What are the odds that any given dove in the world will not be alive one year from now?   1 in 2
This figure appears to remain constant whether or not doves are hunted.

Homing Pigeons Homing pigeons always return home, right? Release a homing pigeon almost anywhere and, unless it is shot by a hunter, killed by a predator, or defeathered by a lightning bolt, it will return to its own nest—or so we and the scientific experts believed until recently.
   A homing pigeon is released at Jersey Hill in New York. What are the chances that it will find its way home?   2 in 5

Something very peculiar happens at Jersey Hill. The air or the ground formation there completely disorients the normally unerring homing pigeon. Pigeons released at Jersey Hill become confused, flying for a time, returning, and wandering about on the ground. Some fly away and become lost. Others take months or even years to find their way home. And no one knows why!

Passenger Pigeons   **A bird flew somewhere over the USA in 1825. What are the chances that the bird was a passenger pigeon?**   1 in 4
In 1813, John James Audubon reported a single flock roosting over a 120-square-mile area. Just 100 years later, passenger pigeons were extinct.

Quail
Life Expectancy   **A quail chick emerges from its shell. What are the chances that this quail will not survive long enough to see the following nesting season?**   4 in 5
Of all pen-raised birds released before the hunting season, 96 percent do not survive to the next breeding season.

Robins
Life Expectancy   **A baby robin hatches. What are the chances that it will not survive one year?**   3 in 4
Of the robins that survive for one year, 75 percent will nest within 20 miles of their birthplace.

INSECTS AND SPIDERS

Prevalence   **There are approximately a million different kinds of animals in the world. If one of them were chosen at random, what are the chances that it would be an insect?**   4 in 5

Bees
Pollination   **An insect pollinates a crop in the USA. What are the chances that this insect is a bee?**   80–85 in 100

Stingers   **Someone is stung by an insect and finds a stinger left behind. What are the chances that he or she was the victim of a honeybee?**   100 in 100
The honeybee is the only insect that leaves its stinger.

Reactions   A person has never been stung by a bee. If and when he or she is stung, what are the chances that the sting will cause a severe allergic reaction?   1 in 250

Such a reaction could be fatal. Anyone with a history of violent reactions will always be subject to similar attacks and require preventive medical treatment.

Beetles

Prevalence   An entomologist is asked to name any one species of insect at random. What are the chances that his or her choice will be a beetle?   2 in 5

Comprising more than a quarter million different species, beetles are the largest order of insects.

Cicadas

Reproduction   A periodical cicada hatches from its egg. What are the chances that it will not mate for at least thirteen years?   100 in 100

Some periodical cicadas are buried alive for seventeen years before reproducing. The periodical cicadas are the world's longest-lived insects.

A periodical cicada stores its fertilized eggs in tree bark. What are the chances that this cicada will die within a few weeks?   100 in 100

Flies

Antennas   What are the chances that the next adult house fly that you see will have an antenna?   nearly 100 in 100

   a many-jointed antenna   35 in 100

Genetics   A male drosophila (fruit fly) with white eyes mates with a female with red eyes. What are the chances that their offspring will have red eyes?   nearly 100 in 100

Mosquitoes

Color Attraction   A mosquito heads toward two people, one of whom is wearing blue and the other some other color. What are the chances that the mosquito will choose as its dinner target the person in blue? 2 in 3

Gender   Someone is bitten by a mosquito. What are the chances that the mosquito is female?   100 in 100

Spiders
Gender   A black widow spider bites a human. What are the chances that the spider is female?   100 in 100

Victims   What are the chances that the victim of a black widow spider's bite will survive?   95 in 100
Drop for drop, the black widow's poison is more deadly than rattlesnake venom, but few spiders carry enough to kill a human.

Webworms
Insecticide Resistance   A sod webworm larva lies beneath a lawn. A webworm-controlling insecticide is applied to the lawn, carefully following the manufacturer's instructions. What are the larva's chances of surviving?   1 in 1,000
But as the sole survivor of the thousand, this unique larva becomes the progenitor of a new strain of webworms immune to the poison applied. Next year another type of poison will be needed. This resistance principle plagues all chemical pest control, whether the targets are giant beetles and roaches or disease-causing bacteria. A poison or antibiotic may be 99.5- or 99.95-percent effective, but the single organism in 1,000 or 10,000 that survives can reproduce to create new colonies of pests.

FISH AND OTHER MARINE LIFE

Guppies
Sex Distribution   A guppy is born. What are the chances that it is male?   1 in 3

Herring
Sex Distribution   Randomly select one herring from an ocean. What are the odds that the fish that you chose is female?   3 in 4

Jellyfish
Lethality   What are the chances that any given resident of Australia

will be killed by a jellyfish this year?   1 in 6 million
The chances drop to 0 if he or she stays away from the ocean.

An individual is stung by an accidental encounter with a Portuguese man-of-war jellyfish. What are his or her chances of dying if no medical intervention is sought?   1 in 1,000
The rare cases of death attributed to Portuguese men-of-war are generally caused by shock.

Lampreys
Spawning   A sea lamprey spawns in a freshwater gravel nest. What are the chances that it will die within the following few hours?
100 in 100

Lobsters
Reproduction   A lobster lays its eggs in the open sea. What are the chances that any given egg will survive?   1 in 10,000
If the eggs are laid in a controlled environment with no predators, the chances are vastly improved to 95 in 100

Octopuses
Bones   What are the chances that an octopus in one of the world's oceans will break a bone this year?   0
An octopus has no bones.

Oysters
Pearls   Imagine that you are lucky enough to find an oyster of the type that produces pearls. What are the chances that you will indeed find a pearl when you pry the oyster open?   1 in 12,000

Porpoises
Sleep   Pick an hour of the day at random. What are the chances that a given porpoise will be sleeping during this period?   12 in 100
Even when a porpoise sleeps, it still keeps one eye open, and half its brain stays awake.

Sharks
Brain   What are the odds that any given portion of a shark's brain is used for smelling?   2 in 3

Captivity   A great white shark is placed in a giant free-swim aquarium. What are the chances that it will be alive a month later?   nearly 0 No white shark has yet lived 24 hours in captivity. Some researchers believe that because ocean water generally contains more oxygen than other water, the shark suffocates when taken out of the ocean.

Risk   What are any human's chances of being killed by a shark this year?   1 in 45 million

Man-eating   A diver sights a shark. What are the chances that it belongs to a species never known to attack humans?   9 in 10

MAMMALS

Bites   What are any given individual's chances of being bitten by a mammal in the USA this year?   1 in 220

Wild   A mammal bites a person in the USA. What are the odds that the animal is wild?   3 in 4

Rabies   A person is bitten by a mammal. What are the chances that he or she will need to be treated for rabies?   3 in 100

Anteaters
Teeth   What are the chances that any given anteater has teeth?   0 Anteaters use their long sticky tongues to carry insects and soft fruits into their toothless mouths.

Antelopes
Diet   A pronghorn antelope begins to eat. What are the chances that the food it chooses is forbs or browse plants?   85 in 100
   cacti   11 in 100
   grasses and grasslike plants   4 in 100
The pronghorn antelope can run faster than 60 miles per hour, making it the second fastest animal in the world. Only the cheetah, capable of bursts of 70 miles an hour, is faster.

Armadillos
Diet   An armadillo eats a snack. What are the chances that the chosen morsel is an insect?   4 in 5

A delectable assortment of termites, cockroaches, beetles, and fire ants are among the armadillo's favorite foods.

Quadruplets   What are the chances that the next armadillo that gives birth will produce quadruplets?   96 in 100

Bats
Prevalence   If you randomly selected one type of mammal from all the types in the world, what are the chances that it would be a bat? 1 in 5

Bears
Parasite Carriers   Scientists capture and examine an Alaskan polar bear. What are the chances that the bear harbors the parasite that can cause trichinosis?   3 in 5

Eskimos always boil polar bear meat. They also avoid eating the liver, which has toxically high vitamin A levels.

Protected   A polar bear roams a vast area of land. What are the chances that at any given moment the polar bear is ambling within protected territory, where hunters cannot legally kill it?   95 in 100

Buffalo
Numbers   Someone walks through a major zoo and wants to look at a great North American buffalo. What are the chances that the zoo has one?   0

Strictly speaking, a zoogoer may be able to see a North American bison, but not a buffalo. The distinction is a technical one: Bisons have horns on the sides of their heads; buffalo horns grow on top. In biological terms, there never were any native buffalo in America.

Camels
Hump   A camel driver prepares his animals for a long caravan trip over the desert. As the animals drink, possibly for their last time for a week, what are the chances that we could find one camel among the team of twenty that stores the water in its hump?   0

Technically, camels do not store water in their humps, though many people believe that they do. Without their humps, however, the camels probably would die of thirst. The hump is made of fat, and when an emergency arises, water contained in the fat is released. It is this extra fat, not an extra container of water, that allows a camel to go thirst-free long after other animals desperately need a drink.

Cats
Taste Buds   Randomly choose one taste bud on the tongue of a cat. What are the chances that it transmits sweet sensations?   0
Cats do not have the ability to taste sweet things.

British Civil Servants   Randomly select a cat from among the 6 million living in Britain. What are the odds of selecting a cat employed by the civil service?   1 in 60
The cat's primary occupation seems to be to catch mice on ships.

Diet   A cat lives in the wild in Wisconsin. What are the chances that its last meal was a bird?   12 in 100
In the wilds of Oklahoma, the chances increase slightly to 14 in 100.

Pets   A person owns a cat. What are the chances that a dog lives in the same household?   1 in 3

Chipmunks
Winter Survival   An adult chipmunk enters a new winter. What are the chances that it will live to see spring?   56 in 100
For young chipmunks, the chances are only 45 in 100.

Deer
Longevity   What are the chances that any given whitetail deer in the wild is more than seven years old?   1 in 50
The oldest whitetail deer in captivity lived to be nineteen.

Points   A yearling whitetail deer grazes along a stream. What are the chances that it has three points on each antler?   26 in 100

four points	17 in 100
one point	7 in 100
five points	1 in 100

A 2½-year-old mule deer buck is spotted in the woods. What are the chances that he has five points on each antler?   16 in 100
Slightly more than one third of the older bucks develop five-point antlers.

Starvation   A deer tries to survive a hard winter in Vermont. What are the chances that it will not succeed and will starve to death?
83 in 100

Dogs
Registered   A dog is registered by the American Kennel Club. What are the chances that the dog is a poodle?   10 in 100

a Doberman pinscher	8 in 100
a German shepherd ,	6 in 100
a cocker spaniel	6 in 100
an Irish setter	4 in 100
a beagle	4 in 100

Eye Disease   What are the chances that any given collie puppy will someday develop an eye disease?   80 in 100
   Shetland sheepdog   5–8 in 100
Collies are remarkably prone to all sorts of eye disorders, but even so, they are not the most susceptible of all dogs. Estimates vary, but the cocker spaniel is said to have an 85-percent risk of developing an eye disorder.

USA   A dog lives somewhere in the world. What are the chances that it lives in the USA?   24 in 100

Pets   What are the odds that a dog lives with any given U.S. family?
1 in 5

Risks   What are the chances that any given pet dog will run away next year?   6 in 100
   will be sent to an animal shelter   9 in 100
   will be accidentally killed   18 in 100

Droppings   A dog leaves droppings along a Chicago street. What are the chances that the dog's owner will remove them?   1 in 20

Research   Pick at random one dog living in the USA. What are the chances that it will die for medical research this year?   1 in 50

Elephants
Tusks   A certain adult elephant has tusks. What are the chances that this elephant is African?   100 in 100
    is Indian   0
    is female   0
The African elephant, the world's largest land mammal, has large ears shaped like a map of Africa. Both varieties of elephants cover their bodies with mud to ward off insect bites and sunburn.

Sleep   Choose any hour of the day or night. What are the odds that an elephant is sleeping then?   1 in 12
With only two hours sleep a day, it's a wonder that an elephant can remember anything.

Foxes
Color   A "red" fox lives in the Northern Hemisphere. What are the chances that the fox's coat is totally black except for some white spots?   2–17 in 100

Gophers
Maturity   A pocket gopher enters the breeding season. What are the chances that the gopher is only one year old?   3 in 4

Groundhogs
Shadow   What are the chances that a groundhog in the wild (as opposed to the Punxsutawney, Pennyslvania, pet woodchuck) will actually emerge from its den on February 2 and see its shadow?
less than 1 in 100
Groundhogs are true hibernators who rarely leave their underground holes before March. Even if a groundhog left its hole on February 2, it is likely that after three months of darkness, it would be too blinded by the light to see its shadow.

Hippopotamuses
Water-dwelling   What are the chances that a given hippopotamus at any given moment is standing or lying in water?   4 in 5

Horses
A horse lives somewhere in the world. What are the chances that its home is in the USA?   11 in 100

Kangaroos
Life Expectancy A kangaroo joey who lives in the wild is seven months old. What are the chances that it will live to the age of seven?
1 in 2
In captivity, more than 75 percent live to this age. At birth, kangaroos are about the size of a bean, but some species grow to nearly 200 pounds.

Koalas
Diet A koala dozes in the warm shade after eating a meal. What are the chances that it ate a leaf from a "gum tree," a type of eucalyptus?
100 in 100
The koala's diet consists solely of the tender young leaves from these trees. Although the teddy bear was modeled on the koala, the koala is not a bear at all, but a marsupial.

Lions
Diet A lion finishes a meal. What are the chances that the meal consisted of only meat or meat and water?   100 in 100

Murders What is the probability that a lion cub in the wild will be killed by another lion?   1 in 5

Hunters A lion successfully catches and kills its prey. What are the chances that the lion is female?   92–95 in 100

Marmots
Hibernation Pick a month at random. What are the chances that the yellow-bellied marmot hibernates during all or part of that month?
2 in 3

Minks
Pelt Sources A processor buys a mink pelt. What are the chances that the mink was trapped in the wild, rather than raised in captivity?
6 in 100

Monkeys

Group Males   A group of howler monkeys lives in the wild. What are the chances that the group has two adult males in it?   1 in 5

one adult male	4 in 5
no adult males	0

Discrimination   A rhesus monkey is taught to do discrimination problems (for example, square peg in square hole). After 250 trials, what are the chances that the monkey will discriminate the next problem correctly?   85–90 in 100

In contrast, cats and raccoons average about 60-percent accuracy on similar problems.

Pigs

Distribution   A pig lives somewhere in the world. What are the odds that it lives in China?   1 in 4   25 in 100

in the USSR	1 in 7	14 in 100
in the USA	1 in 8	12.5 in 100
in Iowa	1 in 40	2.5 in 100

Porcupines

Fir Trees   A porcupine damages a tree in Fundy National Park, New Brunswick. What are the chances that the tree is a balsam fir? 72 in 100

Rabbits

Survival   What are the chances that any given wild hare will still be alive a year from now?   14.7 in 100

Rats

Numbers   Imagine that all the people and all the rats in the world could be put into a hat (Heaven forbid). What are the chances of randomly selecting a rat from this hat?   1 in 2

Scientists estimate that the rat population equals the human population.

Super Rats   A Norway rat, a large aggressive rodent, begins a meal of grain in a Sioux City, Iowa, stockyard. What are the chances that this animal is a "super rat"—one that is immune to most rodenticides? 77 in 100

The World Health Organization advises communities to take emergency measures when more than 10 percent of the rat population becomes resistant to rodenticides.

Food Destruction   Randomly select a bushel of the world's crops. What are the chances that this bushel will ultimately be consumed by rats?   1 in 5

Rat-bite Fever   Pick at random a person living in Bombay, India. What are the chances that he or she will be bitten by a rat this year and come down with rat-bite fever?   1 in 300

Seals
Crab Eaters   What are the chances that any given crabeater seal has never eaten a crab?   100 in 100

Sheep
Distribution   A sheep grazes somewhere in the world. What are the chances that it lives in Australia?   1 in 6   17 in 100
   in the USA   1 in 9   11 in 100

Squirrels
Australia   What are the chances of seeing a squirrel in the wild in Australia?   0

Tasmanian Devils
Toes   A Tasmanian devil, a doglike Australian marsupial, injures a foot. What are the chances that the foot has four toes?   1 in 2
The Tasmanian devil has four toes on its hind feet but five toes on its forefeet.

Tigers
Captivity   A Siberian tiger settles down after a large meal. What are the chances that this animal lives in captivity?   greater than 1 in 2

Distribution   Choose the name of a continent at random. What are the chances that the continent that you chose has wild tigers?   1 in 7
Only Asia has wild tigers.

Man-Eaters   A tiger is born in Asia. What are the odds that it will become a man-eater?   3–4 in 6,000

Vicuñas
Peru   A vicuña (an animal similar to the llama and valued for its fur) lives somewhere in the world. What are the chances that its home is in Peru?   4 in 5

Risks   The vicuña is an endangered species. Yet what risk does any one have of being killed by a hunter next year?   1 in 16
The ancient Incas regarded the vicuña as sacred, though Peruvians today do not.

Weasels
Chicken Houses   An animal raids a chicken house in Michigan. What are the chances that the predator is a long-tailed weasel?   59 in 100

Whales
Canadian Coast   A whale species lives somewhere in the world. What are the chances that the Canadian coast sometimes hosts members of this species?   39 in 100

Wildcats
Distribution   Choose one of the seven continents at random. What are the chances that the continent of your choice has no wildcats? 2 in 7
Neither Antarctica nor Australia has indigenous wildcats.

Wolves
Diet   A wolf dines in Jasper National Park. What are the chances that the animal that it eats is larger than the wolf itself?   4 in 5

Zebras
Stripes   What are the chances that two zebras roaming Africa on any given day have exactly the same pattern of stripes?   0
The stripes on zebras are like fingerprints on people—no two are identical.

Zebus
Efficiency   A zebu in India consumes a quantity of food. What is the

probability that the energy that this food produces in the animal will ultimately yield work or fuel (burnable dung) for human beings?
17 in 100
In contrast, western cattle return only 4 percent of the energy that they consume.

REPTILES

Crocodiles
Reproduction   A crocodile in the Florida Bay area lays her eggs in a nesting mound. What are the chances that at least one offspring will result from this nesting attempt?   65 in 100
   that the offspring will survive at least
      six weeks   50 in 100

Lizards
Poisonous   A lizard crawls across the earth somewhere in the world. What are the chances that it belongs to a poisonous species?
1 in 1,500
The Gila monster, found in the southwestern USA, is one of the two poisonous lizard species in the world.

Sex Ratio   A Komodo "dragon" monitor, the largest member of the lizard family, lumbers slowly across an Indonesian island. What are the chances that it is a male?   4 in 5
This is not because the males are killing the females, but because Komodo eggs hatch four times as many males as females. The severe divergence between the numbers of the sexes currently works against the giant lizard's struggle to survive as a species.

Snakes
Venomous   Pick any snake in the world. What are the chances that the snake is venomous?   1 in 10
In the USA, the chances of selecting a venomous snake are considerably less (about 1 in 63). The coral snake, copperhead, cottonmouth, and rattlesnake are the only four North American snakes capable of killing humans. Despite the low incidence of poisonous snakes, an estimated 20 percent of Americans suffer from ophidiophobia (fear of snakes).

Venom Release   A poisonous snake strikes. What are the chances that the snake will not release any venom?   3 in 10

Risk   A poisonous snake in the USA bites someone who receives no treatment. What are the victim's chances of surviving?   1 in 2

Fatalities   A person dies of snakebite somewhere in the world. What are the chances that the victim lives in India?   3 in 4

Cobra Victims   A cobra strikes rapidly and bites a human. There is no cobra antivenin available. What are the chances that the victim will survive anyway?   9 in 10
Most bites by the Asian cobra and king cobra are nonlethal. The black mamba and taipan, on the other hand, kill nearly all their victims unless antivenin is administered.

Turtles
Survival   A sea turtle lays an egg (which strongly resembles a Ping Pong ball) in her nesting sandpit. What are the chances that the egg will be hatched successfully and that the young turtle will survive for at least one year?   1 in 1,000
The sea turtle is a desirable meal for land predators (dogs, ocelots, raccoons, humans) and sea predators (mackerel and sharks) alike. In some areas of the world sea turtles are protected. The odds given here are for turtles in unprotected areas.

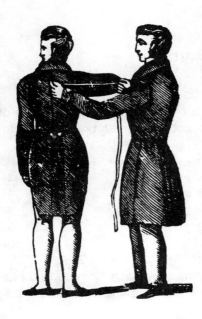

11   The Human Body

The odds in this chapter offer a perspective on the composition of the human body and some of its activities. Some areas chosen for special attention include nutrition, sleep and dreams, weight problems, and life expectancy.

In recent years a popular attention to the body has grown up in addition to the scientific one, and while specialists attempt to prolong life, combat birth defects and genetic abnormalities, and improve our understanding, we are turning our attentions to improving our diets, losing weight, and exercising. The great surge of interest in natural foods and natural healing, body therapies and yoga, dance, dream analysis, self-hypnosis, and such is evidence that people want to explore and perhaps change the odds in these areas.

Here you will find the odds that your muscles are working at only partial capacity, that someone you know has an extra X chromosome, that you will dream about a stranger, and that you will live to see your 115th birthday.

STRUCTURE AND COMPOSITION

Blood

Types   Select at random a person from each of these populations. What are his or her chances of having each of the four blood types— O, A, B, and AB?

	Chances (in 100) of Having Blood Type			
Population	*O*	*A*	*B*	*AB*
Americans	45	41	10	4
East Indians	31	19	41	9
Japanese	29	42	20	9
North Chinese	31	25	34	10
Russians	32	38	23	7

Blood type B is relatively common among Chinese and blacks, yet extremely rare in Native Americans and completely absent among Australian aborigines.

Rh Factor   A person born in England is blood-typed. What are the chances that he or she has an Rh factor (a protein found only in Rh+ blood types)?   85 in 100

The Rh factor is present in practically all Chinese but is rarely found in Basques.

Hemoglobin Cells   What are the chances that any given hemoglobin cell from an adult's blood is a fetal hemoglobin cell (the type present at birth and decreasing in the first months of life)?   1 in 50

Bones

Foot Bones   From a list of all the bones in the human body, pick one bone at random. What are the odds that this bone is in the foot? 1 in 4

Brain

Memory   Someone is asked to provide specifics from a newspaper article that he or she read two days ago. What are the chances that the person will remember the points requested?   4 in 5

Most people forget 20 percent of what they read within two days, 60 percent within nine days, and 74 percent within one month.

Oxygen Use   A molecule of oxygen enters the bloodstream of a healthy young adult. What are the chances that it will be used by the brain?   1 in 5

The human brain requires a steady supply of oxygen to perform its high-speed electrochemical operations. Without oxygen, brain cells will die in approximately 4 minutes.

Pain   A neurosurgeon probes delicately within a patient's brain. What are the chances that the patient will experience any pain?   0

Brain tissue cannot sense pain or heat. The brain, in fact, is so impervious to pain within itself that patients are sometimes wide awake during brain surgery, receiving only a local anesthetic to deaden the pain as the skull is opened.

Cell Replacement   A brain cell dies. What are the chances that it will be regenerated or will produce another to take its place?   0

Cells

Makeup   Randomly select a single molecule from tissue inside a human cell. What are the chances that it will be a water molecule rather than a protein?   18,000 to 1

Water molecules are unbelievably small. It takes about 750 trillion water molecules to cover an area the size of the head of a pin.

Circulatory System

Blood Pressure   What are the odds that any given person's blood pressure is higher in the right arm than in the left?   2 in 3

Aorta Branches   Most humans have three arteries branching off the aorta (the major artery leaving the heart). What are the chances that any given individual has either more or fewer than three arteries branching from the aorta?   35 in 100

Eyes

Legal Blindness   Pick at random one person in the USA between the ages of forty and sixty-four. What are the chances that he or she is legally blind?   2.4 in 1,000

Between sixty-five and sixty-nine	5.0 in 1,000
Over sixty-nine	14.5 in 1,000

Handedness

Interests   A college student is a science major. What are the chances that he or she is left-handed?   1 in 20

Art majors may include as many as 15 percent left-handers. This is consistent with a theory of how the brain operates. The half of the brain controlling the right hand tends to be best at analytical, rational, and verbal thought. Most scientists, who excel at these skills, also tend to be right-handed. The side of the brain controlling the left hand is better at spatial perception and emotional interpretation—just the things that artists are best at.

Crossed Dominance   An individual is generally right- or left-handed. What are the chances that he or she shows at least some preference for (even though perhaps not realizing it) the opposite eye?
13 in 100

Most of us are consistently one-sided in the way that we predominantly use our bodies.

Height

Six-year-olds   Randomly select a six-year-old in the USA. What are the chances that his or her height is less than 3 feet 6 inches?
1 in 20

   more than 4 feet 2 inches   1 in 20

Adults   Select at random a man born in the USA. What are the chances that he is 5 feet 9 inches or shorter in height?   1 in 2

The average height of U.S. women is just under 5 feet 4 inches.

Muscles

Control   Select one of the 650 muscles in the human body. What are the chances that it cannot be voluntarily controlled?   1 in 3

We normally have control over skeletal muscles, those muscles attached to bones. We have little or no control in normal circumstances over our internal muscles. Containing nearly 75 percent water, muscles constitute approximately 40 percent of human weight.

Muscle Fibers   An individual lifts a weight that takes maximum effort. In the muscles being stressed the most, there are thousands of muscle fibers. What is the probability that any specific one of these fibers is working?   3 in 10

At any given moment, 70 percent of the fibers, even at greatest stress, are resting. If all the muscle fibers contracted at the same time, it would create a force powerful enough to rip the muscles from the bones.

Teeth

Prehistoric   What are the chances that any given prehistoric Native American child had dental cavities?   3 in 5

This estimate comes from a seventeen-year-old anthropological study and surprised scientists who believed that Native Americans, who did not eat refined sugars, were essentially immune to tooth decay.

GENES

Eye Color

Light Eyes   Two light-eyed parents of entirely light-eyed background have a child. What are the chances that the child will be light-eyed? 98 in 100

Two brown-eyed parents, each with a recessive gene for light eyes, have a child. What are the chances that the child will have light eyes? 1 in 4

If one parent is entirely of dark-eyed background, the chances of light eyes are nearly 0.

Color Blindness

Pattern   A man is color blind. What are the chances that his sons will be carriers of the gene?   0
   his daughters   100 in 100

Sons can inherit this trait only from their mothers. Daughters can be color blind only in the rare event that both parents carry the genes for color blindness.

Sex Chromosomes

XYY Males   A boy baby enters the world. What are the chances that he has an extra Y chromosome?   1 in 3,000

This extra Y chromosome gives the boy an XYY (as opposed to the normal

XY) sex-chromosome configuration. Such boys usually grow up to be taller than normal. Some authorities have argued that XYY males are also more prone to violence and criminal behavior, though there is intense scientific argument over this contention.

XYY Criminals   Test the sex-chromosome configuration of a man convicted of a violent crime. What are the chances that he has an extra Y chromosome?   1–2 in 1,000
This means that at least 998 in 1,000 men who commit violent crimes are genetically normal. However, the incidence of XYY males convicted of violent crimes is three to six times higher than in the rest of the population.

XXY Males   A baby boy comes into the world. What are the chances that he has two X chromosomes and one Y chromosome—an XXY configuration?   1–2 in 1,000
This is called Klinefelter's syndrome and is usually associated with mental retardation and infertility.

XXY and Retardation   A male has Klinefelter's syndrome. What are the chances that he is mentally retarded?   1 in 4
With even more X chromosomes, the chances of retardation begin to approach certainty.

XXX Females   A girl baby is born. What are the chances that she has three X chromosomes instead of the normal two?   1 in 1,500
This does not seem to cause many problems other than some menstrual irregularities.

NUTRITION

Food Composition
Chemicals   What are the chances that your last meal contained at least one chemical?   100 in 100
All things that we eat and drink are amalgamations of chemicals. Coffee, for example, contains more than 393 chemicals, milk more than 200, and an apple, 227.

Relative Amounts   A person in the USA eats an "average" diet. What are the chances that any given calorie in his or her food comes from fat?   43 in 100
 from carbohydrate   45 in 100
 from protein   12 in 100
Sugar alone accounts for 24 percent of all calories and, along with alcohol, makes up the greater part of carbohydrate consumption. Many nutritionists believe that we would be wise to reduce our intake of these products.

Cholesterol   What are the odds that any given molecule of fat found in food is a cholesterol molecule?   1 in 600

Vitamin B$_{12}$ Choose a fruit or vegetable at random. What are the chances that it contains vitamin B$_{12}$?   0
Vitamin B$_{12}$ is found only in animal products.

Nutrient Use
Calcium   A molecule of calcium is used by the body. What are the chances that it will help build bones or teeth?   99 in 100

Carbohydrates   Someone eats a calorie of carbohydrate. What are the chances that it will be used by his or her brain?   70 in 100
 by muscles   25 in 100

Minerals   A woman consumes a milligram of iron during her last three months of pregnancy. What is the probability that this nutrient will go to the baby?   85 in 100
 A milligram of calcium   84 in 100

Running   A runner begins a long-distance race. What are the chances that the next calorie of energy that his or her body burns comes from a fat?   83 in 100
 a protein   16 in 100
 a carbohydrate   1 in 100
There are a number of dieting fads in endurance running, just as there are in most other areas of life. To date, scientists have not found any particular dietary needs of endurance runners other than a nutritionally balanced diet with adequate calories. During the race, however, highly diluted glucose in a low-potassium solution can prolong the runner's effort and improve per-

formance. It also appears that a strong exercise training session 36 to 48 hours before the actual race will help the runner's performance more than any known dietary approach.

For those who wonder how many more calories are burned by exercising at a faster rate: Speed does not particularly affect the number of calories burned. A person uses about the same number of calories walking a mile in 20 minutes as in running it in one third that time. Weight, however, does affect caloric use. The heavier the person, the more calories he or she uses in any given amount of exercise.

SLEEP AND DREAMS

Amount
Normal Amounts   A person does not complain of insomnia. What are the chances that he or she sleeps fewer than 5 hours a day?
2 in 1,000
    more than 10 hours   20 in 1,000

Infants   Choose a newborn baby at random. What are the chances that he or she will stop waking at night by the age of three months?
70 in 100
    six months   83 in 100

College Students   Pick a U.S. college student at random. What are the chances that he or she averages at least one nap a week?
51.5 in 100
It is not known how many of these take place during classes.

Difficulties
Bruxism   What are the chances that any given individual is a bruxist (a person who gnashes and grinds his or her teeth during sleep)?
1 in 5
Bruxists often are not aware of their habit, but over years of nightly grinding, they can permanently damage their teeth.

Sleep Apnea   A person suffers from sleep apnea (momentary failure to breathe during sleep). What are the chances that this person is male?   98 in 100

Menopause   What are the chances that any given postmenopausal woman will experience sleep difficulties?   2 in 5

REM Sleep
Comparative Amounts   A person is sleeping. What are the chances that, at any given moment, he or she is in rapid-eye-movement (REM) sleep (commonly associated with dreaming)?   24 in 100
Here are comparable chances for other animals:

Opossums	32 in 100
Cats	26 in 100
Chimpanzees	18 in 100
Rabbits and mice	14 in 100
Frogs and turtles	1–2 in 100

Age   A baby less than a year old is sleeping. What are the chances that the child is in REM sleep?   2 in 5
At the other end of the age range, for persons over fifty, the chances are only 1 in 5.

Dreams
Characteristics   A person recalls a dream. What are the chances that total strangers were in the dream?   43 in 100

that the dreamer experienced fear in the dream	40 in 100
that the dream was in color	29 in 100
that the dreamer was alone in the dream	15 in 100

Content   A person has a dream about something in the future. What are the chances that it is a dream about death, disease, or some other major tragedy?   1 in 10

WEIGHT

Underweight
Incidence   A person lives in the USA. What are the chances that this person is "underweight"?   13 in 100

Obesity

Incidence   A person lives in the USA. What are the chances that he or she is obese (is 20 percent or more over ideal weight, according to height)?

Chances (in 100) of Being Obese

	Male		Female	
Age	White	Black	White	Black
12	18.0	9.8	10.0	9.0
14	18.8	12.5	15.3	18.6
16	29.0	13.0	11.7	11.1
21	15.1	8.3	16.6	18.1
30	21.0	12.0	25.9	36.4
40	23.1	16.4	36.5	46.1
50	23.9	13.2	41.9	52.7
60	18.6	19.0	37.8	46.7

Overall, 28 percent of the people in the USA are overweight.

Educational Level   An adult has a high school education or less. What is the probability that he or she is obese?   1 in 3
In contrast, the probability of obesity in a person with a postcollege degree is only 1 in 10.

Thyroid Problems   A person is obese. What are the chances that the excess weight is caused by a thyroid disorder?   1 in 100

Familial   What are the chances that a person will become obese if one of his or her parents was obese?   45 in 100
    if both parents were obese   75 in 100

Infants   If a person's weight at birth was above normal, what are the chances that he or she will be obese as an adult?
1 in 3   33 in 100
    If the birth weight was normal or
        below   1 in 5   20 in 100
Even by the age of six months, the pattern would seem to have started. Infants overweight at six months have more than 1 chance in 3 of being obese adults, while those who are normal or underweight have only 1 chance in 7.

Children A child is obese. What are the chances that he or she will grow up to be an obese adult?   4 in 5

Fatality Risk One person more than forty-five years old is 10 pounds overweight. Another one is not overweight. One dies. What are the chances that the overweight person was the victim?   54 in 100

If the person is 20 pounds overweight	59 in 100
If the person is 30 pounds overweight	64 in 100
If the person is 50 pounds overweight	78 in 100

Reduction Success An obese person begins to reduce. What are the chances that this individual will bring his or her weight down to the normal range and remain nonobese for at least five years?   1 in 20

LIFE AND DEATH

Life Expectancy
Infancy A baby is born live in the USA. What are the chances that he or she will not survive infancy?   15.7 in 1,000

USA A baby is born in the USA. What are the chances that he or she will survive at least two years?   98 in 100
In Peru, 11 percent of the babies born will die before they learn to walk.
  The life expectancy for U.S. males and females is presented below.

Age	Percent of Males Reaching Age	Percent of Females Reaching Age
2	97.9	98.2
3	97.4	98.0
16	96.4	97.5
26	94.4	96.8
36	91.8	95.4
46	86.6	92.3
56	74.9	85.8
66	53.7	73.1
76	25.5	47.6

Middle Age   A man in the USA has his forty-fifth birthday. What are his chances of surviving to age fifty-five?   90 in 100
For men in Sweden, the chances are 95 in 100.

Age Seventy   A woman in the USA turns seventy. What are her chances of reaching eighty?   7 in 10
For men, the chances are only 1 in 2.

100 Years   A person is born in the USA. What are the odds against this individual's living 100 years?   20,000 to 1
There were slightly more than 12,000 centenarians living in the USA on January 1, 1980.

Twins   A pair of identical twins enters the world. What are the chances of both living to age 100?   1 in 1 billion

115 Years   What are any individual's chances of living to be 115 years old?   1 in 2.1 billion
Since our current world population is more than 4 billion, two of our co-inhabitants should achieve this.

Death
Causes   What are the chances that the death of the next person who dies in the USA will be due to heart disease?   37 in 100

cancer	20.4 in 100
a stroke	9.6 in 100
accidental causes	5.4 in 100
a motor vehicle accident	2.6 in 100
pneumonia or influenza	2.6 in 100
diabetes	1.7 in 100
cirrhosis of the liver	1.6 in 100
murder	1.1 in 100
suicide	1.0 in 100

12   The Sexes

In this chapter you will find some odds related to behavioral differences between men and women; most of the odds are related to the variety of ritual and personal interactions between the sexes. The search for a compatible companion is covered, as are the proposal-engagement-marriage tradition, divorce and remarriage, and sexual interactions, pregnancy, and childbirth.

That the odds in these areas are important to many people is clear. Marriage counselors and sex therapists are in business to help change some of these odds. Computer dating services and the plethora of personals in newspapers are attempts to improve on the blind date—or no date at all. Each year millions of dollars are spent to fund a variety of services aimed at sexually active youth.

You may have a personal interest in some of the odds. But no matter where you are in your relation to the sexes, the odds will help you see this level of social interaction in a better light.

DIFFERENCES

Cosmetic Surgery   A surgeon performs a cosmetic procedure. What are the chances that the patient is male?   1 in 5
This is an overall probability. If the surgery is specifically a facelift, the chances are 9 in 10 that the patient is a woman.

Accidental Death   A person in the USA dies by some form of accident. What are the odds that the person is a male?   2 in 3

Telephone Interruptions   A man and a woman are talking on the telephone. One of them interrupts the other. What are the chances that it is the man who interrupts?   96 in 100
When men talk to men, both tend to interrupt equally. The same is true when women talk to women.

Lavatory Messages   A woman writes on a public lavatory stall in New York City. What are the chances that her message concerns romance?   16.6 in 100
   gay rights   8   in 100
   politics   2.4 in 100

Girls' Graffiti   New graffiti has been written on the wall of a high school restroom. What is the probability that it was written in the girls' room?   88 in 100
Girls' graffiti involves mainly love themes, while boys' is largely erotic.

THE SEARCH

Singles Bar   A man enters a singles bar. What are the odds that he really is single?   45–50 in 100

Visiting Prostitutes   Observe the next adult white male that you meet in the USA. What are the chances that he has visited or will visit a prostitute sometime during his life?   69 in 100

Lonely Hearts   A lonely hearts classified advertising service is begun

in the USSR. What are the chances that its next customer will be a woman?   7 in 10
So far only one newspaper offers this service. Like nearly everything in the USSR, it has a waiting list—in this case, a year long. Women are probably not particularly more aggressive in the USSR; it is just that at the moment they outnumber men by 17 million.

PROPOSALS

Location   A man in the USA proposes marriage to a woman. What are the chances that the proposal occurs either in his car or in her home?   1 in 2
Specifically, 27 in 100 take place in his car; 23 in 100 in her home.

Acceptance   A woman in the USA receives a proposal of marriage. What are the odds that she will accept?   1 in 3
The average woman refuses two proposals before accepting.

MARRIAGE

Considerations
First Marriage   A man in the USA has never married. What are the chances that he is twenty-four years old or older?   1 in 2
Half the women in the USA are married for the first time by age 21.6. The median age for first marriage has risen by a full year for both men and women since the 1960s.

Proximity   A couple marries somewhere in the USA. What are the chances that at the time of their first date together they lived within eight blocks of each other?   37 in 100
   within sixteen blocks   54 in 100

Age Pattern   A couple marries in the USA. What are the chances that the bride is older than the groom?   9 in 100
   the same age   19 in 100
   younger   72 in 100

Age Differences A bride and groom are not the same age. What are the chances that the age difference between them is only one year? 22 in 100

two years	21 in 100
three years	15 in 100
four years	14 in 100
five or more years	28 in 100

Of all people who marry in the USA, 2 in 3 choose spouses within three years of their own age.

Religious Factors
Similarities A man and woman decide to marry. What are the chances that they share the same religious preferences? 83 in 100
This figure comes from a study of U.S. whites only.

Interfaith A young person is Catholic or Jewish. What are the chances that he or she will marry outside the faith? 32 in 100
In the country of Andorra, the likelihood of a Roman Catholic marriage is 100 percent because Andorran law forbids non-Catholic weddings.

Escape
Runaway Spouses An adult runs away from his or her spouse (and possibly children). What is the probability that this person is a woman? 1 in 2
Before 1960, the odds were 1 in 300.

DIVORCE

Rate
USA A man and a woman in the USA get married. What is the probability that the marriage will end in divorce? 2 in 5
Married teenagers face a 60-percent risk of divorce.

Teenage Brides A girl marries during her teen years. What are the chances that she will still be married five years later? 1 in 4

USSR A man and a woman marry in the USSR. What is the probability that they will divorce? 27 in 100
The number of divorces in 1975 was ten times the number in 1950.

Divorced Men

Age   A man is divorced and has not remarried. What are the chances
that he is less than thirty years old?   18 in 100

between thirty and forty-four	36 in 100
between forty-five and sixty-four	37 in 100
sixty-five or older	9 in 100

Hazards   Many of us would predict that divorced men would have a
greater risk of accidents, homicides, and suicide. We would suggest
that they may live, on average, somewhat more dangerous lives than
married men. The possibility that there are more maladjustments
among divorced males, possibly leading to interpersonal conflicts and
individual risks, also must be considered. But what can explain these
odds?

Two men less than sixty-five years old live in the USA. One is married; the other is divorced. One will die this year from heart disease,
respiratory cancer, digestive system cancer, stroke, pneumonia, or
tuberculosis—disorders over which we are thought to have little control. What are the chances that the divorced man will be the victim?
69 in 100

Two men younger than sixty-five live in the USA. One is married; the
other is divorced. One will die this year of one of the following causes,
usually somewhat under a person's control: vehicle accident, suicide,
cirrhosis of the liver, or homicide. What are the chances that the divorced man will be the victim?   76 in 100

REMARRIAGE

Rate   A man divorces. What are the chances that he will remarry?
87 in 100
For women, the odds are 75 in 100.

Age   What is the probability that a woman will marry again if she is
divorced before the age of twenty-five?   99 in 100

before the age of thirty-five	94 in 100
before the age of forty	84 in 100
before the age of sixty-five	45 in 100

BIRTH CONTROL

Pregnancy Chances   A sexually active woman of childbearing age uses no contraceptives. What are the chances that she will become pregnant this year?   67–80 in 100

Effectiveness   A woman uses a birth control device. What are her chances of becoming pregnant if she uses an oral contraceptive?
0.3–4 in 100

a condom	0.01–4 in 100
the basal body temperature method	2–4 in 100
a diaphragm	3–17 in 100
foam	3–22 in 100

Vasectomy
Incidence   A man in the USA is married to a woman between the ages of thirty and forty-four. What are the chances that he has had a vasectomy?   1 in 7
This proportion is growing.

Reversal   A man who has had a vasectomy decides that he would like the procedure reversed. A new operation (canalization) is performed. What are the chances that this operation will at least partially reverse the effects of the vasectomy?   7 in 10
The chances of inducing a pregnancy, however, will be lower than if he had never had a vasectomy.

Abortion
Incidence   A woman in the USA becomes pregnant. What are the chances that she will end the pregnancy with an abortion?   1 in 4
In Hungary, 54 percent of pregnant women abort their babies.

Fatality Risks   A woman in the USA is between the ages of fifteen and forty-four. What are her chances of dying from an abortion this year?
1 in 1 million
This is down from the 1963–1967 rate of 5.7 per million.

SEXUAL INTERCOURSE

Orgasm   A woman has been married one year. What are the chances that she has not yet achieved orgasm?   1 in 4
After ten years, less than 10 percent report no orgasmic experience.

Heart-Attack Risk   If a person were to die suddenly from a heart attack, what are the chances that it would occur during intercourse?
1 in 163.5
    during intercourse at home with
      one's spouse   1 in 817.5
In Japan, where these figures are gathered, 80 percent of sudden deaths occur during extramarital affairs.

VENEREAL DISEASES

Genital Herpes
Recurrence   An individual has had the venereal disease herpes simplex II. What are the chances that it will recur?   87 in 100

Gonorrhea
Women   What are the chances that any given woman in the USA has gonorrhea?   1 in 25

Symptomless   A woman has gonorrhea. What are the chances that she is completely unaware of any symptoms?   1 in 2

Syphilis
Homosexuals   A person is treated for infectious syphilis in New York City. What are the chances that the patient is a homosexual male?
55 in 100

Mortality   Choose at random a person living in the USA. What are his or her chances of dying from syphilis?   1 in 1 million

INFERTILITY

Incidence   Two people marry. What is the probability that they will be unable to conceive a child?   12 in 100
This figure may be increasing, partly due to an increase in the spread of venereal disease.

Cause   A couple is infertile. What are the chances that the main cause is the male's low sperm production?   2 in 5

Prognosis   A couple is infertile. What are the chances that the problem can be corrected?   44 in 100

PREGNANCY

Conception   A woman conceives a child within five days of ovulation. What are the chances that she will have a boy?   53 in 100
  If she conceives within two days of
      ovulation   66 in 100

Spontaneous Abortions   A woman suffers a spontaneous abortion during her first three months of pregnancy. What are the chances that the fetus had a chromosome abnormality?   3 in 5

Morning Sickness   A woman becomes pregnant. What are the chances that she will experience nausea as one of her pregnancy symptoms?   68 in 100

Food Cravings   A woman is pregnant. What are the chances that she will have peculiar food cravings at some time during the pregnancy? 64 in 100

Sympathetic Pains   A married woman is expecting a baby. What are the chances that her husband will develop sympathetic physical symptoms during her pregnancy?   11 in 100

UNMARRIED PARENTS

Premarital Conception   Pick one baby at random born in the USA. What are the chances that the child's parents were not married to each other when the child was conceived?   1 in 3

USA   A baby comes into the world in the USA. What are the chances that it is born out of wedlock?   15 in 100
In the USSR, the chances are 1 in 10.

Paternity Suits   A man is falsely accused in a paternity suit. His defense attorney obtains information on the ABO, Rh, and MN blood factors of the mother, the child, and the accused male. What are the chances that this information in itself will be enough to clear the defendant of the charges?   51 in 100

Adoption   A baby is born out of wedlock. What are the chances that it will be put up for adoption?   1 in 10
This is a dramatic change from 1970, when the chances of a baby's being put up for adoption were 9 in 10.

CHILDBIRTH

Mother's Age   A baby is born. What are the chances that its mother is thirty-five years old or older?   6 in 100

Fatality Risk   A woman is pregnant. What is her risk of dying in childbirth?   1 in 5,000

Over Forty   Two women give birth. One is more than forty years old, and the other is not. One dies in childbirth. What is the probability that the over-forty woman is the victim?   3 in 4

Mother's Birthdate What are the chances that any given woman will have four consecutive children arrive on her own birthday?
1 in 17,748,855,000
The *Guinness Book of World Records* reports that Mrs. Teresa Olivares overcame these odds on January 21, 1971.

NEONATES

Birth Defects
Incidence A baby is born in the USA. What are the chances that the infant has a physical defect? 7 in 100

Mother's Drinking Two women give birth. One is a heavy drinker; the other drinks moderately or not at all. One of the babies has a birth defect. What are the chances that the infant with the defect was born to the heavy drinker? 2 in 3
Scientists have not yet found a measurable risk to the babies of mothers who drink less than 2 ounces of alcohol daily.

Sex-Chromosome Abnormalities A baby is born. What are the chances that the infant has a sex-chromosome abnormality?
1 in 400
This is fairly common but of little importance. In most cases the physical or mental manifestations are minor.

Circumcision
Incidence A male baby is born in the USA. What are the chances that he will be circumcised? 83 in 100
    In England   1 in 244
The U.S. rate is expected to fall. In 1975, the American Pediatric Society declared that "there are no valid medical indications for circumcision," though for many people there remain religious reasons.

Complications A baby is circumcised. What is the probability that he will die from complications of the procedure? 1 in 2 million

FAMILIES

Multiple Births
Incidence A woman gives birth. What are the chances that she bears
twins?   6.44 in 1,000
    triplets   1 in 12,000
    quadruplets   1 in 4 million
Nobody knows why, but the colder the climate, the higher the chances of
multiple births.

Identical Twins are born. What is the probability that they are identical twins?   1 in 3

Sex Distribution
Four Children A family has four children. What are the chances that
there are four boys?   1 in 16
    three boys and one girl   4 in 16
    two boys and two girls   6 in 16
    three girls and one boy   4 in 16
    four girls   1 in 16
There is a 50-percent chance of a 3–1 distribution.

SEXUALITY

Transsexuals
Incidence What are the chances that any given man in the USA is a
transsexual (a male convinced that he is actually a female trapped in a
man's body)?   1 in 100,000

Pornography
Arousal A researcher shows a film of explicit heterosexual behavior
to a woman. What are the chances that she will show physiological
signs of sexual arousal?   65 in 100
For men, the chances are 86 in 100.

Sexual Dysfunction
Chronic Vaginitis A woman has chronic vaginitis (irritation, inflammation, and possibly a discharge). What are the chances that this is

due not to recurrent infection but to sexual dysfunction (poor adult sexual relationships due to fears, guilt, and tension)?   1 in 50

Clinics   A person is considering seeking help from a "sex clinic" in the USA. What are the chances that the one that he or she chooses will be legitimate—that is, using scientifically tested methods with qualified staff?   1 in 100

Prostitutes
Force   A woman in the USA is a prostitute. What are the chances that she was physically forced to have her initial intercourse?   23 in 100

Older Partner in Background   A woman in the USA is a prostitute. What are the chances that a person at least ten years older than she attempted sexual play or intercourse with her when she was a girl? 52 in 100
This is dramatically higher than the approximately 25 percent or less found among the entire population.

Homosexual Activity
Prison   A man engages in homosexual activity while in prison. What are the chances that he had no such experience prior to going to prison?   5–10 in 100

YOUTH AND SEXUAL ACTIVITY

Sexual Maturity
Males   What are the chances that any given male child will have experienced a seminal emission by the age of ten?   1.8 in 100
    by the age of eleven   8.7 in 100
    by the age of twelve   22.8 in 100
    by the age of thirteen   56.4 in 100
    by the age of fourteen   87.3 in 100
    by the age of fifteen   95.1 in 100

Sexual Intercourse
Age   What are the chances that any given teenager in the USA will

have had his or her first sexual intercourse by the age of thirteen?
10 in 100

by the age of sixteen	18 in 100
by the age of seventeen	41 in 100
by the age of nineteen	60 in 100

Smoking   A girl between thirteen and seventeen years old in the USA smokes cigarettes. What are the chances that she has had sexual intercourse?   31 in 100
For girls who do not smoke, the chances are only 8 in 100.

Contraception   A young person in the USA has sexual intercourse for the first time at age eighteen or nineteen. What are the chances that he or she uses some form of contraception?   55 in 100
Nearly half the sexually active girls under eighteen do not use contraceptives.

Pregnancy

Risk   A fifteen-year-old girl resides in the USA. What are the chances that she will become pregnant at least once by the age of twenty?
2 in 5

Early   A teenager becomes pregnant for the first time. What are the chances that the pregnancy occurs within one month of her very first act of intercourse?   1 in 5   20 in 100
   within six months   1 in 2   50 in 100
Some authorities argue that, because some girls begin sexual relations very early and are likely to become pregnant soon after becoming sexually active, pregnancy prevention programs should begin before adolescence.

Terminations   A teenage girl in the USA becomes pregnant. What is the probability that she will have an abortion?   3 in 10
   a miscarriage   1 in 10

Complications   A teenage girl is pregnant. What are the chances that she will have complications in labor?   22 in 100
   that her baby will be born
      prematurely   14 in 100

Infant Deaths   A teenage girl gives birth. What are the chances that the baby will die before it is able to leave the hospital?   18 in 100

Collegiate Sexual Activity

Virgins   Randomly choose a student at a college in the USA. What are the chances that he or she is a virgin?   42 in 100
      has had at least five coital partners   14 in 100
Among medical students, 32 percent have had at least five sex partners, while only 19 percent are virgins.

One-Night Stands   An individual is a college student somewhere in the world. What is the probability that he or she will at some time have a "one-night stand"—have sexual intercourse with a partner that he or she will never date again?

	Chances (in 100) of One-Night Stand	
Country	Males	Females
West Germany	17.0	4.2
Canada	21.6	5.9
USA	29.9	7.2
England	43.1	33.7
Norway	32.3	12.5

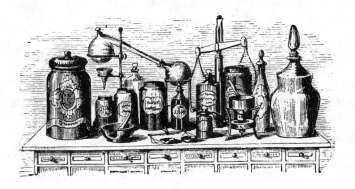

13　Medicine

　　　　Like the chapters on media, crime, and the sexes, this chapter contains odds very different from those of ten years ago. New discoveries in diagnosis and treatment change these odds almost daily. Incidence and risk odds often change, too, for reasons that we can only speculate about. The odds cover a variety of disorders from acne and allergies, through brain disorders, colds, and headaches, to ulcers. Cancers and heart disease are the best represented, reflecting their incidence in our society, but even the plague has its own black moment. A wide selection of probabilities is represented, including those based on incidence, sex differences, genetic backgrounds, and causal factors, as well as odds of dying, survival, and recovery. Special sections present odds in the areas of smoking, medication, and the field of medical practice itself.

　　For persons at high risk for certain disorders, these odds will have special significance. For others, they will be interesting as a sample of what is known about a variety of medical problems.

DISEASES AND DISORDERS

Acne
Incidence   What are the chances that any given teenager in the USA will have at least one pimple during adolescence?   nearly 100 in 100
   will have at least one pimple on any
      given day during adolescence   4 in 5
   will develop severe acne   1 in 50

Treatment   A physician prescribes 13-cis-retinoic acid for a teen-ager's acne. What are the chances that it will help?   94 in 100

Allergies
Food   An individual has a food allergy. What are the chances that one or both of his or her parents also had an allergy?   65 in 100

Plants   Pick an individual at random. What are the chances that he or she is allergic to poison ivy, poison oak, or poison sumac?   4 in 5

Insects   A person is allergic to insect venom. His or her physician advises the individual to receive venom immunotherapy (dilute venom injections). What are the chances that these shots will protect him or her from a severe allergic reaction in the event of an insect sting? 95 in 100

Appendicitis
Gender   A person has appendicitis. What are the odds that the victim is male?   2 in 3

Mortality   A person over forty-five suffers an attack of appendicitis. What are the chances that he or she will die from it?   99 in 1,000
   A person under fifteen   2 in 1,000
Youth and early surgery are the best allies for survival.

Arteriosclerosis
Mortality Risk   A person lives in one of these countries. What is the probability that he or she will die this year of arteriosclerotic heart disease?

Country	Chances in 100,000	Country	Chances in 100,000
Japan	35	Denmark	182
Italy	60	England	193
Switzerland	92	Finland	206
Belgium	95	Ireland	225
West Germany	105	USA	238
Austria	115	Scotland	242
Netherlands	140	New Zealand	247
Norway	147	Canada	260
Sweden	155	South Africa	265
Israel	170	Australia	267

Amyotrophic Lateral Sclerosis

Risk What is the probability that any given individual will develop amyotrophic lateral sclerosis (ALS, a disease that wastes and weakens all the muscles of the body)?   35 in 1 million

Arthritis

Incidence What are the chances that any given person in the USA has some form of arthritis?   1 in 4   25 in 100
    has the most crippling form of
        arthritis, rheumatoid arthritis   1 in 50   2 in 100
Among the elderly, rheumatoid arthritis is much more common than this.

Juvenile A child develops juvenile rheumatoid arthritis. What is the probability that it will go away by itself?   1 in 2
While rheumatoid arthritis rarely disappears in adults, this is not unusual in children.

Treatment An adult is treated for rheumatoid arthritis. What are the chances that he or she will be better off fifteen years from now than today?   35 in 100

Asthma

Children A child in the USA is less than fifteen years old. What are the chances that he or she has asthma?   7 in 100
Asthma is seldom fatal for children, but during acute attacks, it can be quite disabling.

A child less than seventeen years old lives in Canada. What are the chances that he or she has asthma?   1 in 200

Chronic Disease   A child less than seventeen years old has a chronic disease. What are the chances that the disease is asthma?   1 in 3

Hay Fever   A person is an untreated hay fever sufferer. What are the chances that he or she will eventually develop asthma?   3 in 10

Inhalant Steroids   A doctor prescribes an inhalant steroid for an asthmatic. What are the patient's chances of benefiting from the new medication?   85 in 100

Back Pain
Disk Surgery   An individual sees a specialist about back pain. What are the chances that disk surgery will be indicated?   7.5 in 100

Blindness
Preventable   A person becomes blind. What are the chances that the blindness could have been prevented?   1 in 2

Brain Disorders
Elderly   Choose at random one individual aged sixty-five or older. What are the chances that he or she has some form of brain disorder? 15 in 100

Psychiatric Patients   A patient is admitted to a mental hospital for the first time. What are the chances that the person has organic brain syndrome?   1 in 5

Geriatric Patients   A patient in a mental hospital is sixty-five years old or older. What are the chances that this patient has organic brain syndrome?   greater than 1 in 2

Electroencephalogram   A physician orders an electroencephalogram (EEG) to determine whether or not a patient has suffered brain damage. If the patient does, in fact, have some form of brain damage, what are the chances that the EEG will reveal it?   7 in 10

EEG Specificity   An EEG reveals evidence of brain damage. What are the chances that this test can correctly identify the specific brain area affected?   35 in 100

Missed Diagnosis   A neurologist examines a patient who has an un-diagnosed brain disorder. What are the chances that the physician will not discover the problem without ordering extensive tests?
29 in 100

False Signs   A neurologist examines a patient who ultimately will be found to be without brain disorder. What are the chances that the specialist will mistakenly find signs of probable brain problems?
41 in 100

Brain Scan   What is the probability that a brain-scan diagnostic method will correctly identify the presence of a vascular (blood-flow) problem in the brain?   5–6 in 10

Test Risks   A physician suspects that a patient has suffered some degree of brain damage. Two powerful tests—pneumoencephalogra-phy and angiography—can help determine the problem, but each has some risks. For each test, what are the chances that it will accurately detect the presence of brain damage and that it will itself cause more serious damage or even death?

	Chances (in 100) that It Will	
	Detect Brain	Cause Damage
Diagnostic Test	Damage	or Death
pneumoencephalography	90	2.5
angiography	84	4

Psychological Test   What is the probability that the Halstead-Reitan Neuropsychological Battery (a psychological test) will correctly iden-tify a brain disorder?   89 in 100

Aneurysm   A patient develops an aneurysm (an outpouching of an artery) in the brain. Surgery is one form of treatment, but the physician in this case chooses "conservative treatment," and sedates the pa-tient, putting him or her at bedrest in the hospital. What are the chances that the aneurysm will hemorrhage within two weeks?
15 in 100

Brucellosis
Location   A person falls victim to brucellosis (undulant fever). What are the chances that he or she lives in Iowa, Illinois, Minnesota, or Texas?   2 in 5

Brucellosis is transmitted from infected animals. People who work with them—farmers, ranchers, veterinarians, packing-house workers—have the highest risk of infection.

Cancer
Risk   What are any individual's odds of ever developing cancer?   1 in 4

Age Risk   A person is twenty-five years old. What are the odds that he or she will develop cancer during the next five years?   1 in 700

For a person sixty-five, the chances are 1 in 45.

Origin   An adult falls victim to cancer. What are the chances that the malignancy began in the epithelial tissue (the outer layer of cells on the skin and other organs)?   87 in 100

Such cancer is called a carcinoma, and while carcinomas are the most common cancers in adults, they account for only 10 percent of all cancers in children.

Gender   A person develops cancer. What is the probability that the victim is male?   54 in 100

Radiation Therapy   A person is found to have cancer. What is the probability that radiation therapy will be recommended?   1 in 2

Survival   What are a patient's chances of surviving five years after any of these cancers is found?

Type	Average Rate	If Localized	If Widespread
	Chances (in 100) of Surviving Five Years		
Breast	68	86	11
Cervical	64	75	18
Prostate	63	75	21
Bladder	61	75	17
Colon	49	75	9

Stomach	13	42	1
Lung	10	33	1
Pancreatic	1	5	1

Cancer, Bone

Age   A person is the victim of Ewing's sarcoma (a type of bone cancer). What are the chances that he or she is between four and twenty-five years old?   95 in 100

Survival   What is the probability that a person with Ewing's sarcoma will live at least five years following discovery of the disease?
15 in 100

Cancer, Breast

Risk   What are the odds that any given woman in the USA will develop breast cancer this year?   1 in 13

Mammography   What are the chances that any given woman will develop breast cancer in her lifetime if she never undergoes mammography (x-ray of the breasts)?   1 in 14.3
   if she does undergo mammography   1 in 14.1
These figures entered into medical debate in the late 1970s because they suggest that mammographic procedures may actually cause breast cancer in some women (about 2 in 1,000). Contrasted with this small risk is the high accuracy of mammography. A negative mammogram (no evidence of cancer) is accurate in 94 percent of cases.

Symptomless   A woman's breast x-rays reveal cancer. What is the probability that she had no symptoms such as nipple discharge or a detectable lump?   64 in 100

Age   A woman is found to have breast cancer. What is the probability that she is more than fifty years old?   3 in 4

First Pregnancy   Two women are the same age. One first became pregnant before the age of twenty-one. The other had her first pregnancy after the age of twenty-five. One of them develops breast cancer. What are the chances that it is the one with the later first pregnancy?   2 in 3

Mastectomy   A woman discovers that she has breast cancer. What are the chances that she will have a mastectomy?   1 in 2

Reconstruction   A woman undergoes a mastectomy. What is the probability that physicians can provide some form of breast reconstruction?   1 in 2

Second Breast   A woman has surgery to remove a cancerous tumor from one breast. What are the chances that she will develop cancer in the second breast within five years?   4 in 100
    within ten years   6 in 100
    within fifteen years   9 in 100
    within twenty years   13 in 100

Early Onset   Two women, one younger than fifty and the other older, undergo surgery for cancer in one breast. One of the two ultimately develops cancer in the second breast. What are the chances that the victim is the woman who had her first episode at a younger age? 2 in 3

Later Risk   A woman has surgery for breast cancer. Ten years from now, what are her chances of being totally free of any cancer? 1 in 2

Daughter's Risk   One woman has had breast cancer; another has not. Both women have daughters, one of whom develops breast cancer. What are the chances that the victim is the daughter of the woman who had breast cancer?   83 in 100

Cancer, Colon
Risk   In any one year, what is the probability that any given person in each of these countries will die of cancer of the colon?

Country	Chances in 10,000	Country	Chances in 10,000
Japan	2.5	Italy	7
Finland	4	Norway	7.5
Israel	6	West Germany	7.5

Netherlands	8	England	12
Switzerland	9.5	Australia	12
Austria	9.5	Denmark	12.5
Belgium	10.5	Ireland	13
USA	12	Canada	13.5
New Zealand	12	Scotland	15

Cancer, Lung

Asbestos   A person is an asbestos worker. What are the chances that this worker will die of mesothelioma (a cancer of the lungs and internal organs of the body)?   1 in 10
This risk is 1,000 times greater than that for the general population.

Survival   A patient is found to have lung cancer. What are the victim's chances for survival?   97 in 1,000
The National Cancer Institute reports that certain new treatments are achieving better results than traditional methods.

Cancer, Skin

Awareness   Two people contract melanoma (a skin cancer caused chiefly by the sun's radiation). One victim lives in Europe, Asia, or the Americas; the other lives in Australia. One victim dies of the disease; the other survives more than five years. What are the chances that the Australian is the survivor?   2 in 3
The survival advantage appears to be due to Australians' greater awareness of the dangers of excessive sun exposure and their tendency to seek treatment at the first sign of skin trouble. Although Queensland has an extremely high incidence of melanoma, it also has the world's highest survival rate.

Treatment   An individual who has skin cancer obtains treatment in the early stages. What are the chances that he or she will be free of the disease after treatment?   91 in 100

Cancer, Thyroid

Risk   What are any given individual's chances of ever having thyroid cancer?   3.9 in 100,000
Authorities are not sure why, but this rate seems to be increasing, particularly among those between the ages of twenty and thirty.

Radiation   A person received radiation therapy as a child. What is the probability that he or she will develop thyroid cancer?   7 in 100
Radiation therapy was widely given to children in the 1940s. Now it is rare. Thyroid cancer is totally curable by surgery if discovered early.

Cataracts
Surgery   A person has eye surgery to remove a cataract (a clouded spot on the lens). What are the chances that the patient can regain normal vision?   9 in 10

Chicken Pox
Encephalitis   A person has varicella chicken pox. What are the chances that it will develop into varicella encephalitis (a disease of the central nervous system)?   1 in 1,000

Cirrhosis
Alcoholic Risk   A person is an alcoholic. What are his or her chances of developing cirrhosis of the liver?   1 in 10

Survival   If someone with cirrhosis of the liver stops drinking, what are the chances that he or she will survive five more years?   3 in 5

Colds
Rhinovirus   Someone comes down with a common cold. What are the chances that his or her symptoms are caused by a rhinovirus? 45 in 100

Seasonal Risk   What are the chances that any given individual will catch cold or contract some other infection during the winter or early spring?   7 in 10
   during the summer or early fall   4 in 10

Cystic Fibrosis
Life Expectancy   A child is born with cystic fibrosis (a chronic debilitating lung disease). What are the child's chances of living to age twelve?   91 in 100
   to age seventeen   80 in 100

The survival rate shows steady improvement. Earlier studies placed these chances at 80 and 67 percent, respectively.

Heredity   Two carriers of the cystic fibrosis gene have a child. What are the chances that the child will develop the disease?   1 in 4
A child with cystic fibrosis stands only a 50-percent chance of surviving twenty years.

Diabetes
Weight   An adult develops diabetes. What are the chances that he or she was obese rather than thin when the disease was diagnosed? 4 in 5

Heredity Risk   What are the chances that a child of two diabetics will have diabetes as a child?   less than 1 in 10

Parents   A person has juvenile-onset diabetes. What are the chances that at least one of his or her parents is also a diabetic?   11 in 100
For a person with adult-onset diabetes, the chances are 85 in 100.

Diphtheria
Survival   Most people have had diphtheria vaccinations and so are essentially immune to this disease, which begins with throat inflammation and sometimes progresses to damage the heart and nervous system. Imagine, however, that you catch the disease and go to a physician early. What are your chances of surviving?   99 in 100
If you wait five days before seeing a doctor, the probability decreases to 75 in 100.

Epilepsy
Incidence   Choose at random one person in the world. What are the chances that he or she has epilepsy?   3–4 in 1,000

Intellectual Ability   An individual is one of the more than 200,000 people in the USA with epilepsy. What are the chances that this person has above-average intelligence?   1 in 3
average intelligence   1 in 3
below-average intelligence   1 in 3

This is the same distribution as in the rest of the population. In other words, even though epilepsy is a disorder of the brain, it generally does not affect intellectual ability.

Flicker Induction   A person has epilepsy. What are the chances that this person might experience a seizure by watching television?
3 in 100

Treatment   An individual has epilepsy. What are the chances that the seizures can be completely controlled with medication?   5 in 10
     partially controlled   3 in 10

Gallstones
Risk   Choose at random someone in the USA. What are the chances that the individual will have his or her gallbladder removed this year because of painful gallstones?   1 in 550

Glaucoma
Age Risk   What are the chances that glaucoma (a disease causing fluid pressure to increase and damage eye tissue) will develop in any given individual between twenty and thirty years old?   4 in 10,000
     sixty-five years old or older   1–13 in 100
Most victims are unaware that they have glaucoma.

G6PD Deficiency
Heredity Risk   A person is an American Negro. What are his or her chances of having a hereditary susceptibility to suffering anemia or other disorders from several common drugs (like aspirin and sulfonamides)?   1 in 10
This disorder is called glucose-6-phosphate dehydrogenase deficiency anemia. It is rare in other races but is sometimes seen among Mediterranean peoples.

Guillan-Barre Syndrome
Influenza Vaccine   A person gets an influenza vaccination. What are the chances that he or she will develop Guillan-Barre syndrome (a paralysis that is usually temporary but that can be permanent or fatal)?
1 in 100,000

Mortality Risk   If a person does develop the disorder, what are the chances that he or she will die from it?   1 in 20

that his or her muscles will be
weakened for a long time or
permanently   1 in 10

Hay Fever
Incidence   A baby is born in the USA. What are the chances that he or she will eventually develop hay fever?   9 in 100

Headaches
Chronic   Choose a person at random. What are the chances that he or she suffers some degree of chronic headache?   1 in 5

Causes   An individual experiences chronic headaches. What are the chances that they are migraines (headaches that are often accompanied by nausea, blurred vision, and extreme sensitivity to light)?
45 in 100

by muscle tension   45 in 100

Thus, muscle tension and migraine account for 90 percent of chronic headaches.

Children   A child experiences migraine headaches. What are the chances that the child is male?   2 in 3

Adult   An adult experiences migraine headaches. What are the chances that the person is female?   2 in 3

Heredity Risk   A parent suffers migraine headaches. What are the chances that any given offspring will also be affected?   1 in 2
If both parents are migraine sufferers, the chances are 3 in 4.

Heart Disorders
Risk Factors   Select an adult male at random. What is the probability that he has one of these six risk factors for heart disease: smoking, high blood pressure, high blood cholesterol, emotional stress, lack of exercise, obesity?   4 in 5

that he has two of the risk factors   2 in 5

Attack Risks   An adult male has two of these three risk factors for heart disease: high blood cholesterol, high blood pressure, cigarette smoking. What are the chances that he will have a heart attack within the next ten years?   1 in 10

Comparative Risks   A person has had a heart attack. What are the chances that he or she had any of these risk factors?

Risk Factors	Heart Attack Victims	Chances (in 100) by Similar People Who Have Not Had Heart Attacks
Genetic risk	67	40
High-fat diet	53	20
Occupational stress	91	20
Obesity	26	20
Thirty cigarettes per day	70	35
Little exercise	58	60

Coffee   One person drinks more than five cups of coffee each day. Another never drinks coffee. One of the two suffers a heart attack. What are the chances that the victim is the coffee drinker?   2 in 3 Whether the coffee or the personality of the heavy coffee drinker is the culprit is still open to question.

Hypertension   A man dies of a heart attack or a stroke. What are the chances that he had high blood pressure (above 160/95) before the fatal attack?   37 in 100 For women, the chances are even greater—51 in 100. The probabilities become 73 in 100 for men and 81 in 100 for women if all blood pressure readings above 140/90 are considered.

Snoring   A person regularly snores heavily during sleep. What are the chances that this is a danger signal of potential heart failure while sleeping?   1 in 1,000 A sleep disorder, sleep apnea, causes momentary breathing failure in some adults. These people are usually unaware of their problem, but their bedmates are usually quite aware.

Altitude A man in the USA lives at an altitude above 7,000 feet. Another lives at between 3,000 and 4,000 feet. One of them has a heart attack. What are the odds that the one at the lower altitude is the victim?   56 in 100

Marital Status One man in the USA is married. Another is single. One of the two suffers a heart attack. What are the chances that it is the unmarried man?   2 in 3

Physical Activity A man is stricken with a heart attack. What are the chances that he was engaged in strenuous physical activity at the time of the attack?   1 in 25
According to one study, 90 percent of heart attack victims were sedentary when the attack occurred; another 6 percent were working at sedentary jobs.

Imprisonment Two men were U.S. Navy pilots in Vietnam. One was captured and held prisoner. The other was not. Today, one of the men has heart disease or high blood pressure. What are the chances that the man with the disorder was the prisoner?   1 in 5
The lower disease rates in former prisoners are thought to be due to their light diets, heavy exercise, and restricted drinking and smoking during their captivity.

Contraceptives and Smoking A woman between the ages of forty and forty-four lives in England or in the USA. What are her chances of having a fatal heart attack this year if she neither uses oral contraceptives nor smokes?   7.4 in 100,000
    uses oral contraceptives but does
        not smoke   10.7 in 100,000
    smokes, but does not use oral
        contraceptives   15.9 in 100,000
    both uses oral contraceptives and
        smokes   62   in 100,000

Sleep One woman sleeps more than 10 hours a night. Another sleeps 7 hours or less a night. One dies of a heart attack. What are the chances that it is the woman who slept more than 10 hours a night?
89 in 100

Working   One woman less than sixty-five years old has a full-time job outside the home, while another woman the same age is a housewife. One has a heart attack. What are the chances that the victim is the working woman?   1 in 2
Supposedly, women will undergo increased stress as they move into outside employment. However, according to an eight-year study, the stress is not yet showing up in heart attack rates.

Aneurysm   A person has an unruptured abdominal aneurysm (a bulging spot on an artery). What are the chances that he or she will survive with rapid medical intervention?   97 in 100
If the aneurysm ruptures, the survival rate drops to 50 percent.

Survival   A person suffers a heart attack. What is the probability that he or she will survive one more year?   1 in 2

CPR Success   A person suffers cardiac arrest and suddenly drops to the ground. Within 3 minutes someone begins cardiopulmonary resuscitation (CPR). What are the chances that the victim will recover? 45 in 100
In the past, cardiac arrest was invariably fatal.

Emergencies   A person dies of a heart attack. What are the chances that he or she died before reaching a hospital?   57 in 100
This is why many authorities urge people to learn cardiopulmonary resuscitation.

Electrocardiography   Following hospitalization for a heart attack, a patient receives a physical examination and is given an electrocardiogram (EKG, a test of the heart's electrical activity). What are the chances that the resting EKG will show no abnormalities?   1 in 2

Cardiac Catheterization   A patient has a heart disorder. A physician recommends cardiac catheterization (a diagnostic procedure). What are the patient's chances of dying from the procedure?   1 in 50

Coronary Artery Bypass   An individual plagued by angina (chest pains) undergoes coronary artery bypass surgery (a technique bypassing a clogged vessel, providing a detour channel for blood). What

are the chances that the operation will provide total relief?
62.3 in 100

substantial pain reduction	80 in 100
no relief	12 in 100

Within seven years, however, pain has recurred in 37.1 percent of those who have had the surgery.

A male between forty and sixty years old undergoes coronary bypass surgery. What are the chances that he will recover and resume a productive life?   85 in 100
Although the surgery is extremely expensive, it appears to be a good risk for those people disabled by the sharp pains of angina pectoris.

Open Heart Surgery   A person has open-heart surgery. What are the chances that he or she will survive the operation?   89 in 100
Studies yield a range of 80 to 99 percent.

Heart Transplant   A patient undergoes heart transplant surgery. What are his or her chances of surviving at least one year?   4 in 5

Hepatitis, Alcoholic
Recovery   A person has alcoholic hepatitis (a liver disease caused by drinking alcohol). If this person stops drinking, what are the chances that he or she will totally recover normal liver functioning?   1 in 2
It is important to recognize and treat this disorder early because it can lead to cirrhosis.

Hepatitis, Viral
Risk   A person lives in the USA. What are the chances that he or she will suffer viral hepatitis (a liver disease, often with yellowing of the skin) this year?   1 in 3,700
The odds can best be overcome by washing hands after toilet and before meals, and by not using razors, hypodermic needles, or other objects that might have other people's blood on them.

Types   A person develops viral hepatitis. What are the chances that the disease will be diagnosed as Type A (transmitted from fecal material of a carrier, often from lack of hand washing)?   60 in 100

What are the chances that it will be diagnosed as Type B (transmitted by used hypodermic needles, razor blades, or other objects that may transfer the blood of one person through the skin of another)?   25 in 100

The remaining 15 percent are not specified.

Mortality Risk A person contracts viral hepatitis. What are the chances that he or she will die from the disease if it was caused by germs in the environment?   1 in 200   5 in 1,000

caused by drug-abuse injection	1 in 125	8 in 1,000
caused by blood transfusion	1 in 29	35 in 1,000

Huntington's Disease

Heredity Risk A person has Huntington's disease (a disease of the nervous system that results in uncontrollable muscle movements). What are the chances that any given child of this person will also develop the disease?   1 in 2

Even though inherited, the disease, sometimes called Huntington's chorea, usually does not show up until the age of thirty or forty.

Treatment A person has Huntington's disease. What is the probability that some of the symptoms can be relieved by tranquilizers?
1 in 3

Hypertension

Incidence Randomly select someone who lives in the USA. What are the chances that he or she has high blood pressure?   1 in 10

Hypothermia

Incidence A person in the USA is sixty-five or older. What is the probability that he or she is "particularly vulnerable" to accidental hypothermia (a potentially fatal drop in body temperature below 35° C) and should keep the winter home thermostat set no lower than 18° C?
1 in 10

Leukemia

Risk A person lives in the USA. What are the chances that he or she will develop leukemia this year?   1 in 10,000

Survival A child is discovered to have leukemia. What are the chances that he or she will survive at least five years?   62 in 100
This figure is rising steadily. At one time, the life expectancy following diagnosis was ten weeks.

Treatment An adult has leukemia. What are the odds that treatment can provide a remission (a halt in the progression of the disease)? 2 in 3
  that treatment will provide a cure (at least five
    years without the disease)   1 in 10

Lung Disorders
Seasons What are the chances that any given individual will develop a respiratory problem during the winter or early spring?   40 in 100
  during the summer or early fall   17 in 100

Incidence   A person lives in the USA. What are the chances that he or she has a chronic lung disease, such as asthma, bronchitis, emphysema, or tuberculosis?   73 in 1,000
Here is the breakdown by specific disease:
  Asthma   30 in 1,000
  Chronic bronchitis   29 in 1,000
  Emphysema   7 in 1,000
  Tuberculosis   1 in 1,000
  Other   6 in 1,000

Limitations What are the chances that an individual's activities are limited if he or she has chronic bronchitis?   4 in 100
  asthma   17 in 100
  emphysema   45 in 100
  tuberculosis   50 in 100

Measles (Rubeola)
Mortality Risk A person in the USA has measles. What are the chances that he or she will die from the disease?   1 in 1,000
In some less-developed countries, the death rate from measles is more than 20 percent.

Vaccination   A child in the USA is between the ages of ten and thirteen. What are the chances that he or she has at some time been given a measles vaccine?   72 in 100

In one of the most exciting developments of recent medical research, it is now theoretically possible, according to some authorities, to totally eliminate measles from the USA. Already some states have had no reported cases for a year or more.

Measles is generally thought of as a mild disorder. Yet, even though the risk is slight (possibly as low as 1 in 10,000), children can die from it. In fact, before the vaccine became available in 1963, nearly 500 children died from measles each year.

The problem currently standing in the way of measles eradication is that fewer toddlers (aged one to four years) are being immunized than in the peak years of 1973 to 1976.

Meningitis

Treatment   A child develops meningitis and receives treatment. What are his or her prospects for recovery?   9 in 10

New medication has turned the tide on this potentially severe disorder. Five years ago, the survival rate was only 10 percent.

Mononucleosis

Risk   What are the chances that a given individual will suffer mononucleosis (a usually mild disorder marked by tiredness and possibly a mild fever) this year?   1 in 2,632

Antibodies   A student enters college. What are the chances that he or she has antibodies to the Epstein-Barr virus and thus is protected against mononucleosis?   57.5 in 100

Scientists have only recently confirmed that the Epstein-Barr virus causes mononucleosis. Many people become infected with the virus as children. When this happens, the illness is mild and does not develop into mononucleosis. The only people, therefore, at risk to fall victim to "mono" are those who have not developed Epstein-Barr antibodies as children.

This is one reason why developed countries, the USA in particular, have a high incidence of mononucleosis. Because of cleanliness and sterilization techniques, many individuals in the USA avoid the mild Epstein-Barr infection as children, only to develop mononucleosis later on. Most children in less-developed countries develop Epstein-Barr immunity and do not fall prey to the "kissing disease."

Unprotected Risk   A college student has no antibodies as protection against mononucleosis. What are the chances that he or she will fall victim to the disease?   1 in 8
Approximately 1 in 3 infected individuals will have only mild symptoms. Less than 1 percent of victims will suffer serious complications.

Mortality Risk   Mononucleosis is usually a mild disease, but it can have serious complications. If a person does contract the disorder, what are the chances that he or she will die from it?   1 in 3,000

Multiple Sclerosis
Risk   Worldwide, each individual has an equal chance of developing multiple sclerosis (an incurable, progressive disease of the nervous system). What is that chance?   75 in 100,000

Mumps
Birth Defects   A pregnant woman comes down with mumps. What are the chances that this disease will cause her unborn baby to be deformed?   0

Myasthenia Gravis
Respirator   A patient suffers myasthenia gravis (extreme muscle tiredness from very little effort). What are the chances that the patient will eventually need a respirator for help in breathing?   15 in 100
Many patients, however, recover spontaneously. Still, they usually need three to five years of treatment before they get well.

Pain, Chronic
Treatment   A person suffers intractable chronic pain. What are the chances that he or she will be at least slightly helped by acupuncture?
55 in 100
by surgery	70 in 100
by hypnosis	70 in 100
by electrical nerve stimulation	30 in 100

Surgery   An individual undergoes surgery to relieve chronic pain. What are the chances that the operation will still provide satisfactory relief five years later?   1 in 10

Plague
Mortality Risk   A person develops the pneumonic form of the plague. What are the victim's chances of surviving?   1 in 10,000

Pneumonia
Contagion   A school-age child has a *M. pneumoniae* infection. What are the chances that nonimmunized family members will catch this disease?   85 in 100

Mortality Risk   A person contracts pneumococcal pneumonia but does not seek treatment. What risk does he or she face of dying from the disease?   3 in 10
If the disease is treated properly, the survival rate is 95 percent.
   The aged with complicating diseases are at high risk of not surviving this disease regardless of treatment.

Klebsiella   An individual develops primary Klebsiella pneumonia. What are the chances that the person is male?   85 in 100

Poliomyelitis
Risks   A person develops poliomyelitis (polio). What are the chances
that he or she is less than ten years old?   50 in 100
   will die from the disease   10 in 100
   will be permanently crippled   15 in 100
The oral polio vaccine is essentially totally effective in preventing the disease, but as of 1979, almost 40 percent of children in the USA had not yet been vaccinated.

Reye's Syndrome
Survival   A child develops Reye's syndrome. What are his or her chances of survival?   65 in 100
Reye's syndrome can be caused by numerous viruses, each of which carries its own mortality risk. The early symptoms of Reye's syndrome can include nausea, vomiting, unusual belligerence, and disorientation (a child may forget how to perform simple tasks). Rapid medical intervention can increase the child's chances of surviving.

Rheumatic Fever
Heart Involvement   A person develops rheumatic fever. What are the chances that the disease will affect the victim's heart?   3 in 4

Recurrence A person recovers from rheumatic fever. What are the chances that the disease will recur? 1 in 4

Sickle-Cell Anemia
Incidence A black person lives in the USA. What are the chances that he or she carries the sickle-cell trait? 1 in 10
    that he or she will actually be a
        victim of sickle-cell anemia   9 in 1,000

Staphylococcus Infections
Carriers What are the chances that any given individual currently harbors the staphylococcus bacterium staph-aureus? 35 in 100
Usually carried in the nose, the bacterium is a constant danger in hospitals and is constantly battled by hospital employees.

Streptococcal Sore Throat (Strep Throat)
Prognosis An adult develops a sore throat and fever from a strepto-coccal infection but does not seek treatment. What are the chances that his or her temperature will return to normal within 72 hours? 3 in 4

Tay-Sachs Disease
Jewish Incidence A person is an Ashkenazi Jew. What are the chances that he or she carries the gene for Tay-Sachs disease (a disorder often causing blindness, loss of motor control, and seizures in babies, who usually die by the age of three or four)? 1 in 30
Current methods of identification may eventually eliminate this disease.

Heredity Risk Two carriers of Tay-Sachs disease have a child. What are the chances that the child will have the disease? 1 in 4
Amniocentesis is used during pregnancy to identify the disease when both parents are carriers.

Non-Jewish Incidence What are the chances that any given non-Jewish individual carries the gene for Tay-Sachs disease? 1 in 250
Until recently, Tay-Sachs had been considered strictly a disease of Jews. Usually, Jewish people are tested for the gene before they have a child, but non-Jews typically have not been given the tests.

Tetanus
Mortality Risk   A person is a victim of tetanus. What are the chances that he or she will die despite the best medical treatment?   1 in 2

Tinnitus
Incidence   What are the chances that any given person in the USA suffers from tinnitus (ringing, hissing, buzzing, or roaring in the ears)?
3 in 100
Until recently, there was no treatment for this disorder that sometimes drives people to drugs, drink, and even suicide. The American Tinnitus Association now claims that a newly developed "masking" device can help 70 percent of sufferers.

Tumors
Pituitary   An individual has a brain tumor. What are the chances that the tumor is of the pituitary gland?   1 in 10

Retinoblastoma   What is an infant's risk of being born with retinoblastoma (a tumor of childhood often causing blindness)?
1 in 25,000 live births

Brain Scan   A patient has a brain tumor and undergoes a diagnostic brain scan. What are the chances that this procedure will correctly identify the tumor's presence in the brain?   4 in 5

Ulcers, Duodenal
Symptoms   The classical symptom of duodenal ulcer (an ulcer of the duodenum, a pouch just below the stomach) is pain in the upper mid-abdomen, occurring mostly when the stomach is empty, waking the victim from sleep in the early morning hours and disappearing when he or she eats. What are the chances that a person who has such an ulcer experiences these symptoms clearly?   1 in 2
The victim may simply experience indigestion, bloatedness, or other pain.

Gender   What is the probability that a duodenal ulcer victim is male?
9 in 10

Ulcers, Peptic
Referred Pain   A person has a perforated peptic ulcer. What are the chances that his or her shoulder hurts?   1 in 2

Ulcers, Stomach
Risk   What are the chances that any given individual will develop stomach ulcers sometime during his or her life?   1 in 20

Antacid   A person sees a physician for a gastrointestinal complaint. The doctor prescribes an antacid. What are the chances that the patient will still be taking the medication one year later?   34 in 100
   five years later   12 in 100

Healing   A person has a benign stomach ulcer. If he or she carefully follows medical advice, what are the chances that the ulcer will heal completely within twelve weeks?   3 in 4

Recurrence   A patient receives treatment for a stomach ulcer, and it heals. What are the chances that the problem will recur within two years?   1 in 2

Urticaria
Risk   Choose at random someone who is between twenty and fifty years old. What are his or her chances of developing urticaria (splotches of itchy skin, due largely to allergies in children and of unknown cause in adults) this year?   12 in 100,000
Older and younger people have lower rates.

Prognosis   A person develops urticaria. What are the chances that it will go away within three months?   1 in 2
   that it will still be present after
      ten years   1 in 5

SMOKING AND HEALTH

Comparative Risks
Mortality   Two men between the ages of forty-five and sixty-four live

in the USA. One smokes; the other does not. One dies. What are the chances that he is the smoker?   65 in 100

Two men in the USA, a smoker and a nonsmoker, are between the ages of forty-five and sixty-four. One develops terminal cancer. What are the chances that he is the smoker?   68 in 100
    If one develops a fatal heart or
        circulatory disorder   65 in 100
    If one develops a fatal lung cancer   89 in 100

Heart Attacks   Two people are under the age of sixty-five. One smokes; one does not. One suffers a heart attack and dies. What are the chances that the victim is the smoker?   67 in 100
    If the smoker is a "heavy smoker"   78 in 100
Of all smokers who survive heart attacks, 2 in 3 stop or reduce their consumption of tobacco.

Infant Death   Two women deliver babies. One of the women smokes; the other does not. One of the babies is stillborn or dies shortly after birth. What are the chances that this was the smoker's baby?
56.5 in 100

Infant Health   An infant's parents smoke. What are the chances that the child will have pneumonia or bronchitis before the age of one?
17.7 in 100
If the parents do not smoke, the chances are considerably reduced—to 7.6 in 100.

Lung Disease   What are the chances that a chronic lung disease will develop in any given man who smokes?   19 in 100
    woman   17 in 100
For nonsmokers, the chances are 12 in 100 for men, and only 5 in 100 for women.

Two people have chronic lung disease. One smokes two packs of cigarettes a day, while the other smokes none. What are the chances that the smoker will die first?   96 in 100

If the smoker smokes only ten cigarettes a day, his or her chances of dying first are decreased to about 83 in 100.

Other Effects
Models A child has an older brother or sister and a parent who both smoke. What are the chances that this child, as a teenager, will smoke?   1 in 5

If parents and older siblings do not
  smoke   1 in 20

Physicians
Responsibility A smoker visits a physician. What are the chances that this particular doctor feels no responsibility for persuading the patient to cut down or quit smoking?   1 in 4

Compliance A doctor advises a patient to quit smoking. At the next visit, the physician asks about it, and the patient asserts that he or she has stopped smoking. What are the odds that the patient is lying? 1 in 3

Smokers
Persistence Choose at random someone who has at some time or other been a smoker. What are the chances that he or she still smokes?   7 in 10
In comparison, only 15 percent of those who have ever been addicted to heroin are still addicts.

MEDICATION

Effectiveness
Native Drugs A person in a non-Western country is ill and is given a native medicine. What are the chances that the medicine will help? 37.5 in 100
Estimates suggest that between 25 and 50 percent of all native medicines are effective.

New Drugs   The Federal Drug Administration approves a new drug for medical use in the USA. What are the chances that the drug offers "important therapeutic gains" over existing products?   64 in 1,000
More than 70 percent of today's prescription drugs were unknown in 1949.

Morphine   A physician administers morphine for severe pain. What are the chances that the recipient will receive little or no relief from the drug?   3 in 10

Side Effects

Severe Reactions   A patient is admitted to a hospital. What are the chances that the hospitalization was caused by an adverse reaction to medicine?   6 in 100

Hospital Drugs   A patient is in a hospital. What are the chances that medicine prescribed during his or her stay will cause an adverse reaction?   18 in 100

Drug Resistance

Salmonella   A sample of disease-causing salmonella bacteria is isolated in a hospital. What are the chances that it is resistant to six or more antibiotics?   9.2 in 100
This is a 1975 statistic. In 1967, fewer than 1 in 100 salmonella bacteria were resistant to antibiotics. The increasing resistance of bacteria to our therapeutic drugs has caused several authorities to caution against excessive use of antibiotics. The more antibiotics prescribed, they argue, the more chances the bacteria have to develop drug-resistant strains.

Miscellany

Plant Sources   Choose at random one prescription drug. What are the chances that one of its active ingredients was extracted from a plant?   1 in 4

Effects   A person in the USA ingests a prescribed medication. What are the chances that the drug affects primarily the brain?   31 in 100

Tranquilizer Use   A woman lives in England. What are the chances that she will take a prescribed tranquilizer today?   19 in 100
For men, the chances are only 9 in 100.

Pickups   A pharmacist fills a prescription. What are the chances that no one will ever pick up the medicine?   1 in 25

MEDICAL PRACTICE

Second Opinions
Surgery   A doctor advises a patient to have surgery, but there is no emergency involved. The patient obtains a second opinion from another physician. What are the chances that the second doctor will recommend *against* surgery?   17 in 100
Surgeries most often advised against include hysterectomies, dilation and curettages, breast and gallbladder surgery, cataract removal, and varicose vein removal.

The System
Office Visits   A person makes an office visit to a physician. What are the chances that this occurs in a hospital setting?   1 in 4
This proportion may be increasing.

Medical Dollars   A dollar in the USA is spent for medical care of some kind. What are the chances that a doctor receives the money?
1 in 5

Malpractice Suits   An individual files a malpractice suit against a physician. What are the odds that the doctor—not the patient—will win?
4 in 5

Physicians
Psychiatric Problems   A physician practices in the USA. What are the chances that he or she has a psychiatric disorder severe enough to interfere with patient treatment?   1 in 20
Alcohol, drugs, and senility are the most common difficulties among those with psychiatric disorders.

Addiction   What is the probability that any given physician is also a drug addict?   1.5 in 100

Suicide   A physician commits suicide. What are the chances that he or she previously had a drug abuse problem?   25 in 100
   an alcohol problem   40 in 100

Hospitals

Costs   A dollar helps build a hospital. What are the chances that it will be spent on some form of medical equipment that will be obsolete in ten years?   2 in 3

Treatment Problems   A patient is in a hospital. What are the chances that he or she will develop an iatrogenic (treatment-induced) medical disorder?   1 in 5

Injuries   An individual is a patient in a U.S. hospital. What are the chances that he or she will receive a compensable injury there?
7 in 100

14   Mental Health

     As in the chapter on medicine, the odds here deal primarily with common disorders—those with a psychological basis, including alcoholism, depression, mental retardation, suicide, and schizophrenia. Probabilities concerning mental disorders of childhood and adolescence are covered in separate sections. Incidence, risk, and prognosis are the most frequent bases for the odds. Odds related to physiological and psychological evaluation are included, as are those dealing with major treatment techniques.

  Again, those at special risk for any of these disorders will be especially interested in these odds. Others may well be surprised at the prevalence of mental problems in our society—the chances that any one of us will ever be admitted to a mental hospital or will take advantage of the services at a community health center. With the explosion of psychological services as big business and self-help titles as a large part of the book market, some insight into mental health odds will help put this field in perspective.

257

CHILDHOOD DISORDERS

Antisocial Behavior
Incidence   A child in England is ten years old. What are the chances that he or she shows an "antisocial behavior disturbance" (repeated antisocial acts without other psychiatric disorder)?   1 in 25
For ten-year-old boys, the chances are 6.4 in 100, while for girls, the chances are only 1.6 in 100.

A boy receives treatment by a psychiatrist in the USA. What are the chances that the treatment is for "antisocial behavior"?   68 in 100
For girls, the chances are 32 in 100.

   When the antisocial behavior stems from underlying psychiatric disorder, the psychiatrist has several treatment choices at hand. Evidence to date, however, suggests that treatment for such behavior is not effective when no other psychiatric disorder is present.

Autism
Risk   A child is born somewhere in the world. What are the chances that he or she will be autistic (unable to communicate or relate appropriately, showing strange or bizarre behavior)?   less than 1 in 1,000

Intelligence   A child is diagnosed as autistic. What are the chances that he or she will escape lifelong mental retardation?   1 in 4
   will ever have "average" or
      "normal" intellectual abilities   8 in 100

Behavior Problems
Risk   What are the chances that any given three-year-old child will show "moderate" to "severe" behavior problems not due to a medically treatable emotional disorder?   7 in 100

Hyperkinesis
Incidence   A child is between five and twelve years old. What are the chances that he or she shows the hyperkinetic syndrome (excess motor activity, inability to concentrate, impulsivity, and irritability)?
4–10 in 100
This behavioral syndrome, which occurs mainly in boys, has been called minimal brain dysfunction, reflecting the belief of many physicians that a

brain maturation problem causes the behavioral difficulties. There are arguments about this, but certain researchers have produced evidence of mild brain abnormalities in some of these cases.

Medication   A child is diagnosed as hyperactive. What are the chances that he or she will improve if given stimulant medication? 7 in 10

Future   A child is hyperkinetic (restless, impulsive, overactive, distractable). What are the chances that as an adult he or she will be "sociopathic" (will show antisocial behavior and attitudes)?   1 in 5

Self-Injury

Incidence   A child is nine to eighteen months old and not under psychiatric care. What is the probability that he or she will engage in behavior that produces damage to his or her body (including head-banging)?   14 in 100
For children nineteen to thirty-two months old, the chances decrease slightly to 12.6 in 100.

ADOLESCENT DISORDERS

Incidence   A child enters adolescence. What are the chances that he or she will experience emotional problems serious enough to require professional help?   1 in 5
The probability is the same as for adults.

Sleep Difficulties   A teenager is referred for treatment of an emotional disturbance. What are the chances that he or she is experiencing sleep difficulties?   13 in 100
In contrast to adults, more male adolescents than females are referred for sleep difficulties. Fearful, worried, nervous teenagers seem to have more sleep problems than angry, hostile, rebellious teenagers.

Anorexia Nervosa

Risk   Randomly select a high school girl in the USA. What are the chances that she will develop anorexia nervosa (a self-imposed star-

vation disorder with potentially life-threatening weight loss)?
1 in 200
Of girls who develop anorexia nervosa, 10 percent will eventually die from the disorder.

Depression
Incidence   A male between ten and nineteen years old receives a psychiatric diagnosis. What are the chances that the diagnosis is "depression"?   1.8 in 100
For girls, the chances are 4.3 in 100. Both percentages increase with age.

School Phobia
Prognosis   What is the probability that an adolescent hospitalized for school phobia (a severe fear of attending school) will ultimately achieve good adjustment?   1 in 3
School phobics who do not improve with treatment tend to develop other neurotic problems. Strangely, the higher the school phobic's intelligence, the less likely he or she is to benefit from hospitalization.

GENERAL DISORDERS

Alcoholism
Risk   What are the chances that any given male will ultimately become an alcoholic?   1 in 20
For females, the chances are only 1 in 100.

Women   A black woman lives in the USA. What are the chances that she is a "heavy drinker"?   22 in 100
    a nondrinker   51 in 100
Among white women, 7 percent are heavy drinkers, and 39 percent are nondrinkers.

Delirium Tremens   An alcoholic develops delirium tremens (the "DTs"—a frightening reaction of the brain following prolonged heavy drinking, with symptoms marked by horrifying hallucinations). What is the victim's risk of dying?   1 in 10

Treatment   An alcoholic is admitted to a hospital emergency room or clinic and is given no treatment for alcoholism other than "drying out." What are the chances that he or she will abstain from drinking for the next year?   19 in 100
for the next three years   11 in 100

Relapses   A patient is discharged from an alcoholic treatment program. What are the chances that he or she will return to some type of drinking within one year?   86 in 100
This statistic is based on treatment programs that aim for total abstinence.

Spouses   A married man in the USA is an alcoholic. What are the odds that his wife will leave him?   1 in 10
In sharp contrast, 9 in 10 husbands will leave alcoholic wives.

Skid Row   A person in the USA is an alcoholic. What are the chances that he is a skid row bum?   less than 1 in 20

Violent Deaths   What are the chances that any given alcoholic will die a violent death (for example, from a fall, accident, fire, or suicide)? 24 in 100

Child Abuse
Survey   Ask a randomly chosen adult in the USA this question: "Could you at some time injure a child?" What are the chances that he or she will answer yes?   22 in 100
Some 58 percent agree that "almost anybody could at some time injure a child in his or her care."

Incidence   What are the chances that any given parent in the USA has ever kicked, bitten, or punched his or her child?   8 in 100
Not only do some parents show violence toward their children but 16 percent have at least one violent incident toward their spouses in a year's time.

Depression
Risk   What are any one individual's chances of someday experiencing emotional depression severe enough to require medical treatment?   15 in 100

This is a worldwide average, though there are notable differences from country to country. The Scandinavian countries for no reason yet identified (possibly their record-keeping methods) seem to have the highest incidence of depression.

Diagnosis   What are the chances that a patient's emotional depression will be recognized by a physician during a routine physical examination?   9 in 100
Many authorities believe that depression is the underlying source of many visits to physicians; yet it is frequently overlooked.

Retirees   A person is retired and has little social interaction. What are the chances that he or she is depressed?   85 in 100
If the retired person has a great deal of social interaction, the chances of depression are cut by half—to 42 in 100.

Menstrual Period   What is the probability that any given woman during a month's time will be most depressed just before or during her menstrual period?   9 in 10
Of all women, 50 percent have their most depressed mood just prior to menses; 40 percent are most depressed during the menstrual period.

Twins   A person who has an identical twin suffers severe mood problems (serious depression or excitement-euphoria with poor judgment). What are the chances that his or her twin has a similar emotional disorder?   69 in 100
The rate for fraternal (nonidentical) twins is 13 percent.

Treatment   If a person with a depressive illness (sadness, hopelessness, insomnia, apathy) does not receive adequate medical treatment, what are the chances that he or she will die within three years?
11 in 100
   If given adequate treatment
    (electroshock therapy or
    medication)   2.5 in 100
These treatments seem to reduce both suicidal and nonsuicidal deaths.

Prognosis   An individual has a manic-depressive disorder (depression with periods of excitement) that has been successfully treated

through the use of lithium carbonate. If he or she continues to use the drug regularly, what are the chances that the patient will still be well four years later?   40 in 100
    five years later   33 in 100

Divorce A married individual has periods of serious depression without times of excitement and unrealistic gaiety. What are the chances that this person will eventually be divorced from his or her spouse? 8 in 100
If the depressive episodes are followed by periodic excitement and unrealistic gaiety, the probability of divorce grows to 57 in 100.

Suicide A woman in the USA has a depressive disorder or manic-depressive disease. What are the chances that she will take her own life?   1 in 10

Down's Syndrome
Incidence A baby enters the world. What are the chances that it has Down's syndrome (a genetic form of retardation)?   1.5 in 1,000

Survival A child is born with Down's syndrome. What are the chances that the baby will live more than a month?   70 in 100
    more than a year   47 in 100
    more than ten years   40 in 100
Some live to be forty, but beyond that age, these people are at high risk for deteriorative diseases.

Maternal Age Most people are aware that the risks of having a child with Down's syndrome are higher in older women. Exactly what are the risks at different ages?

Mother's Age		Risk
20	1 in 1,923	5.2 in 10,000
25	1 in 1,205	8.3 in 10,000
30	1 in 885	11.3 in 10,000
35	1 in 365	27.4 in 10,000
40	1 in 109	91.7 in 10,000
45	1 in 32	310 in 10,000

Future Risk   A mother gives birth to a child with Down's syndrome. If she later has another child, what are the chances that that child will also have Down's syndrome?   1 in 100

Drug Problems
Cocaine   A person is taken to an emergency room because of a drug-related problem. What are the chances that the patient has been using cocaine?   1 in 100

Flashbacks   Someone uses a psychedelic drug like LSD. What are the chances that this person will experience "flashbacks"?   1 in 4
Studies have found that from 15 to 30 percent of users suffer flashbacks. The risk is greatest among persons who had emotional disturbances before taking psychedelic drugs.

Hallucinations   A person ingests a dose of LSD and hallucinates. What are the chances that the hallucinatory experience includes a religious symbol or image?   72 in 100
   a small animal or a human being   49 in 100

Brain Damage   An individual who has used a wide range of drugs enters a hospital to withdraw from drugs. What are the chances that he or she has suffered subtle brain damage?   45 in 100
Much of the damage is apparently reversible, since after five years, symptoms of brain damage can be found in only 27 percent of these chronic-drug-use patients.

Giles de la Tourette Syndrome
Obscenities   A person with Giles de la Tourette syndrome spews forth a characteristic involuntary utterance. What are the chances that the utterance contains obscenities?   50 in 100
For some unknown reason, about half those persons with this disorder usually utter obscenities while the other half do not.

Mental Retardation
Incidence   A baby comes into the world. What are the chances that it someday will have at least "moderate" retardation (IQ below 50)?
1 in 400

Half these cases are due to genetic defects, most of which are not treatable.

Birth Weight What are a child's chances of being mentally retarded if its birth weight is between 6 and 7 pounds?   2 in 100

is between 3 and 4 pounds	10 in 100
is between 1 and 3 pounds	40 in 100
is less than 1 pound	90 in 100

Risk What are the chances that any given baby will at some time during its life be classified as mentally retarded?   3 in 100
There are about 6 million "mentally retarded" people in the USA.

Child Abuse A parent physically abuses a child. What are the chances that the child will later function intellectually at a retarded level?   1 in 3
This compares to average chances in the general population of about 1 in 20. Boys are more likely to suffer intellectually from child abuse than are girls.

Degree A person is mentally retarded. What are the chances that the retardation is mild?   75 in 100

is moderate	21 in 100
is severe	4 in 100

The mildly retarded individual can receive some simple education and can often hold a job. The moderate retardate can learn to speak and to dress and feed himself or herself but will always need supervision. With severe retardation, the individual is incapable of even toilet training and requires constant, lifelong care.

Prognosis A person is diagnosed as mentally retarded. What are the chances that he or she will nevertheless be able to hold a job, marry, and have children?   89 in 100

Idiots Savants A person is mentally retarded. What are the chances that he or she is an idiot savant (a person with low intelligence, but with unusual skill in some special task)?   1 in 2,000
This is based on institutionalized retarded persons; the rate may be higher among those who live outside institutions.

Phenylketonuria
Incidence   A baby is born. What are the chances that the child has phenylketonuria (an inability of the body to break down phenylalanine, often causing mental retardation)?   1 in 11,500
This disease is largely treatable, mainly by eating a diet low in phenylalanine for at least the first five years of life.

Gene Carriers   What are the chances that any given individual carries the gene for phenylketonuria (PKU)?   1 in 50
The chances that any two people are both carriers are therefore 1 in 2,500.

Heredity Risk   What are the chances that the first child of two carrier parents will be afflicted by PKU?   1 in 4

Suicide
Risk   What are the chances that any given individual will commit suicide?   88 in 100,000

Diagnosis   A person has received a psychiatric diagnosis of depression. What are the chances that he or she will ultimately commit suicide?   15 in 100
Here are the chances for patients with other diagnoses:
Alcoholism	15 in 100
Schizophrenia	10 in 100
Drug addiction (heroin)	10 in 100
Psychopathic personality	5 in 100

Communicating Intent   What is the probability that a person who will ultimately commit suicide will communicate his or her intent beforehand?   69 in 100
by verbally stating intent to kill himself or herself	41 in 100
by vaguely referring to a wish to die	23 in 100
by making an earlier unsuccessful attempt	22 in 100
by putting his or her affairs in order	5 in 100
by showing vague interest in burials and graves	3 in 100

Prevention Service   What is the probability that a person who ultimately commits suicide will first call a suicide prevention service?
less than 1 in 50

Successful Attempts   A person makes a suicide attempt. What are the
chances that the attempt will actually result in death?   1 in 8
If a person tries to kill himself or herself and fails, there is still a 10-percent
probability that the individual will ultimately commit suicide.

Changing Methods   If a person makes a second suicide attempt,
what is the probability that he or she will try a different method from
the first time?   1 in 2

Twins   A person who has an identical twin takes his or her life. What
are the chances that the identical twin will also commit suicide?
17.7 in 100

Gender   A reported suicide victim has no previous psychiatric history. What are the chances that this individual is male?   75 in 100
  If the victim had psychiatric
      treatment   56.5 in 100

Schizophrenia

Risk   A child is born somewhere in the world. What are the chances
that he or she will develop schizophrenia (a psychotic disorder char-
acterized by thinking difficulties)?   1–2 in 100
If one parent has suffered from schizophrenia, the chances increase to 10
to 15 percent. It makes little difference whether the schizophrenic parent or
someone else raises the child; the risk of schizophrenia is the same in
either case.

Hospitalization   A patient diagnosed as having schizophrenia enters
a hospital in the USA. What are the chances that he or she will be
hospitalized at least five years?   1 in 5
In Denmark and Finland, the comparable figure is 1 in 20.

Readmissions   A psychiatric patient suffering from schizophrenia is
discharged from a hospital. What are the chances that he or she will
be readmitted within two years?   1 in 2
Various studies put the return rate at 40 to 60 percent.

EVALUATION

Physiological Indicators
Brain Waves   A child has a psychological disorder. What are the chances that his or her brain waves show an abnormal pattern?
7 in 10

A person has no psychological disorder. What are the chances that his or her brain waves nevertheless show an abnormal pattern?
7.5 in 100

Heart Rate   A youth commits a sexual offense. What is the probability that his resting heart rate is below average for his age?   67 in 100
Among those who commit violent but not sexual crimes, heart rate is below average in 81 percent of the cases.

Psychological Tests
Intelligence Tests   A person takes an intelligence test. What are the chances that he or she will score in the "genius" range?
less than 1 in 100

in the "superior" or "very superior" range	10	in 100
in the "normal" range	50	in 100
in the "retarded" range	2.2	in 100

The term *genius* is no longer used medically or scientifically. Writers who refer to highly gifted people use IQ scores of 140, 150, or 200 as the minimum for what might be thought of as genius.

The most widely used "intelligence" (academic prediction) tests are the Wechsler scales—the Wechsler Intelligence Scale for Children (WISC) and the Wechsler Adult Intelligence Scale (WAIS). The "normal" range on these tests is between 90 and 109.

Scores below 70 on the Wechsler scales are classified as "mentally deficient" among native U.S. residents and may support a medical diagnosis of "mental retardation."

Personality Tests   A psychologist gives a statistically based personality test to a college student. The student's results suggest a diagnosis of schizophrenia. Were the psychologist to report that the patient actually had schizophrenia, what are the chances that such a diagnosis would be wrong, that is, that no schizophrenia would be found during a medical evaluation?   9 in 10

Most psychologists realize that this is a statistical issue and not simply a clinical one. Statistically based personality tests have demonstrated higher accuracy than other tests in identifying the presence of specific psychiatric disorders. But by their very nature, these tests have flaws. For example, 5 percent of all people taking such tests will score in the diagnostic range of a schizophrenia subscale. Yet only 1 in 100 people in the entire population actually has a schizophrenic (psychotic) disease, and the rate among college students is far lower still. Therefore, a psychologist who identifies a college student as schizophrenic on the basis of such a test will be wrong in at least four cases for each one that he or she correctly identifies and, more likely, will be wrong 9 in 10 times. This is why psychologists always try to be aware of the actual incidence of disorders within each group that they work with (college students, psychiatric patients, medically ill patients, prisoners, PTA members, and so on). Incidentally, the psychologist in this case would correctly request medical evaluation; he or she would not try to diagnose the specific disorder.

Draw-a-Person Tests   An individual is asked to draw a person. What are the chances that he or she will draw a person of his or her own sex?   81 in 100

Circle Drawing Direction   A teenager is asked to draw a large circle. What are the chances that he or she will draw it in a clockwise direction?   3 in 10

Spontaneous clockwise drawing is called torque. Some psychologists believe that torque occurs most often in young people with learning or emotional problems.

Interview Techniques

Suicide Appraisal   A psychologist or psychiatrist determines that a male patient is seriously depressed and at risk to commit suicide. The patient refuses treatment, however, and goes home. What are the chances that he will still be alive a year later?   99 in 100

The best scientific methods of suicide prediction cannot identify the one actual suicide among 100 patients most at risk to kill themselves during any given year. The best statistical predictors are psychiatric depression and a previous suicide attempt. The best actual predictor, however, is simply to ask. Most patients, except prisoners and those being evaluated by court order, will be honest about their intentions. The most untrustworthy response is either a flat denial or the statement that "such a thing would never enter my mind."

TREATMENT

Behavior Modification
Use What is the probability that a person who obtains psychiatric help will receive behavior modification as the primary form of treatment?   1 in 10
People suffering from specific (not general) fears, or who think the same thought or do the same act over and over, or who have specific sexual inability are most likely to benefit from behavioral therapy. Other patients will have other methods as the primary treatment.

Refusal If a psychiatrist offers behavioral therapy to a patient, what is the probability that the patient will refuse the treatment?   23 in 100

Hypnosis
Hypnotizability What is the probability that any given person will be unable to be hypnotized?   8–9 in 100
It is possible that a person could become hypnotizable if he or she increased his or her motivation to be hypnotized. People who want to be hypnotized are better able to become hypnotized.

Medication
Antidepressants A person receives antidepressant medication. What are the chances that he or she will show significant improvement in four to six weeks?   65 in 100

Side Effects An adult is treated with antipsychotic medication. What is the probability that this patient will develop tardive dyskinesia (a serious drug side effect that can be overcome if treated early)?
56 in 100
However, the risk is much less than this in younger patients and may be as high as 75 percent in elderly persons.

Psychoanalysis
Use   What are the chances that a given person being treated by a psychiatrist will receive psychoanalysis?   1 in 50

Patients   A person is a patient of a psychoanalyst. What is the probability that the patient is white?   98 in 100
   has a college education   78 in 100

Psychiatrists   A physician in the USA is a psychiatrist. What are the chances that he or she is actually involved in giving psychoanalytic treatment?   1 in 7

Length of Analysis   A person begins psychoanalytic therapy for emotional problems. What are the chances that he or she can complete analysis in two years?   2 in 100
   in three to four years   30 in 100
   in five to six years   48 in 100
   in seven or more years   20 in 100

Psychotherapy
Effectiveness   It is suggested that a given individual should receive psychotherapy. What are the chances that, if he or she does receive the therapy, it will bring about an improvement?   3 in 4

Sex   A person is a mental health professional. What are the chances that this person has had sexual intercourse with one or more of his or her patients?
   Psychiatrists   5 in 100
   Male psychologists   5.5 in 100
   Female psychologists   0.6 in 100
About 80 percent of those who have once had relations with a patient repeat the experience.

Shock Therapy
Effectiveness   A person is depressed to the extent of requiring hospitalization. What are the chances that he or she will show "marked improvement" with electroconvulsive (shock) therapy?   76 in 100
   with drugs   50 in 100

Depressions of old age and manic-depressive illnesses are likely to respond best to shock therapy.

Mortality Risk   A depressed patient receives a series of shock treatments. What are the chances that the patient will die?   1 in 25,000 Untreated, such patients have a 15-percent suicide rate.

THE SYSTEM

Need for Treatment
Police   What are the chances that any given New York City police officer will need mental health attention for an emotional breakdown or a near breakdown this year?   6 in 100

College Students (Egypt)   A male student attends college in Egypt. What are the chances that he will require psychiatric care this year? 28 in 1,000
For females, the chances are only 9 in 1,000.

Community Mental Health Centers
Use   What are the chances that any given person will use a community mental health center this year?   1 in 210

Staff Meetings   Someone visits a community mental health center and asks to see a psychiatrist. What are the chances that the psychiatrist is in a staff meeting?   1 in 4

Medicare   A community mental health center collects a bill for patient care. What are the chances that the money comes from a Medicare or Medicaid program?   1 in 30

Hospitalization
Admission   What are the chances that any randomly chosen individual will be admitted to a psychiatric hospital sometime in his or her life?   9 in 100

USSR   A bed is in a hospital in the Soviet Union. What are the chances that it is being used by a psychiatric patient?   1 in 10

This figure remains remarkably stable over the years because Soviet law essentially dictates how many psychiatric cases are allowed at any given time. No more than 10 percent of all hospital beds may be used for patients with mental disorders. In the USA half the hospital beds are filled by psychiatric patients.

Alternative Support   A person is admitted to a psychiatric hospital. If family and community help had been available, what are the chances that the hospitalization could have been avoided?   84 in 100

Physical and Mental Disorders
Basis   A person makes a visit to a physician. What are the chances that the patient's problems have an emotional cause rather than a physical one?   3 in 5

Concomitant   A patient is being treated for a psychiatric disorder. What are the chances that he or she also needs treatment for a physical disorder at the same time?   28.3 in 100

A person is admitted to a psychiatric hospital. What are the chances that he or she needs medical help for physical as well as emotional problems?   46 in 100
If the person is admitted for alcoholism, drug abuse, or brain syndrome, the probability jumps to 88 in 100.

Incorrect Diagnoses   A person more than sixty-five years old is admitted to a psychiatric hospital. If the staff conducts a thorough case history review and a complete examination, what are the chances that the patient will be found to have a physical rather than psychiatric problem?   61 in 100
Such thorough evaluations are rare.

Patients
Felons   A patient has an appointment at a psychiatric clinic in the USA. What are the chances that he or she has been convicted of at least one felony?   1 in 25

Self-Injury   A person is a psychiatric patient. What are the chances that he or she engages in actions that physically damage his or her own body?   4.5 in 100

Marital Status   A person is a patient in a U.S. mental hospital. What are the chances that he or she has never been married?   48 in 100

15   Science and Education

       Science and education comprise two of the largest enterprises in our culture. Billions of dollars are spent annually to support ongoing work, and hundreds of new research projects and new education programs are screened for funding. Millions of people are involved.

    Science is responsible for countless changes in our lifestyles. Advances in medicine, disease control, materials, agriculture, and manufacturing processes are all results of the efforts of scientists. The odds in this section of the chapter give some insight into the research process itself.

    Education is also far-reaching in the modern world. Each of us has at least some direct contact with organized education. Most of the odds in the education section of this chapter are concerned with the fundamental questions of who gets education and how much.

SCIENTIFIC RESEARCH

Background

Medical Advances   Consider any of the greatest advances in modern medicine (for example, the advent of antibiotics, the polio vaccine, or the discovery of drugs for hypertension). What are the chances that the key, or milestone, scientific article that made the advance possible was a report of basic research?   62 in 100

a report of applied or clinical
   research   21 in 100
a report of engineering and
   development   15 in 100
a review article synthesizing current
   knowledge in the field   2 in 100

From the scientist's viewpoint, there is a difference between basic and applied research. In an applied research investigation, the scientist is nearly certain of what he or she will find—the study is essentially set up to prove or demonstrate a belief. The basic researcher, on the other hand, is uncertain how an investigation will turn out. Although he or she may have a good idea of what will happen, the basic scientist works at the edge of the unknown, attempting to uncover new knowledge.

Researcher Interests   A researcher publishes the report of a completed study that makes a significant contribution to progress in knowledge about heart or lung diseases. What are the chances that at the time of the study the researcher had no direct interest in either of the diseases, but was seeking only "knowledge for the sake of knowledge"?   41 in 100

Nobel Prize

Individual   What would be the chances that any given U.S. scientist would win the Nobel Prize next year?   1 in 256,728
Children of Nobel laureates in science are several thousand times more likely to win this award themselves. W. L. Bragg, G. P. Thomson, Irene Joliot-Curie, and Aage Bohr are Nobel Prize winners who were children of Nobel laureates.

Collaboration   A scientist crowns a professional career by winning a Nobel Prize. What are the chances that he or she worked with collaborators on the prize-winning project?   79 in 100

It is a comment on the complexities of modern research that most projects are team efforts. Early in the history of the Nobel Prizes, only 41 percent of the works chosen were collaborative projects. Team efforts or not, the odds are only 1 in 3 that the prizewinners will share their winnings with their coworkers.

Support

Government Funds   A scientist in the USA is conducting research. What are the chances that the funds supporting the research come from the federal government?   3 in 5
Funds may be dispensed through any of numerous channels.

Investigation

Types   A psychological study of children's development is published in a leading child psychology journal. What are the chances that the study is a laboratory-style investigation?   76 in 100
   one using paper-and-pencil tests   17 in 100
   a natural-observation study   8 in 100

Small-World Investigation   One of the most unusual and surprising fields of research in the social sciences is called small-world investigation. It demonstrates in a remarkable manner how interrelated we all are. Here's how it works: A social scientist identifies a human being somewhere in your country (most studies have been done in the USA and Canada). He or she gives you a message and asks you to attempt to get the message to the "target" person by going through a chain of first-name acquaintances. In other words, the only way you can transmit the message is to go to someone you know—and who knows you—by first name, hoping that your friend can move the message one step closer to the target person. What are the chances that your message will ever reach its destination?   48 in 100
In theory, the real odds may be close to 100 percent. But most people don't spend a great deal of time or effort figuring ways to transmit messages for social scientists. What is remarkable, however, is that the messages that do get through use an average of only five to six intermediaries. In other words, two people who do not have a first-name relationship, or who may never have even heard of one another, are connected by a surprisingly close social network. Although these two may not know each

other, they each know someone who knows someone who knows someone else.

Incidentally, the average person, according to these social scientists, has about a thousand first-name acquaintances.

Research Errors   A social scientist makes and records an observation during a research investigation. The scientist later tabulates the observations and reports them in a professional journal. What are the chances that the researcher records, tabulates, or reports the observation incorrectly?   1 in 100

    that the scientist's error favors the
      hypothesis of the study   2 in 3

Scientists

Affiliations   What are the chances that the scientist who helps produce the next highly influential research report in biochemistry or molecular biology will be associated with the U.S. National Institutes of Health?   12 in 100

with Harvard University	5 in 100
with the Medical Research Council of the United Kingdom	5 in 100
with the Rockefeller Institute	5 in 100
with the Pasteur Institute	3 in 100
with the University of Pittsburgh	3 in 100

Membership   A scientist in the USA publishes a paper reporting experimental or theoretical work. What are the chances that he or she belongs to the National Academy of Sciences?   7 in 1,000

Scientific Writing

Language   A scientist in France works on a research project. When it is time to report the work to the scientific community, what are the chances that he or she will write the journal article in the English language?   61 in 100

Rejection   A psychologist writes a professional paper and submits it to an American Psychological Association journal for publication. What are the chances that the journal's editors will reject the paper? 78 in 100

Rejection rates seem to be highest for review articles (those that summarize existing research). *Psychological Bulletin* and *Psychological Review* reject 85 percent of all material submitted to them.

Citations   A scholar writes an article that appears in a scientific journal. To affect the course of future research, the report must come to the attention of other investigators and be mentioned in their own articles. What are the chances that no other scientist will ever refer to this article?   1 in 4

that the article will be mentioned in
500 or more articles by other
scientists   1 in 20,000

A scientist publishes a report in a journal of biochemistry or molecular biology. What are the chances that the report will be mentioned in more than 550 future reports?   1 in 600

in more than 1,000 future reports   1 in 1,500
in more than 2,000 future reports   1 in 5,500

The average biochemist who publishes three articles a year, for example, would have to work in the laboratory for 200 years to produce one report that would gain wide attention.

Reading   A scientist spends 4 hours each workday reading journal articles. Reading very rapidly, he or she is able to cover fifty articles a day, or 12,500 each year. Meanwhile, someone else randomly chooses an article in the scientist's active field this year. What are the chances that the scientist will have read it?   1 in 10

EDUCATION

Elementary and Secondary School
Brazil   A student starts the first year of elementary education in Brazil. What are the chances that he or she will finish the first grade?
65 in 100

will complete elementary school   10 in 100

USA   A child is born in the USA. What are the probabilities that he or she will complete the eighth grade?   97 in 100

will graduate from high school   85 in 100

Mathematics   Ask a nine-year-old this question: "What is two thirds of nine?" What are the odds that the child can answer correctly?   1 in 8
Even among seventeen-year-olds, only 1 in 4 can answer correctly.

Higher Education

Graduates   A student enters college as a freshman. What are the chances that he or she will graduate within five years?   62 in 100

Football Players   A college student plays on the school football team. What are the chances that during the next five years he will actually earn a diploma from his school?   77 in 100
This is higher than the graduation probabilities for students in general during any five-year period (62 in 100).

Foreign Students   A student attends the Massachusetts Institute of Technology. What are the chances that he or she is a citizen of a country other than the USA?   17 in 100

Geography Majors   What are the chances that a college student will declare geography as his or her major field of study?
less than 1 in 1,000

Natural Science   If a person has had at least some college classes, what is the probability that he or she has taken at least one natural science course?   2 in 5

Grade Inflation   Select a student from a college class in 1969. What are the chances that he or she had an A or B grade-point average?
35 in 100

Select a college student today. What are the chances that he or she has an A or B grade-point average?   59 in 100

Phi Beta Kappa   A person graduated from Dartmouth in the class of 1974. What are the chances that he or she made Phi Beta Kappa?
1 in 4
In the 1980s, only 10 percent of Dartmouth's graduating class will be Phi Beta Kappas. That's a new Dartmouth rule.

Graduate School

Advanced Degrees   A student receives a bachelor's degree. What are the chances that he or she will attempt to obtain an advanced degree?   38 in 100

In 1940, only 15 percent of college graduates continued their education.

Ph.D. Success   A student is accepted into a graduate school in psychology. What is the likelihood that he or she will successfully achieve the Ph.D. degree?   26 in 100

For those in graduate programs in physics and chemistry, the chances are 36 and 51 in 100, respectively.

Medical School

Physicians' Children   A person is a medical student. What is the probability that he or she is the son or daughter of a physician? 14 in 100

Funding   A dollar goes into the budget of a medical school in the USA. What are the chances that it was donated by a drug company? 3 in 100

EDUCATIONAL TESTING

Guessing   A student about to take the Graduate Record Examination (GRE) or the Scholastic Aptitude Test (SAT) has decided that he or she will guess, rather than leave any item blank, when he or she doesn't know an answer. Assuming that the student guesses on every item for which each of the five possible responses seems equally probable, what are the chances that he or she will improve his or her total score over what it would have been had the items been left blank?   1 in 2

If the student decides to guess only on those items from which he or she can eliminate one possible answer as clearly incorrect, his or her chances of improving his or her total score become 57 in 100. Guessing only on items from which two responses can be eliminated would result in a 67-percent chance of bettering a "blank" score, while guessing only on those from which three responses can be eliminated increases the chances to 80 percent.

Overall, then, guessing is the best strategy. For any given item, however, the odds are greater that guessing will hurt rather than help the score.

The explanation lies in the way that the tests are scored. The examinee gets no points for a no-response item and loses a quarter of a point for an incorrect response but gains one full point for a correct answer. Therefore, on any five-choice question, the odds are only 1 in 5 that the test-taker will guess accurately. But, for every five guesses, he or she will come out even—missing four, for a total one-point loss, and getting one correct, for a one-point gain—an even bet. Whenever the test-taker can eliminate even one obviously false choice, the odds clearly favor a guessing strategy.

16　The World

　　　　　　We know more about the peoples and lands on other
parts of the earth than did any generation before us. We also know
that changes are occurring more rapidly than ever before as new
nations are born, nationalism and/or racial or ethnic pride reasserts
itself, Westernization takes place, and scientific "advances" reach
previously isolated parts of the world.

　　For most of us, contact with the rest of our world is mainly through
the news media, but when these sources focus on some area of the
world, chances are that our attention is drawn to a problem, rather
than to a lifestyle or to the unique characteristics of the land itself. The
odds in this final chapter deal with the people and lands of the world
in daily life. Where people live, their customs and habits, age, religion,
language, and background are all reflected in the odds. The geo-
graphical characteristics of various nations are also represented. You
may also become reacquainted with the planet on which we live in the
modern age.

POPULATION

You are a member of the world's population. This makes you one of the 4.3 billion human beings estimated to inhabit this planet in 1980. Your chances, therefore, of being chosen in a lottery of everyone on Earth are 1 in nearly 4.3 billion. Imagine that we hold such a lottery and select one human being from the earth's entire population. What are the chances that the person who "wins" . . . ?

is Asian, South American, or African	3 in 4	75 in 100

By the year 2000, this is expected to rise to 80 percent.

is Asian	3 in 5	58 in 100
drinks coffee	2 in 5	40 in 100
lives in China or India	2 in 5	40 in 100
lives in a country that allows political and personal freedom	2 in 5	37 in 100
is illiterate	1 in 3	34 in 100
lives in a Communist country	1 in 3	34 in 100
eats with a knife and fork	1 in 3	33 in 100
eats with his or her hands	1 in 3	33 in 100
eats with chopsticks	1 in 3	33 in 100
is less than fifteen years old	1 in 3	33 in 100

Of the children under fifteen years of age, 80 percent live in underdeveloped regions. Almost 40 percent of the children in developing countries die before the age of five.

lives in a city	3 in 10	30 in 100

In 1800, less than 3 percent of the people in the world lived in or near cities with at least 20,000 inhabitants. By the year 2025, 63 percent of us will live in urban areas, and 70 percent of the world's population will live on 10 percent of the earth's surface.

supports a family on less than $250 per year	1 in 4	25 in 100
is Christian	1 in 4	25 in 100
is Chinese	1 in 5	22 in 100
is Moslem	1 in 5	19 in 100
has black skin	1 in 6	18 in 100
speaks Mandarin	1 in 6	16 in 100

is Roman Catholic	1 in 6	16 in 100
lives in Europe	1 in 7	14 in 100
lives in a desert	1 in 8	12 in 100
is Hindu	1 in 8	12 in 100
lives in Africa	1 in 10	10 in 100
speaks English	1 in 11	9 in 100
lives in North America or Central America	1 in 12	8 in 100
is Protestant	1 in 12	8 in 100
lives in the USSR	1 in 16	6 in 100
is Buddhist	1 in 16	6 in 100
lives in South America	1 in 16	6 in 100
lives in the USA	1 in 19	5 in 100
has an extra rib	1 in 20	5 in 100
is a man with some form of color blindness	1 in 28	4 in 100
speaks Portuguese	1 in 30	3 in 100
is surnamed Chang	1 in 50	2 in 100
lives in California	1 in 180	
receives ADC (Aid to Dependent Children) welfare payments	1 in 373	
lives in New York City	1 in 568	
plays volleyball in the USSR	1 in 800	
is a woman with some form of color blindness	1 in 2,000	
is a Roman Catholic priest	1 in 10,000	
is an albino	1 in 10,000	
is an Eskimo	1 in 70,000	
is a psychiatrist practicing in the USA	1 in 186,000	
is an Apache Indian	1 in 446,800	
has A-H blood	1 in 1,433,000,000	

Three people somewhere in the world theoretically have this blood type.

A note about population growth: It took eighteen centuries from the time of Christ to achieve a world population of 1 billion people. It will take less than twenty years to add 2 billion more to our present number. Some experts now believe that our total population will stabilize at about 8 billion.

PEOPLES OF THE WORLD

If our lottery were held one country at a time, the various winners would obviously reflect characteristics of their own nations. For each of the countries listed below, what are the chances that its winner . . . ?

Afghanistan

is Moslem	99 in 100
lives on a farm or in a small village	82 in 100
lives in a mountain valley	80 in 100
is a nomad	12 in 100
is a city dweller	5 in 100
is a physician	1 in 18,000

Afghanistan has more than nineteen different ethnic groups.

Albania

is Moslem	70 in 100
earns less than $40 a month	50 in 100

Algeria

is an Arab	78 in 100
is a Berber	20 in 100

Angola

cannot read or write	70 in 100

Argentina

is white	97 in 100
is of European ancestry	90 in 100
can read and write	80 in 100
lives in the Humid Pampa	67 in 100
lives in Buenos Aires	35 in 100
is a physician	1 in 500

Australia

is a city dweller	85 in 100
is an Australian aborigine	1 in 110

Even today, 1 in 68 Australian aborigines has minimal or no contact with white Australia.

Austria

    speaks German   98 in 100

    lives in Vienna   20 in 100

Bahrain

    lives within 25 miles of the sea   100 in 100

    is Moslem   99 in 100

    is an Arab   90 in 100

Bangladesh

    speaks Bengali   95 in 100

    lives in a rural area   91 in 100

    is Moslem   85 in 100

    cannot read or write   80 in 100

Belgium

    speaks Flemish (Dutch) at home   60 in 100

    speaks French at home   40 in 100

Belize

    lives along the coast   60 in 100

    is Roman Catholic   60 in 100

    is descended from African slaves

        brought to British Honduras by

        British settlers   40 in 100

    lives in Belize City   23 in 100

Botswana

    survives on subsistence farming and

        stock raising   95 in 100

    is Christian   14 in 100

Most people in Botswana practice tribal religions.

    is a Bushman   1 in 55

Brazil

    lives in a home with indoor plumbing   38 in 100

    is an abandoned child   1 in 100

Nearly half the people in South America live in Brazil.

Burma

wears a neck coil to increase neck
length   47 in 100

The probability of neck coils depends on gender and age. For women over the age of six, the probability is almost 100 in 100; for men, it is 0. The practice is said to have grown from the belief that neck coils protect women from tiger attacks.

Burundi

belongs to the Watusi tribe   15 in 100
is a pygmy   1 in 100

Burundi is the home of the world's tallest people, the Watusis, who often are more than seven feet tall, as well as the world's shortest people, the pygmies, all standing less than five feet.

Canada

lives within 100 miles of the U.S.
border   75 in 100
lives in Ontario   34 in 100
speaks French at home   25 in 100

Cape Verde

has Portuguese and black ancestors   72 in 100

China

is a peasant   90 in 100
is less than twenty-one years old   63 in 100
is named Chang   10 in 100

Colombia

is mestizo (of mixed white and
Indian ancestry)   60 in 100
is mulatto (of mixed white and black
ancestry)   15 in 100

Congo Republic

is Christian   50 in 100
believes that trees, grass, and
stones have spirits   48 in 100

Czechoslovakia
is a Czech   65 in 100
lives in a home without an indoor
    toilet   60 in 100
is a Slovak   30 in 100
belongs to the Communist party   9 in 100

Denmark
lives on an island   60 in 100
lives on the Jutland Peninsula   40 in 100
lives in Copenhagen   25 in 100
uses antiperspirant regularly   50 in 100
Although 2 in 3 Danish women use deodorants daily, only 1 in 3 Danish men uses deodorant regularly.

Djibouti
is illiterate   90 in 100
is a Somali   49 in 100
is an Afar   39 in 100
is an Arab   6 in 100
is a European   4 in 100

Ecuador
is a descendant of the Incas   65 in 100

Egypt
lives in the Nile valley or delta   99 in 100
This comprises less than 5 percent of Egypt's land area.

owns a car   4 in 100
Most Egyptians travel short distances on foot, and longer distances in overcrowded buses or trams.

Finland
speaks Finnish   93 in 100
speaks Swedish   6 in 100

France

takes a vacation in August   45 in 100

A full 80 percent of white-collar workers take their vacations in August.

wears a bra with size B cups   33 in 100

This probability depends on gender and age. Of French women who wear bras, 69 percent wear a B cup size.

lives in the Paris metropolitan area   17 in 100

Germany, East (German Democratic Republic)

lives in a city   76 in 100
has access to a family car   33 in 100

Germany, West (Federal Republic of Germany)

speaks English   52 in 100

More than 70 percent of West German teenagers speak fluent English.

Ghana

lives in a family of seven or more   50 in 100

Great Britain

lives in a city   80 in 100

England has had a large urban population since the nineteenth century. By 1900, 3 in 4 Britons were living in cities, and the proportion of city dwellers has slowly grown throughout this century.

slept until 10 a.m. last Sunday   25 in 100
slept until noon last Sunday   10 in 100
is named Smith   1 in 100

Greece

lives in Athens   40 in 100

Grenada

is black   52 in 100
is mulatto   43 in 100
is white   1 in 100

Guatemala

is a descendant of the Maya	95 in 100
will eat corn today	75 in 100

Guyana

is an East Indian	56 in 100
is Hindu	34 in 100

Although Guyana is a South American nation, most of its people are of Asian descent. The British brought laborers from India to work Guyanese farms during the mid-nineteenth century.

Haiti

is a descendant of African slaves	95 in 100
lives in a rural area	80 in 100

Honduras

lives in a family whose income is from agriculture	70 in 100

Hungary

is a Magyar	95 in 100
lives in Budapest	20 in 100
is a member of the Communist party	7 in 100

Iceland

is of Norwegian or Celtic ancestry	99 in 100
is Lutheran	98 in 100
lives in the Reykjavik metropolitan area	50 in 100
is an Eskimo	less than 1 in 10,000

Despite what many people think, Eskimos do not reside in Iceland.

India

eats only with the right hand and drinks only with the left hand	84 in 100

The Hindu religion prescribes this eating style.

Indonesia

lives on Java	65 in 100

Iran

is Moslem	96 in 100
is an Arab	80 in 100
is Shiite Moslem	92 in 100

The official religion of Iran is Shiism.

is illiterate	60 in 100
lives by farming or herding	50 in 100
is a Kurd	15 in 100
is a physician	1 in 3,300

Ireland

doesn't use soap regularly	20 in 100
has red hair	4 in 100

The red-headed Irishman has long been a stereotype held by Americans even though it appears to be false.

Israel

is Jewish	85 in 100
was born in Israel	50 in 100
was born in Asia or Africa	27 in 100
was born in Europe	23 in 100
was raised in a kibbutz	14 in 100

Of Israeli air force pilots in 1980, 40 percent were raised in kibbutzim.

Italy

is Roman Catholic	95 in 100
lives in the Po Valley	40 in 100

Jamaica

is black	85 in 100
is Protestant	75 in 100

Japan

lives in a home without a flush toilet	73 in 100
has a high school diploma	73 in 100

More than 90 percent of the adults in Japan have high school diplomas.

lived in a family with an income of less than $4,000 in 1977	12 in 100
lived in a family with an income of more than $20,000 in 1977	2 in 100

Comparable figures for the USA show that 36 percent of workers earn more than $20,000.

Jordan

is a bedouin	2 in 100

Bedouin, once the renowned wanderers of the desert, now face the challenge of urban living. Almost 95 percent of bedouin currently reside in four-walled houses.

Kenya

lives in a home with five or more other people	50 in 100

Homes in Kenya are among the world's most crowded, with half sheltering five or more people. By contrast, the average U.S. household is home for just under three people, as are the average residences in West Germany and Sweden.

Kuwait

is an Arab	85 in 100
is less than fifteen years old	43 in 100

Lebanon

is an Arab	93 in 100
lives in a city	60 in 100
is Moslem	57 in 100
is Christian	40 in 100
is an Armenian	6 in 100

Liberia

is descended from black settlers from the USA	5 in 100

These American-Liberians, despite their minority status, tend to dominate the political and high governmental ranks of the country.

Libya
resides in a family unit that depends
on farming or cattle raising   80 in 100

Liechtenstein
resides in a family unit that depends
on the sale of stamps for its living   4 in 100

Surprisingly, 6 percent of Liechtenstein's national income comes from the sale of stamps.

is a member of Liechtenstein's
armed forces   0

Liechtenstein maintains no armed forces.

Mauritius
is sixty-five or older   3 in 100

Surprisingly, Mauritius has a high life-expectancy rate. Recent advances in disease control, especially malaria, coupled with high birth rates has developed a rapidly expanding younger population. More than 40 percent of Mauritius's population is under 16.

Mexico
lives in a city or town   64 in 100

Almost 98 percent of the cities and towns in Mexico do not have potable water systems.

is mestizo   60 in 100
is less than fifteen years old   46 in 100
relies exclusively on herb doctors or
witch doctors for medical care   33 in 100
is Indian   30 in 100
will make an illegal entry into the
USA next year   1 in 500

The U.S. Immigration and Naturalization Service arrested nearly 75,000 people in 1964, and more than 1 million in 1978, for illegal entry into the country. Of these, 93 percent came from Mexico.

Monaco
is French   58 in 100
is Italian   17 in 100

Nauru

lives within 4 miles of Nauru's
   borders   100 in 100

Nauru has a total area of only 8 square miles. Nauru generates almost all its income from the land, which is rich in phosphates from thousands of years of bird droppings. Unfortunately, this natural resource is expected to be depleted by the year 2000.

Netherlands

lives in an urban area   77 in 100
is Protestant   40 in 100
is Catholic   40 in 100

New Zealand

is a descendant of the Maori, the
   first inhabitants of New Zealand   8 in 100

Nicaragua

is mestizo   69 in 100
is illiterate   45 in 100
is black   9 in 100

North Yemen

is illiterate   84 in 100
has married or will marry before
   reaching the age of nineteen   46 in 100

About 5 percent of North Yemenite girls marry before their fifteenth birthday.

Norway

lives within 20 miles of the sea   60 in 100
lives in a village of fewer than 200
   people   35 in 100
eats at least four meals a day   50 in 100

Eating five meals a day is not unusual for many farm families.

Pakistan

is Moslem   97 in 100
is under sixteen   48 in 100

is over sixty-five   4 in 100

Because so many Pakistanis are young, Pakistan's population is expected to continue increasing rapidly through the remainder of the twentieth century.

Panama
is mestizo   70 in 100
is black   13 in 100
is white   10 in 100
is Indian   6 in 100

Paraguay
is mestizo   96 in 100
is Roman Catholic   95 in 100
speaks Guarani   90 in 100
is part Indian   3 in 100
speaks Spanish   75 in 100

Most Paraguayans are bilingual.

Peru
lives in the mountains   62 in 100

Philippines
speaks Filipino (Tagalog)   44 in 100
speaks English   39 in 100
speaks Spanish   2 in 100
speaks Chinese   1 in 100

Poland
is Polish   98 in 100

In 1939, 69 percent of Poland's people were, in fact, Polish. The rest were mostly Ukrainian (14%) and Jewish (8.5%). The Nazis all but eliminated Poland's Jewish citizens, killing 98 percent of them.

Rumania
is Rumanian   85 in 100
is Hungarian   8 in 100

owns a television set	5 in 100
is German	2 in 100
owns an automobile	1 in 100

Rwanda

depends directly upon agriculture for survival	92 in 100
belongs to the Bahata tribe	90 in 100
belongs to the Watusi tribe	9 in 100
is a pygmy	1 in 100

Saudi Arabia

is Moslem	99 in 100
is Sunnite Moslem	97 in 100
is a nomad	30 in 100
is a physician	1 in 3,000

Scotland

lives in the Lowlands	75 in 100
lives in publicly owned housing	52 in 100
speaks both Gaelic and English	1 in 100
is named Macdonald	1 in 100

Macdonald is the most common surname in Scotland.

South Africa

is black	70 in 100
is colored (mixed race)	9 in 100
is white	8 in 100
is Asian	3 in 100

South Korea

has the surname Kim	16 in 100

This is the most common Korean surname. The most common Swedish surname is Johanssen. In Russia, it is Ivanov; and in the USA and Great Britain, it is Smith.

Spain

lives in a home without indoor plumbing	30 in 100

Many Spaniards still carry all their water supplies from wells, springs, or streams.

is a Basque	6 in 100

Swaziland

was fathered by King Sobhuza	1 in 1,000

Literally the father of his country, King Sobhuza had more than 100 wives, who bore him more than 500 children during his 59-year reign.

Sweden

is Lutheran	97 in 100
is more than fifteen years old	90 in 100
will vote in Sweden's next national election	72 in 100

Nearly 90 percent of Sweden's eligible voters participate in their national elections. This voter turnout is the highest among democratic nations.

lives in an apartment	61 in 100
has access to a vacation home or a boat	24 in 100

Switzerland

lives on the Swiss Plateau	75 in 100

Togo

will die before the age of forty	51 in 100

The Togolese have the shortest life expectancy in the world.

Uganda

lives in a rural area	91 in 100
is a Bantu	72 in 100

Union of Soviet Socialist Republics

lives in European Russia	75 in 100
is ethnic Russian or Slavic	53 in 100
is Ukrainian	18 in 100
is Moslem	16 in 100
is Belorussian	4 in 100

Uruguay

    lives in Montevideo   42 in 100

Venezuela

    lives north of the Orinoco River,
        which divides Venezuela roughly
        in half   90 in 100
    is mestizo   70 in 100
    is white   20 in 100
    is black   8 in 100
    is Indian   2 in 100

Yugoslavia

    is of the Orthodox faith   50 in 100
    is a Serb   40 in 100
    is Roman Catholic   30 in 100
    is a Croat   23 in 100
    is a Macedonian   6 in 100

Zimbabwe

    is black   96 in 100
    is white   4 in 100

GEOGRAPHY

If a meteor were to strike our planet today, what are the chances
that it would hit . . . ?

water	3 in 4	72 in 100
the Pacific Ocean	1 in 3	33 in 100

The Pacific Ocean is large enough to hold all the earth's continents.

the Atlantic Ocean	1 in 6	16 in 100
the Indian Ocean	1 in 8	12.5 in 100
the Eurasian landmass	1 in 10	10.4 in 100
Africa	1 in 17	5.9 in 100
arable land	1 in 20	5 in 100
Antarctica	1 in 35	2.9 in 100
the Arctic Ocean	1 in 37	2.7 in 100

the USA	1 in 55	1.8 in 100
a lake, pond, or river	1 in 100	1 in 100
a person	1 in 40,000	

As Skylab moved toward its fiery plunge to earth in July 1979, NASA scientists reassured a nervous world that the chance of any human being injured was 1 in 150. This is a far larger risk than the estimate for a meteor. Skylab scattered thousands of parts over an area 4,000 miles long and 100 miles wide, presenting a far higher risk than a single meteor. Were the risk of being hit by a meteor equal to Skylab's 1 in 150, one human a year would be killed by plummeting meteorites. As it is, there has been only one documented case of a person being injured by an object falling onto the earth's surface from space, and to date no one has been killed in this manner.

LAND AREA

If the meteor were to strike land (rather than an area covered with water), what are the chances that it would hit . . . ?

the Eurasian landmass	1 in 3	36 in 100
Asia	2 in 7	29 in 100
a desert or wasteland	1 in 4	25 in 100

At the beginning of the twentieth century, less than 15 percent of the earth's land surface was classified as desert or wasteland. Land is classified as desert if it receives less than 10 inches (25 centimeters) of rain a year.

forestland	1 in 4	25 in 100

Ten thousand years ago, half the earth's land surface was covered by forests.

grasslands	1 in 4	25 in 100
Africa	1 in 5	20 in 100
the USSR	1 in 6	16 in 100
North America or Central America	1 in 6	16 in 100
a desert	1 in 6	15 in 100
a glacier	1 in 8	13 in 100
a tropical forest	1 in 8	12.5 in 100
South America	1 in 8	12 in 100
a coniferous forest	1 in 11	9 in 100
a land surface currently under cultivation	1 in 13	8 in 100

Canada	1 in 15	7	in 100
the People's Republic of China	1 in 15	7	in 100
the USA	1 in 16	6	in 100
the Sahara Desert	1 in 16	6	in 100
Europe	1 in 16	6	in 100
Brazil	1 in 17	6	in 100
tundra	1 in 18	6	in 100
Australia	1 in 20	5	in 100
a deciduous forest	1 in 34	3	in 100
wetlands	1 in 50	2	in 100
taiga	1 in 50	2	in 100
Los Angeles County, California	1 in 14,000		
New York County, New York	1 in 1 million		

COUNTRIES

A square meter of area is chosen at random within the border of each of the countries below. What are the chances that the land represented . . . ?

Albania
   is scrub forestland   30 in 100

Algeria
   is in the Sahara Desert   90 in 100

Australia
   is entirely in the Southern
      Hemisphere   100 in 100
   receives less than 21 inches of rain
      a year   80 in 100
   is pastureland   50 in 100
   is cultivated   20 in 100

Austria
   is in the Alps   75 in 100
Some land in the Austrian Alps is farmed. Farming the mountainous terrain is frequently a slow, difficult process, thereby limiting the amount of area

that a farmer can make productive. The average Austrian farm is less than 18 acres in size.

Bahamas
    is on an island that is inhabited   1 in 150
Only 20 of the 3,000 Bahama Islands have permanent human inhabitants.

Barbados
    is sugar farmland   70 in 100

Bolivia
    is forestland   39 in 100

Botswana
    is covered by sparse grass and
        thornbush savannah   84 in 100

Brazil
    is farmland   11 in 100

Bulgaria
    is on a government-run collective
        farm   95 in 100
    is in a city or village   3 in 100

Cambodia
    is covered by tropical hardwood
        forest   50 in 100

Canada
    is farmland   8 in 100

Colombia
    is in the tropics   100 in 100
    is used for grazing animals   25 in 100
    is farmland   5 in 100

Costa Rica
   is forestland   80 in 100
   is farmland   18 in 100
   is planted in such permanent crops
      as coffee, bananas, and cocoa   3 in 100

Cuba
   is forestland   14 in 100
   is farmland   30 in 100
According to law, all Cuban farms are less than 167 acres in size.

Czechoslovakia
   is arable   76 in 100
Nearly 70 percent of Czechoslovakia's arable land is farmed.

Ecuador
   is forestland   74 in 100

Egypt
   is desert land   96 in 100

El Salvador
   touches the Atlantic Ocean   0
El Salvador is the only Central American country without an Atlantic seacoast. Until El Salvador's ruling junta seized huge quantities of farmland in March 1980, nearly half the farmland in El Salvador belonged to fewer than fifty families.

Finland
   is above the Arctic Circle   33 in 100
   is forestland   70 in 100
Finland's forests consist almost entirely of pine (46%), spruce (36%), and birch (16%) trees.

Great Britain
   is in Scotland   37 in 100

Greece
is within 90 miles of the sea   100 in 100
is on an island   20 in 100

Haiti
is forestland   8 in 100
Due to their increasing demand for fuel and land (the average farm size is 2 acres), the Haitian people are clearing the forest at a very rapid rate.

Ireland
is within 70 miles of the sea   100 in 100

Japan
is not cultivated   86 in 100
is forestland   67 in 100

Kenya
is cultivated   16 in 100
is forestland   3 in 100

Kuwait
is desert land   nearly 100 in 100

Lebanon
is mountainous terrain   50 in 100
is cultivated   23 in 100

Libya
is desert or barren plains   95 in 100
is arable   1 in 100

Malawi
is forestland   25 in 100
Mahogany and eucalyptus trees are numerous in Malawi.

New Zealand
is within 80 miles of the sea   100 in 100
is 650 feet or more above sea level   75 in 100

Norway
is mountainous terrain	60 in 100
is above the Arctic Circle	33 in 100

More than 1 percent of Norway's land lies under glaciers.

is forestland	25 in 100
is arable	3 in 100

Pakistan
is irrigated	20 in 100

Pakistan irrigates 75 percent of its croplands and has one of the most highly developed systems of irrigation canals in the world.

Papua New Guinea
is covered with natural unplanted vegetation	75 in 100

Most of this is tropical rain forest vegetation.

Paraguay
is in the temperate zone	67 in 100
is in the tropic zone	33 in 100

Philippines
is forestland	44 in 100
is grassland	38 in 100
is on Luzon Island	35 in 100
is on Mindanao Island	32 in 100
is swampland	25 in 100

Portugal
is cultivated	40 in 100
is in a vineyard	4 in 100

Portugal is one of the world's leading wine producers.

Turkey
is in Asia	97 in 100
is farmland	33 in 100
is forestland	25 in 100
is in Europe	3 in 100

Uganda

is forestland   6 in 100

Nearly 15 percent of Uganda's total land area is covered by lakes.

Union of Soviet Socialist Republics

is forestland   32 in 100
is arable   24 in 100
is desert or semidesert   17 in 100
is treeless steppe   11 in 100
is subtropical   2 in 100

The Soviet Union spreads nearly 7,000 miles from east to west. It stretches from the frozen tundra in the north to the subtropical regions in the south. It spans eight time zones and shares borders with twelve other nations. A substantial portion of Soviet land is devoted to state farms (sovkhozy), nearly half of which are larger than 100,000 acres in size.

Venezuela

is cultivated   3 in 100

Zaire

is forestland   48 in 100
is arable   20 in 100
is under cultivation   1 in 100